KAMP OLYMPIK

KAMP
OLYMPIK

BY
DON BRAGG

WITH
THERESA BRAGG

AS TOLD TO
PATRICIA DOHERTY

AHLP Books
Cherry Hill, New Jersey

AHLP Books
an imprint of Africana Homestead Legacy Publishers
100 Springdale Road Ste A3 #206
Cherry Hill, New Jersey 08003
e-mail: editors@ahlpub.com or book-orders@ahlpub.com

All rights reserved. Published 2008.
Printed and bound in the United States of America.
11 10 09 08   5 4 3 2 1

Most of the poems in this book are reprinted from *Reflections of Gold: A Collection of Poems* by Don Bragg, unpublished collection (1979).

Don Bragg wrote the following six poems specifically for *Kamp Olympik*: "Lures," "The Jersey Devil," "Hovering," "Labyrinth," "Demon Tree," and "Images."

This paper meets the requirements of ANSI/NISO Z39.48-1992 (R 1997) Permanence of Paper.

Photograph on page 1 courtesy of Joe Dougherty.

ISBN 978-0-9818939-3-8
        The Library of Congress has cataloged
        the hardcover edition as follows:

Bragg, Don, 1935-
  Kamp Olympik / Don Bragg with Theresa Bragg as told to Patricia Doherty.
     p. cm.
  Summary: "Don and Theresa Bragg recount their experiences running a summer camp for children in the New Jersey Pine Barrens"—Provided by publisher.
  Includes index.
  ISBN 978-0-9799537-9-8 (hardcover : alk. paper)
  1. Kamp Olympik (N.J.) 2. Camps—New Jersey—Pine Barrens. 3. Bragg, Don, 1935- 4. Bragg, Theresa, 1939- I. Bragg, Theresa, 1939- II. Doherty, Patricia, 1942- III. Title.
  GV194.N5B73 2008
  796.54'220974961—dc22
                    2008001989

Dedicated to supportive parents who made it all possible

Dominick and Yolanda Fiore
and
George T. Bragg

Chapter One

To tell a story and to tell it well. To present a tale, to create a spell.

A woven cloth of embellished scenes. A carpet ride of enchanting dreams.

—*Don Bragg, "Lures"*

With the dog-eared photographs finally arranged on my desk, I leaned back, closed my eyes, and boom! It's 1967—and it's Parents' Day, and the mother who'd backed me up to the bank of the Wading River was a quivering mound of outrage. "Then it's true! You actually let my son jump off an eighty-foot-high platform into *that*!" She pointed with disgust at the river water a few feet away. "It's filthy! Bet it's full of sewage."

"No, ma'am," I told her in my most reassuring voice. "The diving platform's only forty or so feet high, and the water picks up that brown color from … "

But the lady was still thinking sewage and cut in, "You can't even see the bottom. *Anything* could be swimming or crawling around down there. And what's this I hear about my child having to swing through the woods on flimsy little pieces of rope?"

"Flimsy? Now those are one-inch nylon ropes, ma'am. They could hold an elephant. And nobody makes the campers use those swings; it's a privilege!"

Moving still closer, she dropped her voice to a rasping whisper. "What about the campers that went missing during an overnight canoe trip?"

"Nobody's missing." I glanced toward Kamp Olympik's dining hall. Why the hell didn't the lunch bell ever ring when I needed rescuing? "Besides, the kids are crazy about adventures like overnights."

"Heavens," the woman continued. "I've never heard of a camp like this. My son was telling us that the devil drops by regularly and snatches children from their bunks."

"You mean the Jersey Devil?" I managed to laugh heartily. "That's just a campfire ghost story. Besides, it's historical—part of the indigenous folklore. The kids love it."

The camp bell mercifully clanged just then and the anxious mother hurried away to round up her son. The boy's dad stood beside me in silence, rocking back on his heels, his hands in his pockets. He finally murmured rather wistfully, "Think I could take a turn on those rope swings after lunch?"

Putting an arm around his shoulders, I propelled the man toward the dining hall. "Sure," I said. "There're already a few dads out there, but it's trickier than it looks. In fact, see that guy limping toward us? He was just at Tarzanville. Maybe you should ask him if you should try it."

Damn, but we had fun back then. So did the kids who came to Kamp Olympik. Of course, the whole idea behind Kamp Olympik was to give kids a place to have fun for a few weeks during the summer. Me, I'd grown up running wild in the Jersey farmlands and woods—outside all summer long, having a ball, just being a kid. Yeah, training for that Olympic gold medal was the driving force for me as I grew into adulthood, but I think in the back of my mind I always had this crazy dream of giving other kids a taste of growing up out of doors.

Now the summer camp idea didn't entirely surface right after the 1960 Olympics. Following the career paths of other Olympians from Crabbe to Weissmuller, I took my new wife, Theresa Fiore, to Hollywood because I'd been offered the brass ring: the chance to play Tarzan on the screen. You've gotta understand that when I was a kid, I constantly played Tarzan, swinging from ropes tied to trees in my backyard. I credit my early swinging with giving me the upper body strength I needed to become a pole-vaulting champion. It was a major influence in my vaulting success.

So yeah, I jumped at the chance to be in the movies, but let's cut to the chase. Tarzan didn't pan out for me. Despite a contract for six films, litigation over filming rights made it clear the picture we'd started would never be released. So not quite a year after the heady victory in Rome, I was back home wondering how I was going to support my wife and brand-new baby.

My skin crawled at the thought of having to work for somebody else, but you do what you gotta do. I mean, I finally had the family I'd always wanted, and I was damn well going to provide for Theresa and Mark. Okay, so here I am—a guy who hated so much as buttoning his collar—putting on a suit and tie and selling pharmaceuticals to people who seemed like they couldn't have cared less. Talk about learning patience the hard way. My long-suffering butt grew numb as I sat for hours in waiting rooms, grinding my teeth, thinking I'd rather be digging ditches. I even tried my hand at being a repo man until I got shot at when I tried to tow the car of some mobbed-up nutcase. Then I found a job that at least looked bearable: working for the State of New Jersey.

Theresa and I settled our little family in Trenton once I began punching the time clock for the New Jersey Department of Conservation. I guess my degree in finance qualified me for something, since they put me on the team negotiating for the purchase of land contiguous to the Wharton State Forest. I earned the necessary real estate license, rolled up my sleeves, and got going. I lucked out when they assigned Sam De Gasparis as my partner. We became good friends, and I enjoyed our work as we contacted potential sellers around the Wharton State Forest. This was in the area called the Jersey Pinelands, rich in cranberries and blueberries and steeped in American history.

Sam and I had a simple plan of attack. We'd stop for lunch at an old country store, for instance. While we devoured delicious brisket or home-cured ham sandwiches, we'd get talking with the proprietor and turn the conversation to the local landowners and their likelihood of selling land. But there was another constant to these lunches: my borrowing Sam's small change to buy Tastykakes. Those were the addictively delicious chocolate cupcakes made only in Philadelphia. I had to have 'em. Almost every other day, I'd ask for a nickel or dime to buy this tasty morsel. It became such a habit that halfway through lunch Sam would say, "I guess you want your cookie money." After handing over his change, he'd grin, "When you're stinking rich, you'd better pay me back!"

"Sure, Sam," I'd say. "When I get rich enough."

Then one afternoon while on our way to negotiate for a choice piece of real estate, we happened to pass a beautiful parcel of land on the small Wading River. I noticed a FOR SALE sign—a rarity in this neck of the woods—so I had Sam pull over for a minute so I could take it all in. The deeply wooded area was full of the clean smell of the forest and dotted with wildflowers and blueberry bushes. The deep silence of the place was broken only by the sound of a softly running stream. Tarzan might just have found his new home.

"What a great spot for a summer camp," I said, thinking out loud.

"For a guy who can't afford to buy his own Tastykakes, you're thinking big. You got any idea what a chunk of land like that would cost?"

Yeah, I knew, so I dropped the subject. We headed back to Trenton and joined Sam's good friend Dick Maiorino for Italian food. And it always was Italian food when Sam and Dick got together, since they were both *paisans*. The Italian connection kept our friendship growing, especially since Theresa was also Italian. So between the pasta and the vino and the growing camaraderie, the idea for a camp drifted out of focus.

If it hadn't been for my family, it would've stayed out of focus. Sometimes Theresa and I would throw the idea around late at night or on rainy afternoons, the way some people might talk about a luxurious round-the-world cruise. You know, the impossible dream. But then our four-year-old son Mark got into the act. Don't ever tell me that something can be going on in a home, good or bad, without the kids getting wind of it. We were in the middle of dinner—Theresa's lasagna, I think—and I'd just said something about getting a couple of new tires for the car. Out of nowhere little Mark pipes up, "And then are we going to open our camp?" Hearing the words coming out of my son's mouth solidified something in my mind. So maybe running a camp wasn't just a pipe dream.

Of course, whether it was a dream or impending reality, I had to set it aside so we'd survive in the present real world. Then I happened to mention it to a fellow Olympian I'd been pretty close to. I knew he'd be receptive to even a crazy idea because the two of us had once stopped traffic by diving naked off the Hayden Bridge into Oregon's McKenzie River, forty feet below. No, we weren't roaring drunk, either. We just affected each other like that. Anyhow, he thought a camp was a great idea as well: thoroughly workable. Although my friend got involved in other things, having somebody I wasn't related to say I was on to something got my afterburners going. My dad and I started scouting locations, determined to find the best spot for a camp in the whole damn world.

Theresa: *Don's dad, whom we affectionately called Popeye, really got into the notion of a camp for boys. Whenever he and Don would go prospecting for potential sites for a camp, Mark just had to go with them to share the adventure. The little boy always came home excited about the animals he'd seen in the woods and how we were going to go live there. Despite being covered with bug bites, stickers, and all kinds of little scratches, he was happy as a clam. I know he hoped we'd be moving there the next week. It was so cute.*

No location seemed right, however. Maybe I was just being too choosy, but no place measured up to my expectations. There had to be enough high ground, trees, plus someplace for the kids to swim, preferably with meadowland close by. It seemed an impossible wish list. After months of prospecting, I finally found a property in the South Jersey Pinelands I thought looked fantastic, with woods, high ground, and adjacent meadowland. Dad had just been with us for our second son's christening, and I called him and shared the good news. "How about we do a walk-through and look the place over this Sunday?"

Man, he was happy, and he really got into it. "Why don't I bring up the trailer with a couple of horses so we can ride around the entire property?" he said. "We'd cover a lot more ground on horseback." He was so excited about the upcoming trip that he kept calling back that Saturday night to double-check directions and exactly when we'd meet. Unfortunately, on that Sunday, October 16, 1966, we never did tour the property together.

Theresa: *In August of 1966 I had our second son, George Jeffrey Bragg. There were a million Georges in the family already, so we called him Jeff, but there was no doubt he was named for Don's dad. Popeye was so excited about this latest member of the family being named for him that when we had Jeff's christening in early September, he was the first one to arrive, an hour early, carrying an immense teddy bear. On October 15, he phoned to wish me a happy birthday and go over his plans for the following day. Not only was he enthusiastic about riding the property with Don so that they could scrutinize every square foot, he was looking forward to our picnic. I planned to follow him and Don with the children and a hearty lunch. Early Sunday morning, however, the phone rang with the news that Popeye had had a heart attack.*

I remember packing the station wagon while Theresa dressed the children, and then we rushed to Salem Hospital. But my brother was standing in the corridor outside Dad's room. One look at his face, and we knew my father was gone.

Dad—invincible, indestructible, with his massive arms and powerful carpenter's hands. I couldn't believe he was dead. We thought he'd completely shaken off the heart problems he'd had in 1962. Well, that was the end of the camp, so far as I was concerned. That massive heart attack not only killed my father, it killed our plans as well. There was no way that I could make the camp a reality without him. Then I found out I didn't have to.

Theresa: *After we got back from Salem Hospital, I was in shock, but I realized we had to notify Popeye's employer of his death. I found his wallet and forced myself to go through it, looking for his company card. Then I saw something that looked out of place. Folded in among the family snapshots was a neat square of paper. Curious, I opened it, and discovered a series of diagrams with notes scribbled along the margins. I started to refold the paper, then stopped. I realized what I was holding. It was Popeye's layout for a series of cabins for Don's camp. Any contractor could follow his directions and build our cabins. With Popeye's funeral only days away, however, I knew it wasn't the time to give it to Don, so I tucked the paper away. Weeks later, I heard Don tell his brother that he didn't want to even think about a boys' camp; the idea simply had too much of their father in it. That's when I put Popeye's neatly folded square of paper into my husband's hand. As the realization of what it was dawned on Don, tears welled in his eyes for the loss of a father and the rebirth of their dream.*

The plans for the camp! I took those plans and put them in my wallet. Of course, I still needed time to absorb Dad's death, but after a few months my family convinced me that if I could get the financing, then we should make this dream come true. With this morale-building assist from Dad, I knew I could ferret out the money to get things started. Hell, since I had Theresa beside me, I could do anything.

The time I miss you most of all is just before you leave.

—*Don Bragg, "Leaving You"*

Theresa: *Don went after camp financing with the same beady-eyed single-mindedness that I see whenever he's prowling around the kitchen hunting for chocolate, his favorite sweet treat.*

Did I succeed? Damn straight! And I bought that beautiful parcel of land I'd spotted years before when I was begging Tastykake money from Sam. Once I owned the land, I was over the biggest hurdle to starting our camp. When the time came to begin construction, I gave Dad's folded paper to the contractor and said, "Just follow these plans, and we'll have a camp." My father-in-law, along with his Italian buddies, stepped in for my dad and helped me every step of the way. With Theresa, my father-in-law, and the Italian connection backing up my own drive, the dream started to take shape.

One big change I had to make in my new property's topography **was to** create someplace safe for the kids to swim. When Theresa first **saw** the place, her first question was typically practical. "Where will the kids swim? Is that river really safe enough for little kids?"

"It is not." The fifty-foot-wide Wading River was mainly shallow, but its bottom could be treacherous, often dropping away without warning. "But not to worry," I told her. "I'm gonna move the river."

She gave me a wary "God help us all!" look, and headed for the car. But I wasn't as crazy as I sounded. The previous owner had dug a little canal to fill a pond so he could splash around and cool off. No way would this dinky arrangement accommodate my campers, but I planned to enlarge the canal. I'd dredge out the sand and gravel bottom, sloping it to an eventual depth of eight feet, and then I'd have one hell of a swimming area. Besides, I figured I'd have enough sand from the dredging to spread a 200-foot beach for the kids—with a bulldozer's help, of course. Knowing what children will do in any body of water, I planned to add another outlet to the Wading River. That way the water could flow through the swimming area—even if we had a dry spell—and keep things from stagnating. So I hired a crane to come in and raise some hell, and before long I proudly called Theresa to come take a dip in our new swimming area.

She backed away in horror from my creation. "Oh no you don't! You're not getting me in that swimming hole. That water's horrible—it looks like it's been sitting in a ditch for fifty years."

Theresa wasn't exaggerating too much. The locals called the brown, opaque liquid *cedar water,* as if it picked up its color from flowing through the cedar forest. I think the coloration came from the iron in the soil, but whatever it was, Theresa was having none of it.

"Look, the water's perfectly clean," I argued. "It's better than clean. I hear the Indians say this water has incredible healing powers. Damn near miraculous!"

"Fine. Let the Indians swim in it. I'm not so much as sticking a toe into that murky mess. Just imagine what it would do to my white bathing suit. Don, it's the color of iced tea!"

"So don't wear a bathing suit."

"Besides," she continued, ignoring my lack of couth. "The water's so opaque, I'd never know what was in there with me."

"Honey, this is New Jersey. I guarantee there won't be any alligators or piranhas swimming around out here."

"Uh-huh," she said, giving me one last suspicious look before stalking away.

I did have one slight mishap on my way to creating a beach for the kids. The projected beach area was dotted with good-sized cedars, and they had to go. The idea was to take 'em down, then lay them out so we could spread the beach sand over them. That would dispose of the trees and give the beach a little height. My contractor had other ideas, however, once I'd taken down the trees with a chain saw.

"Look at the girth on these logs. They're too large to bury with the amount of sand we're going to have, Don," he said. "We'll have to burn the whole mess of 'em, first thing tomorrow." Then he got in his shiny black truck and headed home.

Okay, that was fine. But time was of the essence, and I thought I should give him a little hand with our project. So I doused the logs with gasoline and set a match to them. As the flames crackled into life, I felt pretty good. We'd be able to spread and level the sand first thing the next day. Then I took another look at my bonfire. The flames were licking greedily over the wood and mounting up to about twenty feet, and I'd only just lit the damn thing. So I'm running around wondering what to do, and I'm beginning to sweat. Here I am in the middle of the Wharton State Forest, and my attempts to accelerate my beach project had resulted in an inferno that was just getting warmed up. I had visions of newspaper headlines: "Pole-Vaulter Reduces New Jersey to Ashes." That idea really energized me, so I started going around throwing shovelfuls of sand on the burning logs, determined to tame the fire-breathing dragon. Next thing I hear is my lovely wife calling, "Don, that fire's pretty big, isn't it?"

I'm nearly blowing a gasket, but I managed to yell, "No shit, Honey!"

"Just so you know what you're doing," she said, and went back into our little camping trailer. Well, the fire roared away, with flames leaping thirty feet or better into the air. I started to feel helpless, since all my efforts had been absolutely futile.

Then I saw the helicopter.

It came buzzing in over the treetops and kind of hovered. I could see the pilot inside, and he started waving at me. So, being a friendly kind of guy, I waved back. Then he waved some more—well, to be honest, he started making these wild gestures, like a chimpanzee on speed. I'm just standing there looking up, wondering what in hell he wanted from me, when I saw a big cloud of something drop from the tail of the chopper. And I kept on standing there watching it come right for me. Yeah, he'd dropped a load of fire retardant on the fire, and I didn't have the sense to step out of the way. Then I realized that I felt like *I* was on fire, and went tearing over to the creek to wash the toxic whatever off my skin, which was burning like the devil. And when I staggered out of the creek, I realized I wasn't done yet. Driving up the road come two or three power fire wagons. These were boxy trucks—not Tinkertoy trucks, but not the big hook-and-ladder jobs either—that were built to navigate anywhere through the forest. So these trucks screech to a halt, and a bunch of firefighters come leaping out and start whaling away at the rest of the fire. They got it out pretty quick and then turned their attention to me.

"How in hell could this have started?"

I picked up my gasoline can. "Well … "

"You started a wood fire with gasoline? My God, have you lost your mind?"

"It's just that I needed to get rid of all this cedar wood to make room for a beach. I'm starting a summer camp, and … "

"Summer camp, my sufferin' butt! You can't have a fire even one-tenth this size without a permit, and they're only issued to a contractor. Let me guess. That would *not* be you, right?"

I kind of scratched my head, thinking, yeah, I guess Joe Peterson, my contractor, had said something about a permit. The firefighter was looking at me like I didn't have a brain in my head. "Hell, you're right in the middle of a state forest. What were you thinking?" He stopped talking for a minute, stared at me, and then said, "You're not from around here, are you? Where're you from, man, the *city*?"

The word spread quickly among the other guys. "Did you hear what this dumb son of a bitch did? He used gasoline to burn off this timber."

They had a good laugh at my expense, but that was okay, because the guy in charge said, "I'm not going to fine you or anything, because you didn't know what the hell you were doing. Just see that it doesn't happen again."

They took away my Smokey the Bear hat that day, but I felt like I'd gotten off easy. However, I still had to deal with Joe Peterson the next morning.

"What the hell happened?" He looked around the area, all cinders and ash. "So the minute my back's turned you start setting things on fire?"

"I was only trying to help," I said by way of an apology.

"Look, not only did I need a permit, I was under obligation to have a bulldozer on-site for fire control." He sat down on a charred stump and gazed around, surveying the potential for catastrophe. "Bragg," he said. "You're one lucky guy. If that wind had changed, you'd have lost your camp in two seconds."

Well, our beach finally took shape despite my close call. And that was pretty much that, except for the fact that Joe Peterson would look at me funny if I picked up anything more menacing than a pick or shovel.

Designing a project such as this from its primitive state to completion was surely an artistic creation in its own right. It also provided Kamp Olympik with that all-important ingredient: a waterfront playground in the wilderness. But like any artist, I was eager to improve on my work. Noticing that a nice stand of towering cedars was growing smack-dab up against the deep end of the swimming area, I knew I had to add a diving platform. I got busy and constructed a three-tier platform with heights of twelve, twenty-four, and thirty-six feet. For safety's sake, I also double-dredged the area below the diving platform. The kids would love it, and since only experienced swimmers could use it, I figured it would also be an incentive for the kids to improve their swimming skills. I thought it also had the potential to become a great arena for Challenge Night among the camp counselors.

So I had the swimming hole, but I still needed to line up enough campers to make the camp viable, and that meant spreading the word about my new endeavor. I volunteered to speak at every sports banquet in New Jersey. I'd start by retelling my Olympic adventures, and then, once the wine and good food had a chance to mellow out the audience, I'd make my pitch for Kamp Olympik. Invariably, I stirred up a whirlwind of intense interest, but then again, these people had had a few. Over forty guys assured me they'd send their kids to Kamp Olympik, so I felt certain I'd have a full roster in no time. Yet at the end of several months of soliciting, I only had ten actual signed applications.

By late May I was really starting to sweat, so I reached out to my buddies. One of them, my close friend Frank Nappi, was completely unfazed by my situation. "Come on up to the Outward Bound camp in Portland, Maine. There's somebody I want you to meet."

So off I go to Maine, where Frank introduced me to a pleasant-looking guy with thinning hair and worry lines around the eyes. "Don, this is the director of summer programs for the Newark School District."

Boy, did I give him a hearty handshake. I launched into a vivid description of Kamp Olympik, but I had to tell the fellow the truth. "Of course the camp's still under construction, but we'll be ready for business by July."

"Okay," he said, "Get the camp up and running by July first, and I'll send you ten kids per session for the entire season."

Hot damn. This was the shot in the arm I'd needed. But the guy was still talking.

"If you can get a solid tutorial program on-site, I might be able to send you even more kids eventually. Combine a tutorial program with what your camp can offer, swimming and running around in the fresh air, and you'll have a winner."

I hadn't given thought one to a tutorial program before, but if it would make Kamp Olympik fly, I was for it. So was Theresa when I told her about it. Of course that meant we'd have to recruit teachers yesterday, but hell, it'd be summer. Plenty of teachers would still be on the prowl for a few extra dollars, so I anticipated no problems. One other thing put a gleam in my eye. Camp Outward Bound had a network of rope swings installed for their campers. I could hardly wait to get home and build a Tarzanville for my camp as well.

Understand, I'd built the original Tarzanville over twenty years before, when I was ten years old. I'd just seen my first Tarzan movie with Johnny Weissmuller swinging out of the jungle, giving his hair-raising yodel. I came out of that movie with a new hero. I went home and pieced some scrap rope together, hauled my skinny ten-year-old butt up the immense tree by our house, and started making swings so I could be Tarzan. Damn, but I had a ball doing that. When the family moved to the outside of town right next to a real forest, I went nuts putting up swings everywhere! Kids came from all around to play on my Tarzanville's rope swings, landing platforms, and tree forts. They loved to play tag in the jungle with Tarzan, and it was a blast for all of us. Yeah, Kamp Olympik would have its own Tarzanville, but it had to wait till I assured the future of the camp.

The work involved in getting the place up and running was almost overwhelming, but I saw it as just another competition: me against everything. I became a multitasking fool, toting up construction costs while schmoozing with school board presidents even as I weighed the aesthetics of latrine building. I had to laugh. Using my athletic ability to win the Olympic gold medal was clearly only the warm-up for my current position as captain of the Kamp Olympik ditch-digging team. Everything started falling into place, and a lot of the credit goes to my special secret weapon, my fantastic wife. If she had to, Theresa could whip the lunatics in Congress into shape and ensure world peace with one hand and make gnocchi with the other, all the while raising some great kids.

And the camp would be all about kids and letting them have some fun. Theresa and I loved 'em, and that would be the backbone of Kamp Olympik's success. Hell, the two of us were truly excited about having a hand in developing responsible and productive adults. We couldn't wait to try our hands at these new challenges—both of us eat up challenges like candy. Anyhow, I immediately went into overdrive acquiring teachers and getting up to speed on reading and math programs. I was ready and willing to do whatever necessary to make this venture a success, even if it meant leading tough city kids in singing "Kumbaya."

Chapter Two

O pening day arrived July 1967 in a flurry of last-minute chores, like remembering where we'd put the toilet paper and telling Theresa's mom that, no, we didn't need fluffy curtains in the cabins. I was calm and cool, but when the kids and their parents started to arrive, I got goose bumps. Parents were excited and obviously felt secure about leaving their children in our care. That in itself was reassuring.

But there was still no sign of the kids from Newark, and the other campers were getting restless. All the campers were hollering that they wanted to go swimming, and who could blame 'em? It was ninety degrees and as humid as only the East Coast can get. So we got suited up, performed the first of many head counts, and raced down to the lake for our first official dip. The kids had just started into the water, when they all turned to face the growing sounds of Armageddon coming from just down the road.

We heard the incredible racket of shrieks and howls and just plain bedlam before we even saw the bus, and when I did see it, I didn't believe my eyes. Yup, it was the kids from Newark. Pop bottles, wads of paper, and shoes were shooting out of the bus like shrapnel from the kids hanging halfway out the windows. As the bus came to a stop, the children came scrambling all over each other to get out the door. After

Campers arriving.

observing the new arrivals, one of my other campers quickly noted the obvious. "Hey, Mr. Bragg. These kids are *black*!" I couldn't see the problem, but to little kids who'd only seen a handful of black faces in their lives, it was kind of intimidating. Once they started swimming and playing softball together, though, the children didn't give a tinker's toot who was black and who was white—they all just wanted to have fun.

Unfortunately, the camp's racial harmony did not sit well with the white moms and dads when they arrived on Parents' Day the following week. With hard mouths and indignant eyes they snatched their children out of Kamp Olympik's clutches, even though their kids were bawling that they wanted to stay. What can I say? I was stunned, but it was 1967, and America was in the throes of racial turmoil, which, incidentally, defined one of the stupidest periods of our history. With the loss of so many campers, I became horribly aware of the possibility that my camp might go under. I was preparing to jump off the nearest convenient bridge when the phone rang. It was the director of Newark's summer recreational programs.

"Hey, Don! I'm in a bit of a jam. There's a major problem with one of the camps I sent some kids to, and we need to switch them to another camp. Can you help me out?"

"Sure," I said dolefully, expecting maybe a couple of campers.

"Great, Don. I owe you one. So expect our twenty kids tomorrow?"

Twenty kids? Hot damn! I exulted silently as I punched the air. "I guess we can squeeze them in," I said, all casual.

"And," he continued, "you'll be enhancing that tutorial program with in-and-out testing, like we talked about, right?"

"Even as we speak." Actually, that wouldn't be a problem since all I needed to do was to hire a few more teachers. Since the summer was still young, I began recruiting again immediately and had the beefed-up program in full swing within a couple of days. O, God bless Newark!

<hr />

After our first three-week session, I knew we were on to something good: the comparison of the tests we'd given the kids before and after their three-week stint showed marked improvement. And it wasn't just our tutorial program that worked a little miracle. A few of the kids who were staying in foster homes were in bad shape emotionally, and it didn't take long to see why. When they took off their shirts for swimming, we'd sometimes see bruises and even burns on their skinny little bodies. Those kids needed extra TLC, and so we tried to provide it—everybody did, from Theresa and me to the counselors and even some of the other campers. Our own children also sized up the situation and began besieging us to adopt all the kids who'd clearly been abused. That unfortunately just wasn't possible, but it really tore up my wife—she's always been the compassionate one. At least we were able to rattle some official cages to ensure these kids were transferred to better homes.

Give me something to think about, a problem to solve that leaves no doubt.

Something monumental, an ultimate endeavor.

—*Don Bragg, "Consumed"*

It didn't take long for the word to spread throughout the New Jersey schools that we had a terrific program. Once school board directors started calling us up to talk about the camp, I felt we were over the first big hump. I couldn't ease up, though. Over the winter I continued to recruit from various school systems, traveling throughout the Delaware tri-state area to the boundaries of New York State. I'd seen the change Kamp Olympik had wrought in our first campers, and I was convinced our program would render any child better equipped to be effective both in school and in life. Hell, what kid wouldn't learn more in a safe, supportive atmosphere rather than in a dangerous city environment? We had a lot of convincing to do, but I believed in our program, so I put my reputation on the line in advocating Kamp Olympik. If the boards didn't come around after several visits, I took to haunting their meetings. Wherever they looked, they saw my forbidding face. "Ah, yes, Mr. Bragg. So nice to see you again," they'd say, looking all guilty and pathetic.

"About Kamp Olympik," I'd say. "There's still time to register your kids for my summer program." In short, I became their worst nightmare, the kind sunlight couldn't dissipate. Sure, most of them caved eventually. Once I had their approval, I was in hog heaven until I realized, however, this was no time for self-congratulation. It was up to me to prove we were as good as I'd claimed.

We had to expand the facilities for the second season, and the reward was more than monetary. We saw these children grow in knowledge and a disciplined way of life. They learned a new way of looking at things, too. To most of our beginning campers, a green tree was a potted plant growing in somebody else's window. And learning? Something for nerds. But after some time at Kamp Olympik, they came to recognize trees as the most beautiful structures in nature. They also realized education was something they needed, and they began to crave it. Damn, but seeing that going on was satisfying.

That first year we'd more or less grabbed people out of the air to get some sem-blance of a staff ready for opening day of camp, and it took us a year or two to give our new hires something resembling professional polish. Talk about a weird science experiment! For instance, this guy who'd worked for a school concession company applied for the position of camp cook. Since he'd cooked for hundreds of students, I thought we'd found our man. Yeah, right. Not only was the food only so-so, our food costs quickly became astronomical. Theresa's mom suggested he make soup for lunch with some of the meat and vegetables, but he ignored her. So I asked him about using leftovers, and his response immediately had me smelling a rat. First he got all snooty on me. "Leftovers? Are you serious? I throw them out, of course." His eyes started looking at everything except me, and then he changed the subject. So I started keep-ing my eyes open. We noticed that when he took a day off and left the grounds, his car seemed to be dragging its belly, like a pregnant basset hound. We were pretty sure he was pilfering the food that he was supposedly throwing away, which somehow never showed up in the garbage. No wonder our food costs were through the roof! So this grease monkey was history, but that meant finding a good cook for next season.

Theresa was an incredible cook, but she had her hands full with the camp and with me. She came from a long line of superb cooks, however, so I decided to approach my mother-in-law Yolanda about taking on the cooking chores for Kamp Olympik. She was appalled at the idea. *"Uomo pazzo!* I've never cooked for anybody but my family and our friends. Cook for that entire camp? You're out of your mind!"

"Yeah, but Yolanda, Sunday dinner at your house is twenty people, minimum. And your food is *fantastico!*"

"Still, so many people!"

"What about our family picnics? We're talking fifty people, and you don't even break a sweat!"

"Why do you keep harping on that crazy idea? I guess my daughter did marry a lunatic." Long pause. "You'd have to get me some help, of course."

We snagged her a couple of cookie boys to assist with food prep, and with the help of relatives, Mama Fiore's Kitchen was born. Though she was perturbed that some campers preferred a PB&J to her homemade pasta, we explained that most of the kids weren't used to three balanced meals a day. It took a little coaxing to get them to try anything different, but Mama's great food soon won them over. And not only the campers. As Mama Fiore's Kitchen became well known throughout all the Jersey school systems, we found that we began to be inspected more and more frequently. We were concerned until we realized that all the school directors merely wanted to have lunch at Kamp Olympik. Not only did Mama serve delicious, healthy food, but she was able to cut costs by an impressive margin. Best of all, her constant presence in the mess hall instantly created a great family atmosphere.

Theresa, who'd gone to camp as a young girl, had helped bring order into chaos our first year with the sensible suggestion that we immediately implement a program for junior counselors—counselors-in-training, or CITs. We had a good supply of candidates, older campers who combined good sense with street smarts. They jumped at the chance of working their way toward becoming counselors, and there sure wasn't anything better to engage their energies at home. These kids made a wonderful contribution to the camp line of command, and we made plans to augment their numbers the second season.

I also had to give thought to the all-important aquatic director. The one who served the first year was a terrific gal with superb qualifications, but she only stayed with us the one year. And we needed someone who was Red Cross certified, since it was the aquatic director who'd certify the counselors in water safety. The counselors needed that certification, too; our camp bible—the rules and regs for children's camps—demanded it. Most of them were already more than qualified, but we needed that official certification. Small problem there: the second aquatic director we hired had invented all his credentials. I didn't uncover his skullduggery until late in the season, so the rest of the team wasn't certified either. Lesson learned. There were no casualties during his tenure, but from then on we followed through and verified all resumes and references before opening day.

Now my Uncle Joe Bragg, who spent the winters in Florida, worked summer nights as a pari-mutuel ticket seller at the Atlantic City Race Track. He was easy to have around, so he started living in our camp trailer and worked into being the camp maintenance man. Then one day we were boasting about everything we'd each done in our lives, and he showed me his Teamster union card. Bingo! That meant he was qualified to drive large vehicles, from trucks to limos and buses. That Teamster card looked as good to me as an Olympic medal. Now we had a bus driver to transport the kids to off-property special events like visits to the shore or the cranberry bogs, or even to a day at the races on Family Day. Uncle Joe liked kids, and nothing rattled him, so if the campers got rambunctious on a bus trip, I didn't have to worry that he'd cuss them out or leap from the bus and go shrieking off into the woods, like one driver almost did.

The forty-acre camp property had everything: meadows, pine forest sprinkled with cedar, and the Wading River, which sighed past Kamp Olympik on its way to the Atlantic. It also boasted something I hadn't counted on: three cabins, two of which were in great shape. It was so nice having something I didn't need to build myself that I felt like a kid at Christmas. One cabin was beyond repair, with rotted wood and varmint droppings throughout, so we razed it and trucked it away to the dump. My biggest need was a place to stow our sporting and aquatic equipment out of the reach of busy little fingers. Even when I'd done that, the cabin had plenty of room to accommodate our arts and crafts center. No, I didn't run the arts and crafts program myself. If I end up in hell, I may spend eternity stringing wax beads and weaving pot holders, but that just ain't my bag while I have anything to say about it. Renée, my oldest daughter, was fantastic at thinking up craft projects, so she took the helm of the A&C activity. The counselors made no bones about coveting that sturdy third cabin, which was made of original cedar logs and shakes, but Uncle Joe eventually claimed it.

Before I built a cabin for my family, I spent a few nights in the third cabin, and it didn't take me long to realize I was not alone. There was a constant, barely audible rustling in the attic, punctuated by a whirring commotion at both dawn and dusk: to me, that spelled bats. One more thing to tend to, but then I realized the upside. Yolanda would be pleased. She'd always sworn I had bats in my belfry.

The next night at dusk, my suspicions were confirmed, as a dusky cloud of bats exited from the cabin's eaves. The damn things were clearly breeding in the attic, so I knew we had to storm the place and clear it out. Okay, next step: call for volunteers.

"So who's up for getting rid of the bats?" I demanded of my assembled counselors. Not a peep out of anybody. "C'mon, they're bats, they're in the cabin, and they need to go somewhere else. Who'll lend a hand?"

"But that might drive them away," a skinny guy we called Jinx finally muttered.

"That's what I had in mind," I shot back, a little puzzled.

"But we kinda like having them around. Why do we have to get rid of them?"

I felt like I was talking to aliens. "Because they're bats." A bat, so far as I was concerned, was just a triple helping of ugly. I'd always assumed God couldn't make up his mind whether to make a rat, a pig, or a bird, so he made this thing with an upturned snout in a squashed face, then added whiskers, pointy ears and teeth, and an outstandingly foul smell. What sane person would want those flapping around in their house? "What the hell's going on here?"

"We play with them," admitted one of the other counselors after a long silence.

I stared at them in disbelief. This was weirdness beyond my comprehension.

"I mean we use them like Ping-Pong balls."

I still didn't know what in hell they were up to with the bats. "Explain."

"Okay, you know how bugs and moths are always circling around the big two-lamp post? Well, the bats cruise in to eat the bugs."

"Yeah," chimed in somebody else. "We swiped some of Yolanda's old brooms from the kitchen, and one of us throws gumdrops up in the air. Then the rest of us wait till the bats' radar homes in on the candy—you know, when it falls. That's when we take turns swiping at the bats with the brooms."

Jinx continued the story. "Right below the light, that's home plate. The idea is to drop a bat, but after three strikes, you're out, and you have to take a turn throwing the gumdrops."

Okay, so my staff was just having fun whacking bats, not freaking out on me. "Terrific, but keep those brooms out of Yolanda's sight." From what I know about what animals do when they're startled, the bats would be doing their share of dropping, too. I had no intention of scrubbing bat shit out of broom straw, no matter what Theresa's mom said. The bat game developed into a nightly ritual for the counselors, for the bats kept coming … and coming. And we owed all our fun to the congenial breeding ground lurking under the eaves of Uncle Joe's cabin. It was hard on the brooms, but there were no losers in the bat-the-bat contest. It also built a camaraderie among the counselors that gave them a leg up in dealing with the kids. And the bats either liked the gumdrops or the quick rubdown with the brooms. Like I said, everybody was a winner.

Uncle Joe wasn't too keen on the bats, however, so when he took possession of the cabin, he slept with a baseball bat at his side. When the chittering above him became deafening, he'd pound on the wall with his bat. This shut up the bats, but it also shook loose a shower of bat shit. Before too long, he moved to the trailer behind the dining hall, and I didn't blame him. Uncle Joe was the Bat Cabin's last full-time tenant, but we continued to use it for storage and for sleepover guests we didn't like too much. I guess we were pretty sadistic. After we watched the unwelcome guests go into the Bat Cabin, we'd set up chairs in front of the dining hall and make bets on how long it would take for them to come screaming out. When they did, we laughed till our guts ached.

Uncle Joe and family at the "Bat Cabin."

Theresa: *Don's story about the bats is typical of the crazy things our counselors would do, but they also did a great job with the children, giving them both home- work support and companionship in the evenings. Don and I, of course, were there for the campers 24/7. Since I had four kids of my own, I couldn't help but cuddle the tearful little eight-year-olds when they were trying so hard to be brave. Giving them big hugs and talking to them in a mommy sort of way usually did the trick, and they returned our affection with a vengeance. All I—or any other woman—had*

to do was walk across the compound during free period, and a crowd of kids would
descend on us, fighting to see who could get the closest. It was a privilege for all of us
to give these children that extra shot of nurture and intense mentoring to help them
achieve more in their lives.

Yeah, it was rewarding, but geez, it sure took a lot out of the staff, since we had to monitor each kid like mama hawks. Some of these children were coming up against constraining rules for the first time in their lives, so we had to be flexible as well as vigilant. And no rule book prepared us for the insanity the kids were able to churn up. Their more fiendish habits included jamming up the hoppers in the bathroom with anything that wasn't tied down or on fire. And they loved sabotaging a neighboring cabin just before inspection, so their victims would get stuck with cleaning the bathrooms (and they wouldn't). Throwing stones was also a favorite pastime—nothing vicious, just doing something to be doing something. But we had to come down on the kids with both feet on that one. Of course, no stone that actually hit somebody was ever thrown by a camper. No, it was always a combination of Bigfoot and a visitation of some demonic clan. It wasn't exactly that the kids were lying. I think they wanted to believe that they hadn't done anything bad, so they actually bought the wild tales they told. Hell, I believed them myself. Once I saw a kid whip a rock across the camp that whacked another kid in the head. So I grabbed both campers and brought them into the dining hall. "This youngster needs first aid," I announced. "He got hit in the head by a rock, and *this* is the kid that threw it!"

So the kid that threw the stone starts in, "Please, Mr. Braggs. I kinda heard this noise, and I look up, and here's a stone flying through the trees over the dining hall, and it goes and hits Jimmy in the head. He's my pal, and I'd never hit him with some dumb stone." And he starts bawling. Now I *saw* the kid throw the stone, and I'm almost believing he didn't do it. That's gotta be some twisted corollary to Murphy's Law! Of course a few campers never really did adjust. Used to a totally freewheeling environment, they found my rules preposterous, the structure of camp routine unbearable. "What do you mean, make the bed? That's my mom's job." Or, "I never go to bed this early. I'm up 'til one or two o'clock!"

"Not at Kamp Olympik, you're not!"

Not being able to do what they wanted when they wanted absolutely killed some kids. "Don't feel like school. Gonna take out one of the Hondas instead." Of course the rules weren't just for our convenience. Structure and discipline were as necessary to the kids' education as books and pencils. A few campers became such pains in the butt, however, that I shipped them back home. As the bus rolled away, I heard them yell, "We're finally outta jail. We're not cleaning no more stupid cabins." Okay, you can't please everybody. But the next week, when the bus delivered substitute campers to fill the contract—guess who's on the bus? Yup, the campers who'd thought I was a nasty backcountry drill sergeant from hell.

"Why'd you come back, if Kamp Olympik was so horrible?" I asked.

"Mrs. Fiore's food," said one.

"The cool motorcycles and swinging in the trees."

The others said, "I dunno," and stared at me like *I* was crazy. I guess the fact that they were bored out of their gourds back home made plenty of food, unusual activities, and just plain fun look damn good.

One thing we learned fast was that it was pretty much a full-time job making sure the kids stayed put. The deep woods presented a temptation to wander off, and if a child was homesick, he seemed to think that a five-minute walk would bring him back to his house in Newark or wherever. So we kept our eyes open day and night. Which is why all of the staff looked like extras from the film *Night of the Living Dead*.

We featured a chocolate-brown pony, Choo-choo, in one of our classes that first year, but he required year-round care. In fact, if we weren't shoveling food into him, we were shoveling away little gifts from his hind end. It was more than we could handle. But even while Choo-choo was with us, I created something the kids liked even better than the pony. Upstream and immediately contiguous to the camp was a two-acre island I also owned, just loaded with towering old cedar trees. Some of them were fifty feet high and

Choo-choo (pony) with Don and son Mark.

boasted a diameter of two feet, and they reminded me that I'd decided to create a special playground for the Kamp Olympik kids. If the Outward Bound camp used a series of rope swings to boost their campers' agility and self-confidence, I could do the same or better for our little guys.

And so Tarzanville lived again. To gain access to Tarzan's island kingdom, the campers followed a narrow path from the beach to a tall cedar at the edge of the camp property, maybe twenty yards from Tarzanville Island. It was an easy climb to a log spanning the intersecting river. The kids crossed the log, aided by a rope suspended about three feet above and parallel to it as a guide rail, and once they crossed that log, they arrived at the commodious crotch of a stalwart cedar, the takeoff point for the first rope swing.

Of course, installing the swings was no slam dunk. The trees in our cedar lowlands were tall but had no large spreading branches to attach the ropes to. It was up to me to provide what God had left out. Targeting all the trees within ten feet of each other, I proceeded to create my own branches. My idea was to suspend a log or a pipe between the trees, wrapping the center of the suspension with pieces of inner tube to eliminate friction on the rope. There was no way I was going to replace the damn ropes every other week.

Counselor balancing on log over stream.

Do you know what it's like to climb to the top of a fifty-foot tree? Damn scary. I wondered what would happen if I fell. Would I be lucky and go splat on the ground below, or would I get impaled someplace painful on a branch halfway down? I wasn't being paranoid, either. Not only did I have to get to the top of the tree, I had to drag a substantial log or pipe with me, which was damn near suicidal if there was any wind. Most of the counselors turned varying shades of green when I asked for help, but one actually volunteered to give me a hand. It was Barry Ross, whose dad was Olympic distance runner H. Browning Ross. This Olympian had offered me my first scholarship in pole-vaulting to St. Joseph College when I was a junior in high school. A great guy—and Barry took after his father. Barry eventually became assistant director of the camp and my all-around confidant, but I think at the time he might've wondered

Counselor swinging on Tarzan ropes.

why he'd volunteered to leap around in a tree with a wild man named Bragg. As we worked on the highest and longest swing, a stiff wind kicked up. In the top of the tree where we were perched, it felt like a baby hurricane. With our tree swaying wildly, it was all we could do to finish our job. We managed to jam each end of the pipe close to a stumpy branch on each tree, and then we fastened them to the main trunks. This was not too hard, and easy to get right. But we had one last fun chore to accomplish.

"We have to climb out and attach the rope right in the center," I said.

"What do you mean *we*?" demanded Barry.

"You're younger and more agile, and I weigh more than you do."

"You're older and wiser," he countered, then we laughed, because we both knew we were bullshitting each other.

"Hey, we've lashed this pipe securely, and I'll steady it," I assured him. "Besides, I'm right here. If you have trouble, just reach out a hand, and I'll pull you in."

"Like hell you will. I know you: you'll save your own neck first."

Giving me a fearsome look, he began inching out onto the pipe. But as he attached the rope, the wind roared into high gear, and the pipe began to pitch and roll like a kayak in heavy surf. I hung on to the pipe with everything I had: hands, legs, feet, but it kept on bucking. With the job done, Barry wriggled back to the top of our cedar, and I pulled him to safety. I couldn't believe the courage he'd summoned up to perform such a feat. When we finally got out of that damn tree, we were both shaking and near collapse due to the constant strain of working in the treetops.

It took us a week to complete the first swings, though Tarzanville eventually boasted eight rope swings, three platforms, plus six logs suspended between trees as landing stations. Then came the fun part. I had five or six counselors hang on to each rope in turn. That tightened the knots but, more important, it verified the weight support of the superstructure as well as the test poundage of the ropes. That was vital.

I remember when my dad had decided to check out the safety of my original tree swings. I'd pieced together sections of that hairy rope—sisal, they call it—and Dad gave it an emphatic thumbs down. He carried two pieces of the sisal up the tree to make a double thickness, tied the rope to the tree, and swung off to test it. Now I weighed about fifty pounds, maybe, and my dad was pushing two hundred. So he swung out, and he looked mighty fine until the rope snapped like twine—which is what sisal pretty much is. I was really impressed by his landing. I'd had no idea I had a father whose body could bounce all over the yard like that. It was the last time he came anywhere near my swings, though, so it all worked out fine, except for the doctor bill.

But when I set up Kamp Olympik's Tarzanville, I took a leaf from Dad's book and ran the route to make sure the ropes were coordinated mechanically. There was more to designing Tarzanville's rope swings than just sticking ropes on trees. The ropes had to be adjusted so they'd swing perfectly, like pendulums, so I checked them out myself before any kid got near them. I had to engineer each swing properly to ensure a smooth transition, log to log. Since Tarzanville's inhabitants came in all sizes from half-pint (the youngest campers) to big galoot (me), I knotted the ropes to provide grips at varying intervals to accommodate different heights. That prevented anybody from losing their grip and just slipping down the rope to the ground eight or ten feet below. Kids figured out right away which knot to use; it was a foolproof system. For balance, we also tied a parallel rope just above the suspended logs that made it easier for the little kids. Of course, you might miss the damn platform. If you did, you'd have to slither down the rope and climb the tree again. There was an eight-foot corridor cleared between each log or landing station, and fortunately we kept collisions with trees to a minimum.

The landing stations were points of transfer to other rope swings, and this network could handle a dozen or more little Tarzans at the same time. When we completed Tarzanville, campers could climb up a tree, walk a log, and begin swinging throughout the woods. As they got into the spirit of Tarzanville, two cabins would launch frenetic games of tag, with plenty of showing off and crashing into trees. The entire camp would pick sides and cheer or razz their airborne buddies.

Don testing Tarzan ropes.

Though the kids loved swimming, canoeing, and basketball, until I introduced the Honda 50s, Tarzanville ruled supreme as their favorite activity. And you didn't have to qualify to swing on the ropes, whereas the kids had to pass a safety test before taking out one of the Hondas. Thirty years later, after I sold the camp, I visited Tarzanville, and damn if I didn't spot several rusting pipes still tied to the tops of a few trees. Man, did I feel proud! Looks like Tarzan did a good job of construction with the help of nylon rope. It lasts forever.

At the start of each session, I'd introduce the assembled kids to the Tarzanville concept. Trumpeting my Tarzan yells, I'd swing around the rope course, and then drop down in the midst of the kids. They'd be standing there with big eyes and mouths wide open, and I'd hear comments like, "Did you hear that guy? He really must be Tarzan. *Wow!*" Stuff like that would keep me chuckling all day.

Though it wasn't my first priority, I also constructed a pit for pole-vaulting exhibitions. I doubt most of the new kids had the slightest idea of what pole-vaulting might be, but they caught on quick. It was funny to see them grabbing six-foot-long sticks to try vaulting over a blueberry bush or a caterpillar or a frog. When they succeeded without landing on their cans, they'd strut around all proud, which really tickled me. It reminded me of my earliest attempts at vaulting in the lot behind Weinberg's furniture store, where I learned by jumping over ditches and clotheslines using the discarded bamboo poles they used to roll rugs around in the old days.

After that first year, we started to tighten up and streamline camp operation. As soon as the children arrived, we pounced on them with the
Metropolitan tests. It was kinda cute the way some little kids would
swear they were in sixth grade just to be with their brothers, but we had to determine
their grade level pronto. The tutorial program we developed became a stunningly
effective way of disseminating quality education—fast. We needed fast, too. We had
three weeks to give them the foundation they'd need for the most important and vulnerable years of their lives.

But there were no stuffy desks at Kamp Olympik. We sat the kids down outdoors
at picnic tables instead, and they instantly expected a good time. Who the hell can
stay grumpy at a picnic table? Congregating around the tables under the spreading
branches of shade trees, the kids were comfortable and relaxed and open to instruction. The youngsters seemed to enjoy the more concentrated approach, with a solid
hour of reading each morning and an hour of math after lunch. Each one had his own
book, but the books played second fiddle to the relationship between the kids and
the teachers. The counselors did some of the tutoring, the campers that could helped
the ones that couldn't, and the certified teachers concentrated on those who tested
way below par. Our methods were not only efficient in helping the kids learn, they
also produced excellent test results at the end of each session. Under our system, the
kids improved an average of eight-tenths of a grade in math and six-tenths of a grade
in reading, which is pretty damn good for three weeks. Of course, they didn't get
sidetracked with history or social studies. The kids had a limited attention span, so I
made sure that nothing distracted from our main objectives of reading and math. It
was amazing what a little one-on-one instruction can do. Our results impressed the
hell out of the respective school boards and qualified us for the all-important Title I
funding, the backbone of our camp income. And that was after only one year. Damn,
I was good!

Valuing maturity, I'd decided to go with counselors eighteen to twenty-one years of
age the first year, but it didn't work out, big time. I'll tell you one good thing my early
concentration on athletic superiority did for me; it kept me away from booze. These
young counselors were at the age when drinking was the supercool thing to do. They
saw nothing wrong with devoting all their spare time to skipping off to Atlantic City, a
mere thirty miles away, to tie one on and sow wild oats. I saw plenty wrong with it.

"Where the hell you guys been, and what have you been into?"

"Come on, Don. We just had a little fun in Atlantic City. And we haven't been into
anything. Don't know whatchyur gettin' at."

"Gimme a break. I smelled the beer on you halfway across camp."

"Why're you making this big stink over a few beers? We'll be fine for the first head
count tomorrow."

And I thought I'd been pissed off before! "None of you booze hounds are in any shape to monitor kids *tonight*. You get your day off. Any other time I expect you bozos to stay in camp and hang out with the kids. Got it?" Hell. If there'd been an emergency, we'd need all hands on deck and on their toes, not weaving around, unable to find the damn latrine.

Well, when we restricted their road trips, these weasels began pooling their funds and having a buddy pick up beer for late-night carousing. Having even a few counselors bombed out of their skulls wasn't what I had in mind, so the following year we decided to recruit younger counselors.

We reached out to several athletic directors and coaches of surrounding high schools and asked them to recruit us some counselors. I wanted dedicated athletes, yeah, but they had to be good students and fairly straight arrows as well. So we started building a team that enjoyed the outdoors, liked sports, and thought hanging out with an Olympic champion was cool. With everybody more or less on the same page, we were able to create ingenious challenges between the counselors as well as between their individual cabins. We featured speed and distance races, dives with varying handicaps, basketball, and canoe races. The kids also loved it when we'd drop them off throughout the forest in teams of two and let them practice woodsmanship by finding their way home. This kept them extremely busy and motivated not only as individuals but also as a group, and it sent morale sky high. These fifteen- and sixteen-year-olds did a great job, despite a glitch or two at the onset.

When they showed up that second year, they were really feeling their oats. Feeling their oats? Hell, they were drunk with power and decided to try and impress *me* with that fact, if you can believe it. They arrived on a Friday so they could get their bearings before the campers showed up, and right off the bat, here they come, telling me how their vacation schedule should be programmed. "We get Monday off, right?"

"Are you out of your mind? You guys get one day off for every week of work. You're lucky. My wife and I don't get any holidays. Hell, we don't even get any breaks!"

"Yeah, but we think we should get this Monday off."

"Oh, really? Well, your day off comes after you've worked for a week. Welcome to the real world."

"No fair!" Well, I'd wanted younger kids; it looked like I'd gotten 'em. They huddled for a minute, then declared, all smug and sure of themselves, "Then we're going on strike."

"That's okay with me," I smiled. "Just clear off of camp property. Call your parents or whoever, but leave the camp." I stopped smiling and roared, "Now!"

Some of the kids were ready to back down, but their spokesman wavered forward. "Are you kidding? The camp can't function if we leave?"

"What jackass told you that?" I asked, looking as malevolent as only I know how to do. "I'll get a skeleton crew together, and they'll do your work until we can recruit. I'll take control of a couple of cabins and sleep with the campers. The counselors-in-training will man the other cabins. So get going; we don't need you." Now the last thing I wanted to do was to sleep on a pint-sized canvas bunk with my feet sticking out a country mile—not with my bad back—but I continued to shovel it on. "My son, Mark, my brother, and our nephews will take care of the smaller campers. Rich and Barry will handle the rest. So go on and call your parents. The phone's in the mess hall."

They huddled for another union meeting, then came back with, "Okay, but we want … "

"No buts. Case closed," I thundered. "Stop telling me what you want. In fact, stop talking. The ten of you can just leave." No one was going to tell me how to supervise my business, especially not some young wet-behind-the-ears kids.

Well, you've never seen anybody get their butts down off their high horse so fast.

"Aw, please, don't send us home. We'll do what you say."

I think I managed to look magnanimous as I accepted their apology. At the very least I kept my profound relief from showing. I'd avoided a huge pain—in the back—but I would've happily eaten nails to call their bluff, regardless of the inconvenience or indigestion. I dismissed the counselors with this parting shot. "Since you've finally shown some maturity, you can have two days off after the first week." So much for personnel problems … thank God I'm the boss.

My son Mark and my nephews did in fact become counselors and my daughters became the arts and crafts instructors. Our youngest son Jeff was way too young for official responsibility, but he just blended in with the campers during their activities. You could always see my kids bustling around, acting like staff members. With my brother Georgie cruising by now and then to give a hand, the family enterprise was truly taking shape.

Chapter Three

One skill we quickly mastered was how to unload the buses while retaining some semblance of sanity. Our head count had to be exact or we'd have confusion from the get-go. Three buses usually arrived together, and with only one counselor assigned to each one, we didn't have a chance. Even when we unloaded them one at a time, it took several of us per bus, because when we opened the bus doors, it was like unscrewing a jar of grasshoppers: the kids would go leaping all over creation. Some would start running and wouldn't stop 'til a counselor tackled them. Once we got them straightened out and into the bathroom for a pit stop, we'd assign campers to cabins according to age for easier socializing. Boy, the way they lied about their age so they could stay with their friends or family! However, we'd found that even one older child in a cabin could make bullying an issue, and we didn't want our campers intimidated. We even separated brothers to ensure the playing field was even for all campers. Once we caught on to this distribution system, the camp ran more smoothly.

Of course, we soon figured out we had to frisk our campers upon arrival.

Understand, these were mainly good kids, but some of them brought mighty peculiar objects to camp, sometimes out of fear, sometimes because they wanted to look like a big deal to the other campers. So we had to pat down everyone for contraband: matches, cigarettes, weapons, and the occasional stash of pot. Now and then, the counselors would find knives, brass knuckles, or other instruments of destruction on a few of our little darlings. I got such a kick out of seeing how shocked the counselors were, like they'd all grown up in Mayberry or someplace. They sounded like disapproving mother hens when they informed the kids that the confiscated implements of mayhem would be returned upon their departure from camp, not before.

Next, we'd give out freshly sanitized sleeping bags. Did I say sanitized? If we were lucky: more often than not we had to destroy the ones used by bed wetters. Nearly daily, we had to scrub and air the bunk beds of the younger campers, but I couldn't blame 'em. Hell, most of them lived next to terrible things going on right in their neighborhoods; no wonder they got the piss scared out of them at night. And having somebody else coming down hard on them was the last thing they needed. Luckily, the beds were removable and constructed with heavy-duty canvas, so we were able to cope.

As the camp increased in size and numbers, other new problems surfaced. We were now dealing with kids from neighborhoods or towns that'd made war on each other on their home turf. Though it stimulated a healthy competitiveness in the games we played throughout the day, it also fueled night attacks on cabins of rivals. Of course we stepped up night patrols, but the minute the counselors focused their flashlights on suspicious noises, they'd see little groups of kids presumably on the way to the john, smiling and waving. I sensed immediately they looked too damn innocent not to be up to something. Nothing was definitely amiss, however, except that the camp population was continually en route to the latrine until the wee hours of the morning. Since we saw nothing indictable, we ignored our misgivings.

Once we started repairs in the off-season, however, we'd find socks filled with stones stuck way up on the roofs of the cabins. Since we were reasonably certain the squirrels hadn't left them up there, we had a pretty good idea of what some of those kids had been up to on the way to the latrine. Boy, staying ahead of their wicked little minds really kept us on our toes. It was worth it, though.

Our constant surveillance not only kept us current with camp maintenance, it ensured that the young campers could enjoy the camp unafraid. Their camp experience became what we'd intended: a fun, carefree time. We also added more advanced activities for the older campers to keep them out of trouble. I believe that good kids can get into mischief when they're bored—I know I did. To fine-tune the program for the older campers, we added overnight canoe trips and established a later hour for their bedtime. Since they got to stay up later, these kids could play hoops with the counselors and on occasion beat them. It was to harness

Don and campers preparing for canoe trip.

some of the more disciplined older campers' restless energy that we'd originally created a counselor-in-training program. The CITs did a great job, and Theresa and I watched them growing up day by day. It was great! They couldn't wait to become counselors, so they snapped up any extra responsibilities I asked them to undertake. They considered it a special treat when they got to fill in on the counselors' days off, a test run under the supervision of a staff member. Eventually these CITs became not only part of our staff, they became competent young men. We are proud to say that many boys passed through the trees and streams of Kamp Olympik and went on to become prominent citizens.

One guy who helped with this very positive transformation was Nick Werkman. I'd met him during a basketball game with some of my younger friends when we were living in Trenton. The younger guys liked me on their team because, though I could rebound and hold my own on defense, I had no illusions of being a star. When I got my hands on the ball, I always passed to somebody else in position to score—which usually happened to be Nick. I wasn't surprised when I found out he was not only a star player at Seton Hall University, but also the leading scorer in the nation in his junior year. He was in the top three as a senior: a superb athlete. Anyway, the two of us became good friends, and I sort of became his mentor during and after college.

Back then, I was heavily involved in politics and thought I might well have a future in that field—so long as the Democratic candidate for governor won. Perhaps by painting an overly rosy picture of how far we could go in politics, I talked Nick into working with me on a project to support my party's gubernatorial candidate. Since the candidate's speeches had been getting a chilly reception, I recruited some well-known athletes to introduce him at each of his campaign stops. Once my program was implemented, our candidate's speeches were much more enthusiastically received. Nick and I were both ecstatic, and when our guy was elected governor, we were sure we'd be going places in politics.

Yeah, right. All my years of athletic competition failed to prepare me for the vicious feeding frenzy that ensued as the party faithful vied for jobs in the new administration. Hell, it was like a pack of hyenas tearing into a dead carcass, and neither Nick nor I made the cut when the law of the jungle was in force. Needless to say, we both were very disappointed, and I'd say Nick felt a little betrayed by me. I remember assuring him, "Look, if anything materializes in the future, I won't forget you."

The ironic look he gave me told me he didn't take my assurances seriously, but I meant what I said.

During my stint working for the state I'd met and become good friends with Steve Farber, a special assistant to the governor. By the time I got Kamp Olympik off the launchpad, Steve had become special assistant to the president of Harvard University. An acquaintance of his was leaving Boston for a position at a brand-new state college under construction near Atlantic City.

"Just how far from Atlantic City are we talking about?" I asked.

"Down in your neck of the woods, in the South Jersey Pinelands," Steve said. "My friend doesn't know the area, and he asked if I knew anybody who could help him recruit personnel, so I gave him your name. Hell, you know everybody."

So Steve's friend dropped by the camp with his assistant, and we started thumbing through the various job descriptions. Then one line of print jumped off the page at me. "How about this one for the athletic director? Hell, I'd like a crack at that one myself."

The guy looked me over. "You really mean that?"

"Could I take one day a week off during the summer? I need to keep an eye on my camp."

"Not a problem. The school's basically closed during the summer." He glanced at his notes. "Of course, you'd have to hire your own people: your staff, the basketball coach, et cetera."

"Yes!"

I found out Nick was teaching and coaching high school basketball in North Jersey. When I called him up and said "Hi, Nick, how ya doing?" I nearly laughed out loud, because his voice absolutely crackled with suspicion.

"Fine, how are you doing?" he responded in guarded tones, clearly wondering what the madman from Penns Grove wanted now.

"Remember how I promised I wouldn't forget what you did for me back in Trenton? Well, it's payback time: I've got a job offer for you."

There was dead silence on the line. I think if he could've sniffed my breath through the wires for traces of too many martinis, he would've. "What in hell are you talking about?"

"Nick, how would you like to become a college basketball coach and an assistant director of their athletic program?"

His voice impatient, Nick snapped, "Quit fooling around, Don, I'm not in the mood for it."

"Yes, but …"

"Now look," he cut in severely. "I've just bought a new home near Toms River and the mortgage plus the commute is killing me, so take your practical jokes and … "

"That's less than an hour away from here; much easier than Newark. So what do you say?"

More silence. Then, "Are you offering me a coaching job?"

"You'd have to interview with the other administrators, but basically, yes." Knowing his dedication and his knowledge of basketball, I wasn't being glib: I believed in him.

So Nick came to the college for an interview, and of course he aced it. I'd paid off a long-overdue obligation, and the college acquired a first-class basketball coach. Both of us being highly competitive, it didn't take Nick and me long to resume our athletic rivalry. We really got into a one-on-one basketball competition that basically didn't stop. One day after a game I commented that we were just about even in the series.

"We were," said Nick with a grin. "But I'm leading now."

"Oh, yeah, smartass?" I grinned back, not believing an iota of what he'd said.

"Yup. We were tied at 671, then I got on a winning streak. So I'm ahead."

That was typical of the meticulous attention Nick gave his sport. He was a great guy, and the staff gladly welcomed him to the Kamp Olympik basketball venue. Nick and I teamed up with three other counselors against our resident giant—6' 8" Doug Kemble—and a bunch of his local buddies. Talk about competitive! The testosterone flowed unchecked, and despite our friendship, sometimes we'd really get into it over a contested block or accusation of traveling. Occasionally Theresa and her mom, Yolanda, would call a time-out and present us with something delicious to eat. Then and only then did the wound-up competitors start to chill out and act normal, at least until we'd start razzing each other without mercy again. Who could eat Yolanda's stuffed-veal roll with a stony face and an angry heart? Nobody, that's who. Thanks, Yolanda—you saved us from athletic Armageddon.

One of the things that kept us going during the grueling basketball competition was our wildly enthusiastic audience. The campers couldn't get enough of our games, and cheered noisily for Kamp Olympik's team. We won more than our share, which kept camp enthusiasm high. But, God almighty, it was hot. Playing in the humid hundred-degree heat, we were burning up and dehydrated. I do believe we experienced the beginning of actual meltdown. But playing at Kamp Olympik, we found quick respite in the cool river only fifty feet from the court.

Every so often, my old friends Sam and Dick would visit the camp to watch the games and—being Italian—to eat Yolanda's delicacies. One time, while Sam was hoisting a forkful of pasta, he said, "These basketball games of yours are a helluva lot more exciting than what I've seen in the semi-pro leagues in Trenton. Why don't you sell tickets for the games?"

"That's right," continued Dick in the same vein. "And you could charge extra for a picnic of fresh-steamed corn, pasta, crabs, and clams. You'd make a fortune."

"No way," I said. "We're just amateurs having fun and trying to kill each other. Let's not spoil it."

That was the day I had a little surprise for Sam. Right in the middle of chow, I presented him with a stack of boxes and a large piggy bank. The boxes were full of Tastykakes and the piggy bank was full of change: payback for his support of my Tastykake habit during leaner days. Sam laughed his head off, got kind of teary, and then drank a fast glass of Chianti to help himself recover. Seeing him with that piggy bank was pretty satisfying. Then I looked across the table and saw Nick, and knowing I'd given him a nudge to the job he was born to do was frosting on the cake.

Though he never joined the Kamp Olympik staff, Nick was there for those kids—and they really idolized him. He gave them talks, and not just about sports. Because of his reputation as such a dedicated athlete, the kids listened intently to what he had to say about self-discipline and self-respect. If ever he saw an opportunity to help a kid turn his life around, he took advantage of it. Period. That was how Nick conducted himself, and Theresa and I will always be grateful to him for that.

With the growing reputation of our camp, we were booked for what I considered our capacity—a hundred campers—for our third season. Just two days before opening day, however, I got a call from the Jersey City school system. "More kids? Sure, I'll take 'em," I said, answering on autopilot. "How many?" I nearly dropped the damn phone when I heard the magic number.

"Just fifty."

I was barely able to squawk out "Terrific" before hanging up. A second later I was frantically dialing my father-in-law, Dominick. "Dad!" I bellowed. "Get the Italian Connection out here fast! I gotta get three cabins built in two days!"

"Not to worry," he said. "That's plenty of time. Just let me make a few phone calls." Theresa's dad was a terrific guy. Generous and loyal, he was a great father and a fine man who really knew how to live. He could take more pleasure in a honey-ripe fig or glass of cool water than some other folks seem to find in pedigreed furniture or fat stock portfolios. I remember one time, right after Theresa and I got back from Hollywood and I was looking for work, we were staying with Dominick and Yolanda. I was getting ready for an early morning interview, when Dominick said, "It's cold out there. How 'bout a cup of coffee before you leave?"

"Thanks, I'd love one." So I went into the kitchen, saw two cups on the counter, and grabbed one. After the first swallow, my eyes crossed, as fire enveloped my head. I really thought my eyeballs were gonna ignite. "Dominick, what in hell's in this mug?"

He came running over and handed me the other cup. "Sorry, I guess you got mine." He took a swig of his concoction and let out a contented sigh. "I work on the railroad out at DuPont, and it gets cold as hell. So I need a little something to warm me up."

"Warm you up? It's a miracle it doesn't *blow* you up!" The next morning I watched Dominick stir up his extraordinary coffee. He took a coffee mug, and in went the Seagram's 7, gurgle, gurgle, gurgle. Then he added a like amount of anisette. Taking a steaming pot of espresso, he carefully administered a teaspoon or two. As he took his first sip, he looked up with a twinkle in his eye. "Like I said, I like to stay warm." I was fortunate to have this remarkable human being on my side.

Anyhow, as I waited for the pros to come help with the cabins, I became more and more frantic, aware that seconds were ticking away. "Screw this," I finally said, and started assembling the lumber and cement blocks. An amazing amount of crap is needed to build even one cabin, and I had to drag every damn piece of it over to the building site. It was hot as hell, and I was sweating like a horse. To make the chore even more fun, gnats were starting to stick to me. But still no sign of Dominick.

Okay, I told myself. How hard could it be to build a cabin? No harder than winning an Olympic medal, right?

Wrong.

I knew *how* to pole-vault. The floor beams were 2' x 6" studs, so I laid them out flat, nice and neat, then placed the cement blocks under them. I didn't know what the hell else I was supposed to do with 'em, but my handiwork looked damn peculiar to me. So I walked around my project, squinting at it from different angles. Maybe it was just that the cement blocks weren't adequate, I decided. So I start dragging over even more blocks. By this time sweat was pouring out of me into my eyes, making them burn. I grabbed a handy rag, an old T-shirt, actually, and made a bandana out of it. The bandana kept the sweat out of my eyes, but it didn't do a thing to keep off the biting insects that formed a dingy haze around me. Wonderful. Now I had to divide my time between heaving the blocks of concrete and swatting the deer flies and mosquitoes that had decided I was their lunch. So here I am, grunting and groaning while lifting the blocks, dancing around hitting myself all over to keep off the damn bloodsuckers, with this raggedy-ass bandana flapping around my ears. When I'd gotten everything into position, I stood back and surveyed what I'd done. It looked like I'd created my own Stonehenge in a scrap lumber yard, but it was the best I could do. I was just picking up a hammer when I heard this snickering behind me. I turned around, and damn if Dominick wasn't standing there, his hands clasped behind his back, shaking his head in disbelief. Pete and Mike, a couple of his *paisans*, were with him, doubled up with laughter.

"What in hell are you doing?" demanded Dominick. "Is that supposed to be a building?"

Mike stared dubiously at my creation, and then brightened. "I know! It's an out-house for rats!"

Dominick took a closer look at my construction technique. "Thank God we got here before you started nailing this mess together."

Pete Italiano, in his heavily accented English, got down and started rooting around in the dirt, poking here and there. "Holy mackerel, Don! You got the damn boards turned all cockeyed. Backwards, every one of 'em. The joists go up and down, not flat and side-ways. Don't you know anything? It's a good thing you pole-vault better than you build."

Little did Pete know that he was building the cabin where his son would eventually be counselor. Joey was just like his dad, and through the inherited qualities of respon-sibility and dedication, he eventually became assistant director of Kamp Olympik. Not only was Joey a great right-hand man to have around, he was also a budding athlete, though not quite operating at his full potential. I designed a unique weight-lifting pro-gram for him that gave him the boost in strength and speed he was looking for. He returned to the University of Pennsylvania to become the captain of the football team. Yup, he was a remarkable young man.

Anyhow, Dominick and the Italian Connection had a good hardy-har-har at my expense, but I had nothing to say. How could I, standing there, a sweaty mess, all covered with dead bugs, feeling nothing but relieved. The first team had arrived. A few counselors had also wandered over to enjoy watching my ego get its butt kicked, so they immediately got recruited as well. Before we knew it, the half dozen of us were studding up the sides and preparing to lay out the roof. In about three hours, we'd framed the cabin, which was now ready for shingles and screens. At this rate we could easily assemble the three cabins by our two-day deadline. When we felt we couldn't nail one more board, Mama Yolanda kept us going with fantastic meals: homemade pasta, Jersey corn, stuffed peppers, tomato salad, and to top it off, fresh clams from the Jersey shore. Man, that woman knew how to cook! Her great meals made us feel richly rewarded for our labors. On the morning of the third day, all the cabins were camper-ready, and we started hollering, "Bring 'em on, Baby!"

My work wasn't over once the cabins were ready. We'd carefully planned for the needs of a hundred campers. Now fifty more youngsters were about to descend on us. Extra food and supplies, more staffing—and I had to have it all *now*. Otherwise, we'd be up the creek with no paddle and only half a canoe. I got on the horn, did a little bellowing, made a few creative threats, and got it done. Though kids were packed into Kamp Olympik like cones on a pine tree, we were loving every minute. Because of the unexpected influx of campers, Dominick stayed on to help Yolanda in the kitchen. She was now cooking for more than 180 people three times a day. This was a little bit more than the Sunday family picnics, but I was careful not to mention that fact to her. What a jewel that woman was! We couldn't have managed without her.

Dominick and Yolanda prepping meals.

Yolanda: *I know!*

It was a funny thing about the love-hate thing between Yolanda and me. When push came to shove, either one of us would've given an arm up to the shoulder for the other. But all one of us had to say was one simple sentence, and the other would start lobbing thunderbolts. Dominick would stand listening to us go at it hammer and tongs, and he'd finally throw up his hands. "Will you two crazy people please grow up and stop acting like kids? You should hear yourselves carrying on like two spoiled *bambini*! Shut the hell up!"

I'd usually respond with something gallant, like, "Sure, Dominick. But it's ladies first, right?" No, that didn't do much to defuse the confrontation, which I think both of us kind of enjoyed.

But another thing about Yolanda: she was terrific with the kids. We had one little guy, Angelo, who was mentally challenged. He was a cute little kid with a grown-up face. His counselor was going nuts trying to keep tabs on him. "He disappears the second I look the other way. I've never seen any camper who could give me the slip that fast."

"Don't worry about Angelo," I said. "He'll be at the dining hall." Angelo loved to hang out with Yolanda, who always had milk and cookies and maybe a hug for him. I was never really worried about Angelo, because he and his big brother Danny had some kind of mental telepathy thing going on. The brothers were both scrappy little buggers, tough kids who'd had to take care of themselves in a rough neighborhood. If anybody started picking on Angelo, not only would Angelo be all over him, but his brother would appear out of nowhere, and Danny could beat the tar out of just about anybody he came up against, no matter how big they were.

I'd hear kids saying, "You mess with Angelo, you deal with his brother, big time." Danny really loved his little brother and was always there for him. That was kind of cute, and it really got to Theresa, who's all motherly and such. Anyhow, one day, while Angelo was paying Yolanda a visit, she started having him do little things like setting the table, putting out baskets of bread, keeping an eye on the replenishment of dishes on the dinner line.

Now we regularly assigned kids to dining hall duty, and they'd take turns working their shift. Some of them really took to it, and they'd always be yelling, "Hey, Mr. Bragg. Lemme work the dining hall, please?"

And somebody else would start complaining, "Hey, cheater, you already had it twice this week. I wanna have a turn, too!" The kids seemed to crave having these little responsibilities, so they could swagger around and brag on how Yolanda said they'd done a good job.

Well, Yolanda took the time to teach little Angelo the entire dining room routine: the setup of the hot table, proper placement of the silverware, the whole deal. Once the little guy got the pre-meal drill down pat, he got after the waiters like a junkyard dog, barking at them, "Put out a ladle with that. Get more bread in that basket, and fix that spoon. You got it upside down."

And the older kids would say, "Okay, Angelo," and they'd do whatever Angelo told them, as if he were their supervisor. Hell, why not? He knew what he was doing. So for a while we were the only camp on the eastern seaboard with a pint-sized maitre d'. If any waiter gave him any crap, all he had to do was start hollering "Yolanda!" and the unruly waiters toed the line.

The kids did a great job. The dining hall might have been chaotic during mealtimes, but twenty minutes after the campers left the hall, the waiters would have everything neat, with the bread and condiments put away and the floor swept. That was Angelo's doing. If you did a lousy job, you'd hear from him … and his big brother.

Once I mentioned to Theresa what a great guardian angel Danny was to his little brother. "You don't know the half of it," she said. "The boys' parents have the same level of disability as Angelo, and Danny is the one who holds the entire family together." So it kind of got to me at the end of the first session when hard-as-nails Danny started crying.

"Please, Mr. Bragg, can't we stay? I don't wanna go home." And I had to look at this kid and tell him, no, the next session was booked solid. Okay, Danny and Angelo got on the next bus out of camp, and I thought that was that.

The next day, the buses pull in with the next session's campers. As usual, there were a few no-shows, so I arranged for a van to pick up some more kids the following Monday to complete the quota. And when Uncle Joe drove the van into camp, who's sitting in it but Angelo and Danny. Angelo was sitting in the front seat next to Uncle Joe. The kid has this ear-to-ear grin, and he yells, "I called shotgun so I got to sit in front with Uncle Joe." It was great to have the boys back in camp, and when it was time for the third session, I phoned the city's summer camp director. "Don't worry about Danny and Angelo, I'll keep 'em here for the next session for free."

That's the kind of thing you do when you work with children. The kids get into your heart and stay there.

Years later, after I'd sold the camp, Theresa and I worked for the Special Olympics, Eunice Kennedy Shriver's labor of love. So after the main field events, I was looking for Theresa, and there she was getting hugged by a young man who was showing her his trophy.

"Don, look who's here," she said, with tears starting to sparkle in her eyes. I didn't recognize him at first, but then the young man gave me the lopsided grin I knew so well.

"Angelo," I boomed, hugging him. "Great to see you again." At this point, another guy ran up to congratulate him.

"Where'd you learn to run like that?" he demanded, thumping Angelo on the back.

Beaming at the guy, Angelo looked at us and shouted at the top of his lungs, "At Kamp Olympik!"

Talk about making our day! We experienced a surge of emotions almost impossible to control, with a slight teardrop escaping, a telltale sign of how much we loved that kid.

We eventually added bunkhouse-style accommodations that slept twenty comfortably, and our fabulous construction team accomplished that practically overnight. The camp really seemed to be getting up steam for a good run.

As the camp grew, I realized it was our little bit of heaven. Located in the South Jersey Pinelands on forty acres, it lay adjacent to the Wharton State Forest, a 100,000-acre parcel with pine forest uplands and wide stands of Jersey white cedar in the swampy lowlands. How I loved it. To me it felt like a virgin forest, but that wasn't quite so. Years before, savvy colonists shipped the white cedar, so well-suited for boat making, back to England to outfit the Royal Navy. At one time bears and mountain lions roamed this vast wilderness, but folks told us they'd disappeared years ago.

And then one night Theresa came running in from taking the kids to the movies. "Honey, a black panther jumped out and ran across the road right in front of me when I was driving onto our property."

I quickly calmed her down. "There haven't been panthers in these woods for years. It must've been a big pussycat—somebody's pet." Then I heard some of the local hunters talking about an immense dark cat they'd sighted.

"Oh, yeah, we spot him every now and then. Can't nobody get near 'im, though. It's probably a mountain lion."

"Wait a second," I said. "Mountain lions aren't black."

"No, but their coats turn dark in the winter. At night, that winter coat'd look black."

I never did mention the mountain lion sightings to Theresa. I thought we'd all breathe easier if we maintained the fiction of a great big black pussycat with two-inch fangs and claws to match.

There were all kinds of interesting things going on in the nearly quarter-million-acre Pinelands, composed mainly of the Wharton State Park, and I wanted my campers to sample as many of them as they could. One of the campers' first outings was to a glassblowing exhibition at Batsto Village, a former stagecoach stop on a plantation at the southern edge of the park, right on the road to Philly. The area had boasted the country's first glassblowing industry as well as substantial ironworks during our Colonial and Revolutionary periods. Those disappeared along with the oak that the settlers used for their houses and barns, but at least the kids could see how they used to make glass.

As soon as we arrived, the campers charged past exhibition shelves of handmade glass and crowded around to see how in hell you blow glass.

They were fascinated by the process, and watched with barely restrained excitement as this old fellow blew on his long pipe, forming a wobbly bubble of molten glass. When the bubble started to morph into a beautiful bowl, one boy reached toward the shimmering sphere, but I grabbed his arm. "It may look pretty, but that glass is heated to about 900 degrees, and it'd burn your fingers right off."

"No shit?" he whispered. I'd never heard that expression uttered with such reverence.

After they'd seen the artisan crafting so many beautiful things, they ran back to the gallery of art glass and checked out the display. I could hardly pry them away: they hung around scrutinizing the bowls and goblets and such, like connoisseurs shopping at Tiffany's. It really surprised me to see them all absorbed in something they hadn't realized existed a few hours before.

My campers were also taken with the forest itself. Despite the loss of the oaks, it hadn't changed much, except for the size of the trees, since the virgin trees had been felled long ago. What did survive in abundance were the pines on the higher ground and the lowland cedar down in the swampy areas. Unfortunately, the red upland cedar is getting mighty scarce nowadays. I remember taking a chunk of it and showing the kids the red strip that went through most of the inside grain of the wood. "Beautiful, isn't it? They'd use it in clothes closets and cedar chests and for shipbuilding," I explained.

One of the kids from Newark got all excited by that. "Hey, my mom's got a trunk like that in her bedroom back home!"

Another kid asked, "Did the Indians make their canoes out of cedar?" How the hell did I know, but I had to find out the answer for them real fast.

It was fantastic seeing the kids turn on to learning about things like different kinds of woods, grinding corn in a gristmill, and turning logs into lumber at the sawmill. They'd bring it all back to camp, and I'd hear them talking about how you had to pull the lever for the water to start turning the mill wheel. "Man, that was cool. Pretty neat, huh?" All their enthusiasm made the headache of organizing field trips entirely worthwhile. These expeditions seemed to wake up something analytical in the kids, a desire to know why. One night at campfire, a kid I'd have described as hard-bitten asked, "Why does some wood burn brighter, but doesn't last so long?" So I told him about the difference between hardwoods and softwoods, and I had the kids' attention for damn near half an hour. Don't you dare try to tell me kids from the inner cities have a limited learning capacity!

They pored over the differences between the insect- and rot-resistant red cedar, which outlasted most other woods, and the plentiful lowland cedar with its creamy grain shading toward yellow. And they noted the pleasing fragrance of the cedar wood with delight. While the cedar trees still left in the area lack the impressive girth of their forebears, they do have sufficient height to serve as insect-impervious cedar poles, so they're harvested regularly. I mentioned this to the kids, just offhand. I was pleasantly surprised when they'd point out a cedar and ask, "That's a cedar, right? It'd be good for one of those cedar poles, I'll bet."

I pointed out that I learned the hard way that even hard cedar fence posts are vulnerable to a ground worm unless you coat them with creosote starting at ground level and then down another foot. I'd kept an eye out for that malevolent worm because it could start a premature rotting process. But despite my watchfulness, I had to pull out most of the posts I used and redo the job after several years. To clear land for camp activities, we'd had to cut down a dozen large cedars that were over three feet in diameter. We cut them down with regret, but we did harvest some beautiful wood from them.

We weren't the first by any means to take out cedar trees from the area. In order to create the cranberry bogs, the farmers removed all the trees. I heard the kids commenting about what a job that must've been. They were right. The marshes could never support heavy equipment, so they had to use mules to extract the felled trees. The next step was constructing dams to control the stream essential for irrigation: cranberries tend to be thirsty. Each dam had a spillway box, at least three feet wide and constructed of cedar to resist water decay. There were grooved sides on the front, which received the 2" x 6" planks that slid in at various heights. These planks would be adjusted to ensure sufficient water for the cranberry vines' growth in spring and summer and to flood the bogs in the autumn to protect the berries against frost. I loved these bogs. When we constructed our permanent home, we located it on a source bog that had been flooded to become a good-sized lake. The fishing was fantastic, since the former bog was inhabited by large pickerel and huge catfish. Migrating swans and Canada geese also made it a stopover in spring and autumn. It gave me a thrill to look out our living room window and see this wildlife-filled panorama.

The kids from the inner cities were fascinated with the box gates because you could actually make sense of how the water level was controlled. I'd hear them saying things like, "Okay, then they'd adjust these in the springtime to let the water out."

"What for?"

"You turkey! Springtime's when things grow. How'd you like to grow in ice water that's all the way up to your ears?" The Kamp Olympik kids preferred hands-on learning to the dry atmosphere of the lecture hall. For instance, they got a real charge out of seeing exactly how farmers used scoops to harvest the berries in earlier years. The scoop was a fingerlike piece of equipment that you'd grasp and plunge into the vinelike cranberry bush, and the kids saw the problem without being told. "Hey, that's no good. It's shakin' half the berries onto the ground. Who thought that dumb thing up?"

"Is that how they get cranberries today?" They were happy to learn that serendipity led to a better method of harvesting. One canny farmer was watching when the bogs were flooded and noticed the ripe red berries that had fallen into their vines now floated to the top. They'd gather the berries into one corner of the bog, and then transfer them via conveyer belt to a large truck waiting on the dam. From there it was a short hop to the Ocean Spray processing plant. The kids, now evidently well-versed in things cranberry, nodded their approval. "Okay, I can see them doing that."

"Yeah, the old way was bogus, man!"

I was sorry my campers never got to see what happened to the berries in the fall. People would flock to the Pines just to watch the harvesting. The magnificent scarlet berries glittered in the water from the reflected sunlight, and it was beautiful to see. But the kids were pleased enough with not only getting to drink cranberry juice, but also seeing how it was made. Something interesting to tell the gang back in their cities of concrete and stone.

Campers in sack race at Batsto Village.

One minor problem surfaced after our cranberry field trip, however. So taken with the idea that healthfully tart red berries just grew on bushes for the taking, some kids started popping anything they found hanging on a bush or tree right into their mouths. Sometimes they'd grab blueberries, but sometimes they didn't. I'm all for an experienced woodsman living off the land if he wants to, but if my kids started browsing in the forest, they were in for some nasty surprises. We didn't have anything like water hemlock that I knew of, but I was pretty sure there was inkberry around. So I'd say to the kids, "Don't eat *anything* you find growing on the bushes and trees around camp. Some things that look good could give you a bellyache, a bad one."

And they stood there looking at me like I'm the Grinch.

One enterprising little boy wrote me a new page on foraging, though. The kids loved to get a hook and line and go fishing, and they'd sit there along the river bank, real serious, twitching their lines every so often. They'd use anything they found around for bait: a leaf, a peanut, a little chicken bone. Nobody caught anything, but they didn't care. Then one day I heard all this commotion, and some of the fishermen came running up. "Guess what? Levander caught himself a *fish*!" From the way they were carrying on, I expected Moby Dick's big brother. So here comes little Levander, holding up this pint-sized perch.

"Man, that's some neat fish," I told him. "What did you use for bait?"

"I got it off a bush. Didn't put it in *my* mouth. Put it in the *fish's* mouth. That's okay, right, Mr. Braggs?"

"That's just fine, but what was it?"

"I caught him with a blueberry!" he said, standing there all proud of himself. "So blueberries make good fish bait, huh?"

"The best, Levander," I said, keeping a perfectly straight face. Those kids were great.

Theresa: *We never had a nurse on the property, but I placed a well-stocked first aid kit in the dining hall, so we'd be ready for every conceivable emergency. I was always on call to patch up their little cuts. The children who especially enjoyed the extra attention quickly became my regulars. They'd come running up, so upset over some little scrape, so first thing, I'd comfort them. After that, they'd sit there happily as I cleaned the cut, swabbed on Merthiolate, and stuck on a Band-Aid. For the rare medical emergency, we'd take the child to the doctor in Hammonton, twenty minutes away.*

Sick call was a yes-or-no deal, actually. Theresa was terrific at spotting any really sick kids, and those who were got medical attention immediately. Thing was, a trumped-up bellyache was an easy cop-out to escape duties such as toilet or trash cleanup. So she'd tell any suspicious cases to rest quietly and come back at lunchtime. "Then you'll get to visit the doctor and his needles at the hospital," she'd say brightly. Boy, did a lot of kids get well in a hurry. In fact, Kamp Olympik had more miracle cures than the Mayo Clinic.

But the first several days of camp were rough for some kids, especially the few who'd experienced limited structure in their young lives. We had to plan camp activities according to the schedule that experience taught us would work. Man, were some campers shocked when they realized they couldn't swim or play basketball whenever they felt like it. For safety's sake, and so as not to jeopardize the integrity of the tutorial program, we didn't dare deviate from the overall camp schedule. Hell, if we'd have done that, there'd have been chaos, and I doubt we'd have ever gotten the session back on track. Besides, we wanted to guarantee each camper a nice mix of learning, chores, sports, and crazy fun, whether they wanted to be well-rounded or not. If the weather was hot or inclement, we'd throw in an additional swim period, but the core tutorial program was never compromised. Since camp life was a whole new deal for these kids, we had a few comments like, "I don't need this kind of BS. I can go home and let Mom boss me around." Maybe some seriously entertained thoughts of taking off for home, but we had an unbeatable ally right in the forest surrounding Kamp Olympik that made sure the campers stayed put. In addition to our four-footed friends like deer, possum, and skunk, there were stories about a two-footed—and apparently cloven-hoofed—creature known as the Jersey Devil. This beast stalked its prey in the Pine Barrens even as we entered the twenty-first century: just the thing to induce little campers not to stray too far from camp.

I first met the man who had firsthand knowledge of this phenomenon when I was out digging post holes for the cedar fence on a blistering afternoon. I stopped to mop the sweat off my face and here's this elderly gentleman walking up to me. He said he was doing a survey for the township, but he looked at my pickax and asked, "You need any help?"

Like I said, it was hot, and I was sweating like a horse. "Sure," I said. "I pay by the hour. Know anybody who's a good worker?"

He surprised me by saying, "I know me! I'll just go home, change my clothes, and be right back."

The guy was serious, but he was at least seventy, so I begged off. "Thanks for the offer but it's about quitting time." Hell, I didn't want to give the poor guy a heart attack.

He moved away with a twinkle in his eye. "If you ever do need help, just come find me. My cabin's down the road a piece by the big cranberry bog."

That was the beginning of my relationship with this fine old gentleman named Fred Brown. He'd drop by the camp from time to time, and, if I primed him with a cup or two of coffee, he'd start telling stories. He'd hunted with the bow, not a gun, and in the old days, he'd been a hunting guide for professional people who'd come down from Philly to the Pines to hunt. Anyhow, one day he was leading a group around a cranberry bog into the deeper woods when a flock of geese came cruising by, ready to land on the flooded bog.

"I hauled off and drew back my bow and let that arrow fly, and I pierced the lead goose right through the neck. It dropped into the bog, and I waded out to fetch it. When I pulled it up, I saw I had me a fat goose and a three-foot pickerel fish on the one arrow. That was fifty years ago, and nobody else has ever snagged a goose right out of the air *plus* a trophy-sized pickerel with the same arrow."

He slapped his thigh, and looked around with an impish grin on his face and his trademark twinkle in his eye. Another friend of mine who was visiting poked him in the ribs. "Fred, whatcha got in that cup besides coffee?" We all laughed, but Fred just gave us this steely look and his eyes got kind of dark and mysterious.

When shadows come where pines have stood, appears a demon from within the wood. Its phantom face becomes defined from knots of branches and arms of vines.

—*Don Bragg, "The Jersey Devil"*

"You're not from around here, are you?" I shook my head, and he settled comfortably into his canvas-backed chair. "You ever hear of the Jersey Devil? Well, you're about to, Son, right from the horse's mouth." My friend and I exchanged looks but didn't start razzing him, since we wanted to hear the story.

"My great-great-great-grandmother was a midwife. You know—she helped bring little ones into the world. Well, late one night she was helping out with a birth at the Leeds' farmhouse. It was Mrs. Leeds' thirteenth child, and the lady was having a hard time of it. A storm was raging outside and inside too, what with Mrs. Leeds screeching and carrying on. Midwife Brown told her to pray to God. Mrs. Leeds started moaning, 'This is no child of God but of the Devil.' Old gram didn't pay her any mind until the child was finally born. Danged if the baby didn't pop out and start jumping around like a cat on a griddle. It had a stubby tail and hair all over its body.

"The creature grew much faster than any normal child, and was always doing mean, hurtful things right from the start. It started attacking everybody in the Leeds family, so they kept it in the attic, tethered to the chimney, until one day it escaped up the chimney. From that day to this, havoc has reigned in this forest. It started with pigs, chickens, and sometimes dogs being mutilated on neighboring farms, and nothing has ever been absolutely safe in this forest from that day to this. And that," said Fred, with the round-eyed innocence of a baby, "is the most honest rendition of that story you'll ever hear!"

We watched him for a second or two with straight faces, but immediately collapsed with laughter, literally falling off our chairs. I was delighted. Camp stories abound, but to have one with a feasible historical foundation in our campers' backyard made it even better. I couldn't wait to tell this particular yarn around our campfire. It became a staple at the beginning of every session, and it pretty much put the kids' hair on end. Talk about keeping the campers in their beds! They wouldn't stick their noses out of their cabins at night, not to prowl the woods, not to raid neighboring cabins, not even to visit the latrine. So you could say the story did backfire to a degree. Since nobody would get up to take a leak at the latrine on nights when the Jersey Devil tale was told, we invariably awoke the following morning to an epidemic of bed-wetting. So here comes a new camp rule: after Jersey Devil campfires, everybody had to take a brisk run around camp and then hit the latrines before bed. *No exceptions!*

Fred Brown, the old yarn spinner, did in fact collaborate with a writer named McPhee on a book called *The Pine Barrens*. While I'm sure McPhee used Fred as a detail man and source of local color, I heard that Fred's wildest stretches of imagination never made it into the book. It's a shame, too, for Fred's fantastic stories of Wharton Forest could make any best-seller list.

Chapter Four

Any time Fred Brown dropped in for a visit was a welcome respite from the rigors of running a camp, especially my least favorite chore, dealing with hiring and firing. Like any business, we had turnover among the staff, and selecting new counselors and camp staff was precarious, to say the least. We'd learned the hard way that resumes, references, and even personal interviews could be deceiving in the extreme. Only job performance told the true tale of competence. Even if we liked an employee, we had to be hard-nosed. A nice guy who wasn't doing his job put the campers at risk in a potentially dangerous environment. But, man, I hated interviewing applicants. We'd get guys who expected me to pay them so they could work on their tans; grouches who clearly hated kids; and occasionally even hippie types who smelled bad and were so high on drugs their eyes moved independently of each other. I didn't know people could do that. But of all the interviews I suffered through, there's one that sticks in my mind. I'd placed a newspaper ad, and in response to it, here comes a very large Asian gentleman with his retinue. Okay, to be fair, his mom and two brothers, but it still put me off. He climbed out of the car and introduced himself. "Hi, I'm Rich Cheung," he said, affably. One look, and I was sure he'd be at a disadvantage at Kamp Olympik. The man weighed at least 240 and didn't appear to be in the best of shape. Even getting out of the car seemed to tax him. I ran through a description of his responsibilities and job demands with a sinking heart, while he stood at military attention.

"Relax, Rich," I said, and he stood easy, but still alert. "I've gotta be honest with you. You're gonna be tearing around the camp chasing kids in twenty different directions at once. Can you move at top speed in ninety-plus-degree heat with humidity soaring over 70 percent?"

He looked me straight in the eye and said, "I can handle anything the job demands." He must've seen the doubt in my eye, for he continued, "Just try me for one week. If I don't meet every one of your expectations, I'm out of here, no questions, no arguments. I'll be gone."

It didn't take me a week to realize that Rich was the most productive guy I could have hired. Efficient and tenacious, he became assistant camp director the following year, when his two brothers joined us. Within two years Rich was the camp director under Theresa's supervision when I was busy off-site. His efficiency was so astounding that I hired him without hesitation to assist me at Stockton State College on the staff of the athletic department.

It was after Rich arrived that Kamp Olympik acquired the S.S. *Noah's Ark*. One day while picking up fresh produce and fruit from the local farmers' market I spotted a spiffy forty-foot boat just sitting high and dry in some farmer's front yard. The craft boasted a nice little cabin topside and a wraparound deck, and it got me thinking. Made of metal, the craft would be impervious to decay and seemed like a sound investment as a novelty for the campers to play on. Our kids from the city would go wild at the opportunity to climb aboard an actual boat, I decided. So after some heated negotiations, the farmer and I finally reached an agreement. I'm glad we haggled over price, since it cost me half again as much to transport it to the camp. Once we arrived triumphantly with the boat in tow, I wasted no time getting it launched. Boy, was I proud of myself. Then I took another good look at my vessel. First I wondered why it was listing; then I watched helplessly while it majestically sank. So much for my great deal. Old Zeke the farmer sure put one over on the city dude, namely me.

A friend of mine was good enough to bring over his tractor and haul the boat up onto a sandy area adjacent to the water. Once we'd hoisted it on a sawhorse-like structure, it adapted well to land, especially after I installed a ladder on the back for climbing up to the deck. After disqualifying promising names such as *The Adventurer, Pursuer,* and—my favorite—*Paradise Lost*, the campers and I decided the best name for this vessel was *Noah's Ark*. The little boat was never without its share of campers playing pirates or whatever, so I figured I'd made a good buy after all. You should've seen the way they handled the wheel, and I heard them shouting out nautical commands: "Right full rudder." "Landing craft away." "Man the pumps." I've no idea where they picked up that language—probably from some old pirate movie or war movie.

Our souls seem suspended as they sail and soar like dancing doves that

flutter and float upon the wings of winds.

—*Don Bragg, "Hovering"*

One constant at the camp was the head count, because we had a good idea what our little campers were capable of. At mealtimes, and especially at the beach, we constantly checked to make sure nobody was missing. Well, one evening at dinner time, we took a head count. Sure enough, Cabin 3 was missing a camper. Hurriedly we assembled the counselors for a search party. After some fruitless hunting through the woods, somebody short tugged on my shirt. "You won't find him in the woods. Pee Wee's going to Florida."

"He's *what?*"

Gently we interrogated our informant. "Did Pee Wee's parents pick him up without checking with us?"

"Um, no, he's going on a boat."

"Who picked him up?!"

"Nobody. He's sailing out tonight on *Noah's Ark*."

Without a word, the staff sprinted to the beach area, and there on the boat, spinning the wheel like Mark Twain on the Mississippi—all intensity and concentration—was Pee Wee. When my heart stopped pounding, I recalled Pee Wee's earlier days at camp. Before he adjusted to camp life and started enjoying himself, he'd run away several times a day. We'd found a unique way to restrain him, however. Pee Wee had come to camp bearing an enormous suitcase, so big that it weighed more than he did. Since the camp director wasn't about to go chasing after Pee Wee to bring him back to camp every two minutes, he suggested we tie Pee Wee's suitcase to his waist and make sure we used childproof knots. I agreed: that should at least slow him down.

Now, like most summer camps, we used the buddy system for an immediate alert if anyone wandered off, and sure enough, one day when we checked the kids before swim period, Pee Wee was AWOL. His swimming partner raised his hand kind of tentatively. "Pee Wee's not here," he announced.

No kidding. "Did he take off for the mess hall?"

"I don't think so."

"Did he go back to his cabin?"

"I don't think so."

Deciding the child had given up his entire store of information, I barked, "Okay, counselors, fan out and check out the arts and crafts area, Tarzanville, and the latrine."

The little voice interrupted. "He won't be any of those places. He's runnin' away from camp. He told me so!"

Tearing my hair in frustration, I scrutinized the camp area until I spotted the gouged-out tug marks left by a suitcase that was plainly heading for the main road. Calculating the time he'd been gone and the probable drag effect from the suitcase, we figured he couldn't be far off. Rich leaped in a car and lit out, following the trail. The youngster would be just down the road, I reasoned—that suitcase weighed a ton. Well, some time elapsed before we received a call from Rich way out on the main road by Mick's Country Store. He said, "I don't know how he did it hauling that suitcase, but the kid traveled over a mile. Maybe he should get a merit badge or something!" So attaching an anchor to Pee Wee didn't completely cure him of his wanderlust, but it severely limited his range.

Like I said, some campers take a little time to adjust, but they usually do. Pee Wee sure did. Before that session of camp was over, he merited the Camper of the Week award. Go figure.

Years later, after I'd sold the camp, I came back to my old stomping ground. I hardly recognized the place, since some of the buildings that had been its mainstay had been altered by the elements or torn down. Even *Noah's Ark*, the old boat that I'd installed as a landlocked play structure for the kids, had been washed into the main course of the river by heavy rains. The boat evidently kept afloat for a while before foundering a little ways downstream, but it was just a wreck now. It kind of made me sad seeing it sitting there, partially submerged, its hull covered with the graffiti of passing boaters.

Anyhow, it was late summer when I paid my visit, and scores of canoes were drifting past, heading towards Mullica River and Great Bay and the ocean. Sometimes the canoers would beach their craft on my side of the river to stretch their legs or have a smoke. I'd get to talking with some of them and they'd start spinning stories of the mysterious intrigue that once ruled the river. When I'd built Kamp Olympik, I knew it was on the original site of a deer camp that had been owned by Old Man Stong. But I hadn't known that it was reputed to be at the heart of a drug ring whose empire stretched like a spiderweb through the Pinelands. The drug dealers had the run of the place until the state forest rangers added two and two and started keeping an eye on the motorcycle gangs who were regularly riding into the forest.

So these guys are sitting beside their canoes, smoking, and talking in these hushed voices, all impressed with what they thought they knew. "These hoods usta boat up from the ocean, sneak up the Mullica River to the Wading River, and rendezvous right here where we're standing, at Stong's old deer club."

"No!" I said. "In this very spot?"

"Yes! They'd land their cargo of drugs, and the biker gangs would get it to buyers. They always timed their deliveries to the high neap tides, so they could get their boats through. Pretty slick, huh?"

"Uh-huh."

"Yeah! Well, the smugglers had a showdown with the state forest rangers. There was a huge shootout. They arrested a whole bunch of guys, the ones who couldn't get away on their cycles. But one of the drug guys got killed." The voice dropped to a hoarse whisper. "Some people say his ghost still hangs around."

"I see," I said. "And you're sure about this?"

Then the guy got real adamant. "I can prove it. Look right over there. See that old boat? That's what draws the dead guy's spirit. It's the boat that carried the drug runners' cargo."

So here's this wild-eyed guy from Poughkeepsie, pointing to the ship of the damned. That's right, it was the old *Noah's Ark*, the vessel I got out of some farmer's front yard. I walked away chuckling, wondering if stories of this ghost ship would be repeated and magnified around glowing campfires all through the Pinelands. Move over, Jersey Devil. Here comes the midnight boat to hell! Boy, would Pee Wee, her first captain, have gotten a kick out of that.

Talking of Pee Wee, it was natural that Rich Cheung was the one who'd brought Pee Wee back when he and his suitcase had taken off for home. Rich tended to do whatever he set out to do. Having a man like Rich at my shoulder made my job possible, since he was proficient at so many things. He reported to Theresa and worked well with her, but he also executed to the letter every request I ever gave him concerning camp operations. He also absorbed my work ethic of concentrating on the task at hand regardless of the obstacles. Hell, half the people who can't figure out how to solve a problem just haven't been keeping their mind on what they're doing, at least that's my take on it. "Take the energy you'd spend on excuses and pour it into solving the problem instead," I'd say. And Rich listened. One day, for instance, on my way out to my job at the statehouse in Trenton, I told him to reinforce a bulkhead near the swimming beach. Because of heavy rains, the boarded-up bank was being undermined. If we didn't shore it up immediately, we could lose the entire section, including the rope swing and platform that campers used to launch themselves into the river.

I outlined the plan of attack for him. "Fill burlap sacks at our sand hill, then use the pickup truck to cart them the hundred yards to the river. No sweat, right?" As I drove away, I wondered if Rich would be up to the task. When I came home, the job was done to perfection.

Theresa: *I kept an eye on Rich from the dining hall, and it was like watching the Coyote in a Roadrunner cartoon. Everything that could go wrong, did. First he corralled some campers as volunteers, but only by promising them a king's ransom in candy bars. As soon as the kids dug into the sand, though, all the doggone handles broke off the shovels. Without missing a beat, Rich handed the campers buckets,* *and they started scooping the sand into the sacks. Before you knew it, the truck was almost full. When they'd crammed the last sack onto the truck, I assumed Rich was home free, but before the truck moved two yards, the rear axle broke. Next time I looked out the window, Rich and the kids were carting the sacks to the beach in the wheelbarrow. I hadn't realized it, but eight kids plus one wheelbarrow is a recipe for a wobbly disaster. At this rate they'd be at it till Christmas, I thought. The same thought evidently occurred to Rich, because he made a kind of sled by lashing the canvas from an extra bunk bed to two poles. They dragged the sacks off the truck, staggered over and dumped them onto this triangular sledlike apparatus, then dragged the contraption to the river. It was like watching the Three Stooges running amok at the Iditarod dogsled race, but they got the job done. And the children were so proud of themselves!*

So it was mission accomplished, and not an excuse in sight. After hearing Theresa's report on the day's misadventures, I knew I'd made the right choice for camp director.

Being a counselor was no walk in the park. Tearing around the camp all day on the heels of the ten little fiends in your care was like running a daylong marathon. As camp director, Rich had even more to do. He finally convinced me that if he rode the Honda 90 around camp, he could more than double his supervisory capacity, and I figured he'd earned it. The rest of the staff began clamoring for Hondas as they moved up the camp hierarchy, but only Rich merited his own wheels.

My other star employee was Barry Ross. He'd started out as a counselor but after a few seasons became our assistant camp director. In addition, I could count on Barry to sail into camp with a fresh crop of potential counselors at the beginning of each season. For the most part, they were athletes with an appetite for a job with taxing physical demands. Just what we needed.

Our camp was functioning well with 200 campers, and I calculated we weren't even at full capacity yet. One year, a few days before our opening session, Barry brought along his friend Dave Miller to observe our camp operation. Barry and Dave were transferring to the nearby state college where I'd recently become athletic director. It was really a kick to see the two of them together. They were both outwardly kind of quiet. Barry was small, not over 5' 8", and his buddy Dave was at least 6' 5". They kind of reminded me of George and Lennie in *Of Mice and Men*. That was not only due to their respective size, but also because Dave usually had a

Dave Miller, Don, and Barry Ross.

kind of bewildered expression on his face. Barry'd get an idea and tell it to Dave, and then he'd say, "So what do you think, Dave?"

And Dave, looking confused as hell, would think a minute, and then he'd say, "Uh, okay, Barry."

See what I'm talking about? Right out of Steinbeck!

Now Barry had kind of beady eyes, but when he looked at you it was like he was always in a fog a million miles away. He also had the habit of standing there with his mouth hanging open. I said to him once, "I have the perfect job for you. Go on over to the dining hall and work with Yolanda."

Barry looked at me like I'd lost my mind. "*Yolanda*? What in hell for?"

"Because with your mouth always hanging open you'd make a great fly trap, and you know how Yolanda hates to have flies buzzing around her kitchen." Then he'd get all indignant and start giving me grief. But though Barry was basically a quiet guy, he was persistent as hell. He was a distance runner like his father, and he could—and did—go all day long. I liked both Barry and Dave; they were very respectful and accommodating, and both turned out to be productive as hell, but I'm getting ahead of my story. When they first showed up at camp, Barry was trying to recruit his buddy as a counselor, and I informed Dave he was welcome to sleep and eat at the camp if he handled camp repairs for a few hours per day. But he told me he'd decided to go for the big bucks in the lucrative Atlantic City construction game.

Had he indeed? I had other plans for him. So I asked him all casual and laid back if he could do a few little repairs around camp before he started his construction gig. When he said "Sure" I knew I had him. Dave spent the next morning rehanging doors and replacing screens and such, and I saw to it that he'd worked up an appetite before I led him into the dining hall. Yolanda served us homemade lasagna, eggplant parmigiana, and a huge mixed salad—fantastic food. As Dave filled his plate, Barry innocently piped up, "Neat thing is, I get this great chow free. I guess meals will really eat into your Atlantic City paycheck, huh, Dave?"

I eyed the immense piece of cheesecake on Dave's plate. "Nah," I said. "How much could hot dogs, greasy fries, Philly pretzels, and all the cotton candy he can eat set him back?" We continued to double-team the poor guy after a quick game of basketball. We lounged in the shade of the whispering pines as Dave absorbed the backcountry silence and the murmur of the river.

"It's so peaceful here," he said at last.

"It's kind of peaceful in Atlantic City," I ventured. "Course, working construction *you* won't get to enjoy it. Between the jackhammers and the bulldozers grinding their gears, you won't be able to hear yourself think. But the money's great, right, Dave?"

Suffice it to say he hung around to help out on opening day and stayed on with us as a counselor. He was a handy guy to have around.

By the sixth season, we had campers from the Newark, Jersey City, Bergen County, and Philadelphia recreation departments, and we were ready to welcome all registered campers, when our friends in Newark threw us a curve. The day before opening, I hear I'm getting fifty more campers, and I had nowhere to put them. We were in the process of building a new bunkhouse, but that wasn't anywhere near finished. Besides, I'd need an extra hand or two to deal with the unexpected influx of kids.

But then I reasoned that Dave could take care of the overflow of kids. "All you'll have to do is supervise our experienced junior counselors; they'll deal with the campers," I told him. "It'll be a snap." I believed me, too. Since we'd be able to shoehorn twenty of the younger kids into the existing cabins, Dave would only have to deal with thirty. Besides, the CITs were good kids and knew their job. Well, we handed out sleeping bags to the unexpected campers and announced, "Guess what? You get to sleep out under the stars!" The kids went wild at this news, and happily spread their sleeping bags around the campfire. One by one they all drifted off to sleep, so I went to join Theresa and our kids in our cabin.

Next thing I knew, there's this clap of thunder right over my head and the heavens are opening their floodgates, releasing a deluge of biblical proportions on the unsuspecting heads of our neophyte campers. Yelling for Barry and my brother Georgie, I charged over to where Dave and the CITs were trying to collect the campers, difficult since some of the kids crawled farther into their sleeping bags and bit anybody who tried to drag 'em out. A few feisty youngsters had some choice names for me because I let it rain, while others charged into the woods for cover, with the CITs hot on their heels. Eventually, we herded the campers over to the pole-vaulting pit that, luckily, was covered with a large canvas tarp. When we'd shoved a pole into place to create a makeshift tent, they had a nice dry shelter. I'd just gotten into dry clothes when I hear more cries of woe, this time coming from the vaulting pit. The sloping sides of the tent had channeled the rain right into the pit, and the kids were literally back in the soup. The old neighborhood was probably looking pretty good to the sodden kids by the time I led them into the dining hall, which I erroneously thought would be a cozy refuge.

What I hadn't counted on was Theresa's mom. Yolanda looked up from her pre-dawn breakfast prep with fire in her eyes as we slopped into the dining hall.

"What are you doing barging in here in the middle of the night? And with all these children! They should be in bed."

"You're telling me!" Of course the kids had fanned out and were into everything. I grabbed one who was attempting to climb into the oven and relieved another of a gallon jar of *pepperoncini*.

One look at a dozen kids diving for a platter of pastry, and Yolanda lost it. "Out of my sweet rolls! In fact, out of my kitchen!" She glared at me. "You too, *stunade*!"

"Yeah, Yolanda, but see, there's a terrible storm outside, and there's no place else they can go."

"This for your terrible storm," she said, indulging in an expressive Italian gesture. "I'm getting breakfast for two hundred, so I don't need a mob of kids underfoot." I started to explain that thirty kids isn't exactly a mob, but she picked up an immense frying pan and began swinging it like an ax.

The kids were looking upset, so I foolishly opened my big mouth. "Ah, Yolanda, why do you always make a humongous big deal out of nothing?" Oops. With a strangled yell, she heaved this ten-ton skillet at my head while releasing a rush of blistering Italian. I ducked the missile, but came up kind of pissed off. After all, I was the good guy here. So now I had a choice to make. I've never been one for etiquette, but I was pretty sure putting your mother-in-law into orbit was frowned upon. So I did the next stupidest thing: I slammed my fist right through the door. At that instant, a bolt of lightning crackled into the tree just outside, cutting it in two. Faced with a crazed white lady heaving heavy objects, a camp director evidently intent on demolishing the building, and lightning bolts turning trees into kindling, the kids bolted out the back door, terrified. I'd have gone with them, but I had a small problem. Yeah, punching through a door felt real macho, but now my hand was trapped by the splintered wood.

As I pulled my lacerated hand free, Yolanda exploded. "*Stunade*! Now you're getting blood all over my kitchen!" Fortunately Dominick was there to intervene before the raging storm outside became the least of my problems. I headed for the door, grateful that thunder and lightning were all I had to contend with. So, cast out in the storm again, we made for the nearest building: the bathhouse. It was a fairly large facility, and it was at least dry. But it still was the bathroom. Amid comments like "I don't have to sleep with the toilet at my house," Dave got the campers and their soaking-wet sleeping bags inside. Thank God it was over eighty degrees, or we'd have had pneumonia to contend with. With the kids out of harm's way, I went back to my cabin to meditate on the joys of running a camp. The lightning continued to crackle with menace; the thunder was God's kettledrum; and the noise of the rain hitting the corrugated metal roof sounded like boulders being bounced out of hell. It continued to rain, but the thunder and lightning eventually rolled away inland, so I went to check on the kids again.

It was quite a sight. Dave was sprawled against the wall with one elbow on a toilet, sound asleep, with the kids all huddled around him like a pile of puppies. As I watched, Dave's elbow slipped, there was a splash, and he stopped snoring long enough to growl, "Shit!" Silently, I withdrew. I didn't need to comment further on this glorious night: Dave had just said it all.

I'm happy to announce that Barry and my brother slept in the director's cabin and stayed nice and dry. Barry said Georgie kept up a running imitation of me reassuring Dave. "Don't worry, Davie boy, it's just a couple of hours a day, that's all I'd ever ask of you. It's a piece of cake. Honest." The two of them fell asleep with stomach cramps from laughing. I'm glad somebody did.

Well, the next day Dave and his crew of highly motivated campers finished the new bunkhouse, so everyone was happy, especially Dave, who became a permanent senior counselor. He told me he liked the feeling of being a leader and taking good care of his campers, which was a damn lucky thing for me. It was also an omen of things to come. He had aspirations for a singing career, and after the summer camping season I gave him some advice and a few introductions to help him on his career. He became fairly successful, but he surprised the hell out of us all when he became a minister along with his buddy, the Reverend Barry. You can never tell about people—how they start out and end up are two different stories.

Especially in Kamp Olympik's early years, as Theresa and I worked our tails off to get our enterprise off the ground, I sometimes wondered what in hell we'd gotten ourselves into. But I didn't wonder for long because the youngest campers had an incredibly endearing habit. I'd be hurrying across camp, and I'd feel a little hand encircle mine. Though I always had a lot on my mind, it was always refreshing to hear the innocent comments of the younger kids. The T-shirts they wore said DON BRAGG'S KAMP OLYMPIK, so of course they called me Mr. Braggs. One time a little one came up to me, grabbed my hand, and stood squinting up at me for a minute.

"What's happening?" I asked. The little guy kind of frowned.

"Mainly good, Mr. Braggs, but we're scared of those whip birds. Will they really come and get you at night?"

"Now who told you that?"

"My counselor says they'll fly down and put a serious whippin' on you if you leave the cabin at night."

"Not at all," I said, making a mental note to have a discussion with his counselor. "They're called whippoorwills—they're beautiful birds, and all they're doing is talking to each other at night."

"Even when they're sayin' 'whippoorwill, whippoorwill?' That's not about beating on anybody?"

"Nope, that's just how they got their name. It's only peaceable talk between God's creatures."

"Then I don't gotta be afraid of them?"

I gave his shoulder a little squeeze. "Not at all."

"And I don't have to keep my head inside my sleeping bag? Boy, it gets hot in there."

Chuckling a little at the relief on his face, I said, "You live in the city. Is it different out here in the woods?"

"A lot different. Back home there was noise all night. Here it's so quiet. It was kinda spooky at first, but it's real cozy when I get all wrapped up in my sleeping bag." He frowned again. "Lots of things are different. Good different."

"Know what I like best?" I replied. "Not having to stay inside a building with no fresh air or the nice smell of pine trees. And not having to walk on asphalt and concrete all day; I like the way the earth cushions my feet."

"The beach sand feels good, too." He shrugged expressively. "I don't know why, but it does."

"The sand kind of covers up your toes and takes care of 'em while you're busy having fun," I said. "It's almost like sand gives your toes a hug. That what it feels like?"

The little guy's face lit up with a smile of ten thousand watts at least. "That's it. That's just what it feels like."

"And now, run over and join your cabin at the softball field."

"'Kay, Mr. Braggs. See ya!" He sped away, yelling, "Hey, guys, listen to this. They're not gonna whip us!"

That brief moment digs deep into our reason for living. Were there rewards in running a camp that never appeared on a spreadsheet? Like you wouldn't believe.

By the sixth year, the camp was functioning efficiently and all seemed well. We had nearly 300 campers, and we were close to capacity, with campers from Newark making up half of the total. The real miracle worker was Yolanda, who was now cooking for nearly 350 hungry people, counting staff. A quantum leap from the fifty she'd fed at family picnics. Though she still insisted she was just a good home cook, her expertise eclipsed that of any professional chef. The backbone of her ingenious concoctions was the fresh produce from the Jersey farms. Most of the campers arrived thinking eggplants and celery were space aliens, but after a few days of eating her healthy and delicious meals, the tough "I only eat burgers" kind of kids were clamoring for Yolanda's vegetable dishes. Her homemade sauce Bolognese soon became the talk of the Pinelands, and it elevated camp fare into the five-star category. God help anybody who purloined a juicy beefsteak tomato or a handful of olives from her prep table without permission, though. Even the toughest kids learned that if you messed with Mrs. Fiore, the fur and the pots and pans would start flying. Apart from that, everything seemed under control as we looked forward to our seventh season.

Then one evening Theresa dragged me over to the television. It was two days before our opening session and here's a news flash from Newark. Rioting had erupted in parts of the city, and we stared helplessly at the TV as images of tanks entering Newark's main streets to the accompaniment of rifle fire flicked across the screen. All those kids we'd gotten to know at camp were in the middle of this war zone, and we couldn't do a thing to help them. And then the governor made a speech.

"The situation we have here is truly perilous," he intoned in a graveyard voice. "As of today, we're halting all government programs in the city of Newark to ensure the safety of our citizens." I was in shock as I realized that our entire camping program was in jeopardy. I'd already hired the staff, purchased supplies, including all the perishable items for the kitchen. If the state's support evaporated, I'd sustain a financial blow from which the camp might never recover. But nothing keeps me down for long, so I began plotting my next move.

I was far from helpless. Come on, I knew the present governor; I'd helped him campaign for office. Of course, he had an entourage complete with guards trailing him constantly, so getting past them to bend his ear would be iffy. I had an ace in the hole, however. I knew that the governor parked his vehicle in an out-of-the-way spot behind the statehouse—a propitious place to have a quick word with him. The next morning, I loitered in the attack area, attracting the attention of several state troopers who wanted to know what I was up to. Luckily, a couple of them recognized me from when I'd revised their State Police Academy physical fitness program a few years before. "Hi, good to see you again. Actually, the governor asked me to drop by so he could have a word with me before he went into the statehouse. You know how he is."

They sort of bought it, and said, "Okay, Don, but make it snappy. With the riots, he's got end-to-end appointments and meetings all day." Their attention span must have been at low ebb, because when the guy finally arrived, they got all officious and brushed me aside. Well, I wasn't having any of *that*! Elbowing forward, I bellowed the governor's name and waved frantically.

Looking nonplussed, he said, "Don, what in heck are you doing here?"

"I gotta talk to you. Won't take a minute."

"Why don't you walk me to my office?" he suggested. "Now what's on your mind?"

"What's this I hear about cancelling the city's summer program? That would include the grant for Kamp Olympik."

"'Fraid so," he muttered, stepping around a piece of flapping newspaper blowing toward us. "I don't know what else to do."

"Listen, the best way to keep the kids safe is to get them out of the city. They need a time-out to swim, to play in the woods where they'll just be kids, not targets. And our tutorial program delivers the goods. They need Kamp Olympik, don't you agree? Governor? *Governor?*"

As he was walking away, I heard him mutter, "Darn it all, Don. This situation is so dog-gone frustrating!" like he was talking to himself. Had he heard me at all? I couldn't tell.

The next day, after I'd chewed my nails up to my elbows, I heard that the governor had announced that all summer programs with sites outside the city would proceed expeditiously. So camp was on! Talk about cutting it close … this drama played itself out just hours before our opening day. Somebody up there was working with us, and I think my dad had a direct connection.

Upon the arrival of the Newark buses at camp, everyone applauded like crazy, especially the staff members who knew they still had their jobs. Then Uncle Joe, who was driving the lead bus, came leaping out screaming and yelling. "Don't ever, *ever* ask me to do anything like this again. They were shooting at us, Don. Next time you ask me to drive into a war zone, get me a freakin' tank!"

I checked out the bus, and damn if there weren't bullet holes, two in the back and one on the side. My first thought was that the kids would be traumatized, but they weren't mainly chattering about bullets. For the first time in many of their lives, they had new stuff. They all had new clothes and shoes, even though they weren't the right size. Many sported new watches or showed off portable radios. One camper bragged on his new television and hi-fi record player. But when I looked closely, I could see the shadow of fear in their eyes. I tried to visualize what it had been like for these children as they struggled to articulate their horrendous ordeal. Once they got talking, one couldn't stop talking about the gunshots in the neighboring apartment building, another kept repeating how scary it felt like to look outside and see tanks keying their guns in on the snipers. The youngest ones tearfully told of sprinting up and down hallways trying to get to the back exits, thinking somebody was going to shoot them any second. The craziness of it all terrified them, but we assured them that here at Kamp Olympik they were safe. You could see calmness stealing over them as the day went on, and by the time they walked to their cabins, they were indeed happy campers. It sure made us feel good knowing we could give them a safe haven, even if just for a short time.

T hat year my family and I moved permanently to the camp, and the entire property became our playground. Once the camping season was over, the weather was still warm enough for both swimming and riding the Hondas along the forest trails. The camp provided fantastic fun, but also served as a base for interesting nighttime ventures. My brother Bill—half brother, actually, but we didn't see the difference—and his friend Duke came down with their wives for a holiday weekend, so all of us Braggs took them to a famous restaurant called Zaber's just outside of Atlantic City. Since Zaber's lobster dinners were legendary, we each had one of the huge, succulent crustaceans, and the adults imbibed Zaber's-sized martinis, which were triple in size. To this day I maintain that the combination of seafood with the vermouth in the drinks was responsible for what followed. Anyhow, we were all feeling pretty frisky by the time we got back to camp, and when Bill asked what we could do for excitement, I dreamed up some after-dinner entertainment. "Look," I said. "It's been raining for days, and the river's running high and fast. Let's drop some canoes in the river near our cabin and go downriver. It should be a wild ride." Everybody gave their boisterous approval except my sensible wife, who gave me the "leave me out of this, kiddo" look as she collected the younger children around her.

"And then we hike back?"

"Nah," I said. "Theresa can come pick us up … if we survive." They were all laughing like the dickens, which should have warned me that our brains weren't running at full bore.

Seeing the Wading River up close and personal, I realized just how fast the water was moving. "Okay, guys," I said. "Everybody into life jackets. That river is really traveling."

Somebody said, "I'm a fantastic swimmer. No way I'm wearing a sissy jacket!"

Another voice piped up, "Yeah! We'll be safe in the boats."

"Uh-huh, if you *stay* in the boat. With the river so high, the branches of some trees are barely clearing the water. They could knock you out of the boat, and you'd be swept away before we could fish you out."

But the guys insisted. "No life jackets. D'you think we're chicken?"

"Okay, so you're not chicken," I said. "My son and I can stay ahead of you with the flashlight. That way I can warn of any low-hanging tree limbs."

"No problem," came the inebriated chorus. But my son Mark was dubious.

"Dad, are you sure this is a good idea? It's awful dangerous with the river moving so fast."

Now it was my turn to say, "No problem. I'm a professional." That struck me funny, and I burst out laughing. Once we pushed off from shore, though, I wasn't laughing anymore. Several minutes into our lunatic adventure, I realized that with the speed of the river and the limited visibility—even with the aid of our flashlights—we'd gotten into a dangerous situation. My brother and his wife were in the boat immediately behind me, and I heard him shout. "I'm pulling over."

"What the hell for?"

"I have to light my pipe." Brilliant, I thought. This was no time to do a Sherlock Holmes impression. His next comment was even more profound. "Uh, Don? Where'd you put the riverbank? It's gone."

"About four feet directly under your butt. The river's flooded over the banks, remember, Doofus?"

He fussed around with the pipe, and finally got it lit, so I assumed he was happy. Now I hear from Duke, back in the third boat with his wife. "Man, this is tricky. If you relax for even a second, some branch smacks you in the face." So there I was looking over my shoulder at him, all solicitous, and I turn back around into a left hook from this massive branch. As it hit me upside the head, yet another huge tree limb rammed the canoe, and damn near tossed my son and me into the drink.

Righting the canoe, I hollered, "Bill, watch out. This branch is a killer." Just then Bill and Dee started yelling, and I saw a flashlight somersault up in the air and splash into the river as his canoe capsized. I couldn't see a blessed thing, just what sounded like the drowning gasps and gurgling shrieks of fifty people. If they were capable of that much racket, I figured they were okay, and I got set to scoop them up when the current dragged them past our boat. Yeah, right! I glanced up in time to see a tree appear out of the dark, and the damn thing proceeded to knock all hell out of the canoe, flipping it over like a toy.

I bobbed to the surface and realized I'd wear myself out if I fought the current, so I started bellowing for everybody to head for the side of the river and find the damn bank. Mark quickly scrambled to safety, but I was barely able to catch hold of branches to avoid being swept downstream through the dark forest. Naturally, both Bill and I gave vent to some colorful howls of outrage. Not relaxing my death grip on the branch, I looked around and saw Bill's wife, Dee, standing a few feet away in three feet of water, her hands on her hips, laughing her head off. "Why don't you two knuckleheads stand up and quit hollering? It's shallow here." Feeling like an idiot, I clambered to my feet with an assist from my tree limb and stood next to her on the submerged bank of the river. This was more like it.

"Bill?" I called.

Choking with laughter, Dee pointed downstream, and there was my brother, hanging on for dear life to the branch next to the one I'd just turned loose. "You mean that waterlogged raccoon over there?"

The sight of him broke me up, too. Not only was his hair plastered down in true drowned-rat fashion, his teeth were bared rodent-style as they clenched determinedly to that dumb pipe that jutted out from his teeth upside down. God, he looked silly. When we'd stopped laughing enough to talk, Dee said, "Bill, for God's sake stand up and get out of the water."

What she said made sense, or would've if Bill had been standing on the bank with us. Turns out he was beyond the bank in the deepest part of the river. Trying to look dignified he lurched away from his branch and promptly sank with his beloved pipe still clamped between his teeth. The pipe managed to poke itself out of the water for a second or two like a submarine's periscope. Damnest thing you ever saw. Ten seconds later Bill surfaced, already ten feet away, minus his pipe, and screaming for help. Thank God he'd managed to grab a slender branch that dipped well out into the river, but I didn't know if it would hold him for long.

Getting to him was like wading through soupy cement, but I finally reached him and hauled him on to the submerged bank. You'd think he would've been grateful to be safe in knee-deep water, but not my dear brother. "She did it! You heard her tell me to stand up, didn't you?" he roared. "She's always had it in for that pipe, and now she's killed it."

"Don't worry," I consoled him through my guffaws. "Some possum is probably smoking the damn thing right now." That got him laughing, and the three of us stood there dripping, laughing like drunken sailors, which I guess we were.

We finally realized it might be a good idea to see what happened to Duke and his wife. When we found them, I could've cheerfully strangled them both. They were pulled to the side a little ways downstream laughing like hell.

"When you fell in, I hit the tree, but we swerved past you and in toward the bank. I grabbed a tree branch and steadied the canoe so we didn't tip over."

"How nice for you." I was beginning to feel chilly, and his dry clothes and cheery attitude really pissed me off.

"Damn it all," said Duke. "I thought a shark had Bill from the way he was carrying on. I was about to go after him when I saw him grab a branch just upstream of us."

"I lost my best pipe," Bill wailed to the unsympathetic night.

Ignoring Bill's grief for his lost companion, Duke said, "Man, if I'd only caught your little escapade on film, I could've sold it to the Comedy Show of the Week for a small fortune. You guys were a scream."

Duke might have the luxury of sitting there and bemoaning the jackpot he lost for the lack of a camera, but I had to decide how to get us back to the camp. Two canoes were halfway to the Atlantic Ocean by now, and we were still in water up to our waists on the wrong side of the river. Other than that, we were in great shape. My son scared the hell out of me by jumping into the one remaining canoe to help ferry the idiot grown-ups to the other side. I was pretty sure we were out of the woods, so to speak, because I knew there was a path paralleling the river that would lead us back upstream to the camp. We found it, all right. Problem was, this path is now under at least three feet of water.

"Don't worry," I lied. "I could get us home blindfolded." So they're following me, all trusting, and the next thing I know Dee was hollering that the water was up to her neck. That's my drawback as a guide. I tend to forget that everybody's not 6' 3", and we were apparently marching right back into the river. "Okay, back up some, and we'll try again." It took us an hour to wade back to camp from our botched adventure. We could have been lost the whole damn night, with all the wrong turns we'd taken. I can't tell you how good it was to see the camp lights glowing through the trees. We hastily started a campfire, throwing on wood till the blaze started warming us.

Theresa, the smart one, hadn't left to pick us up yet. "I thought your trek would take you a good two hours, if not the whole night," she said pouring cups of hot coffee and passing round a bottle of brandy to revive us. "I guess, considering the possibilities, you made pretty good time." Of course everybody had to tell his version of our adventure around the campfire, and from the way the tale got embellished, you'd have thought we'd been on the Amazon River fighting off headhunters. What a great weekend! Kamp Olympik forever!

Chapter Five

I've told you what a great guy Barry Ross was, but he sure got into trouble with me that first week of camp. See, he'd brought two other counselors with him from his hometown. That was Barry, always talking up the camp, always recruiting.

However.

I was holding down a bunch of jobs during our stint at Kamp Olympik. So whenever I had to supervise the late shift at my health club in Cherry Hill, over an hour away, I'd get back to the camp around midnight. I'd try to ease in quietly and would immediately begin a circuit around the entire area, especially the cabin section, to check the pulse of the camp. This one particular night, as I approached the cluster of cabins not that far from the back entrance, I heard a noise that suggested somebody was having more fun than was appropriate at that hour. I crept closer. There, kicking back behind the first cabin were Barry, his two friends, plus a couple of other counselors. I hung back in the dark and listened.

"Man, this is the life," Barry was saying. "The kids are great; we've got weights to work out with; we can train in the evening and then take a nice swim. What a great job!"

Just then somebody said, "Hey, Barry. Pass me another beer."

Without waiting to hear more, I came flapping out of the woods and chewed out everybody. "What the hell is this? Didn't I tell you that beer is *out*? This is a camp for kids, not a frat house." But the nonchalant way they were eyeing me told me I hadn't gotten through to them, which really ticked me off. "That does it! You guys have a choice. You can get up off your sorry butts and run a hundred laps on Piney Road, or you can pack up and head out, and I do mean now." Piney Road was a dirt path that ran through the pine trees for about the length of two football fields—200 yards in round numbers one way. It was hellishly dark, especially on a moonless night like this one.

All but one of the guys kind of slunk off with comments like, "What's his problem. It's only beer." Barry, however, stood up and headed for Piney Road. He was already running before he disappeared into the pines, monitored by a senior counselor to count the laps. Anyhow, by this time it was about one in the morning, and all I wanted to do was crawl into my bed. But no, I had to stay on the collective rears of these nit-wits and see they got packed up. Needless to say, I wasn't about to show these sullen brats much mercy as they dragged their bags toward the dining hall.

"Where do you think you're going?" I demanded, blocking their way.

"In there to phone for somebody to pick us up, dumbass," one of the little guano heads snickered. "Or do you want us to use the phone in your cabin?" So I was in the presence of comedians!

"Excuse me, gentlemen, but the phone you're going to use is that way." I pointed toward the dark road leading toward Mick's Country Store. "It's only a little over a mile, but I suggest you get your butts going. These woods turn mean after midnight."

You should've seen the way they hustled out of there, looking over their shoulders, nervous as cats on a phone wire. I trailed them with my pickup truck, and to add a little spice to their early morning walk, I'd occasionally flick off the headlights to scare the living daylights out of them as they stumbled along in the dark. I think every monster they'd ever conjured up around the campfire crept along beside them. That made me feel all warm and happy inside.

They slept in the woods until their parents picked them up, and I could hardly wait for the irate calls from their indignant parents. I was really primed. However, nobody made so much as a peep. Maybe mom and dad were as upset about the drinking as I had been. I was heading to my cabin and my sleeping wife when I remembered I still had to deal with Barry. I had to laugh just thinking about the guy. So far as we could see, he wore the same bathing trunks every day, and they had that miserable cedar water stain all over them. At least we all hoped it was cedar water. He looked like wolf boy, one of those feral kids that wandered out of the woods somewhere.

He was still running laps, and his watchdog was laughing. "What's this about?" I asked, almost too tired to give a damn.

"The poor guy stopped dead after about twenty laps and says to me, 'Tell me the truth. I'm fired, aren't I?' 'Could be,' I said. 'Mr. Bragg's pretty steamed.' So he started jogging off, then he came back and asks, 'If I'm fired, why in hell am I running my butt off out here where the Jersey Devil drools in the middle of the doggone night? It's pretty damn scary out there all by yourself.' And I said to him, 'Hell, Barry. Don fires all of us every so often to improve our character. It's part of his charm. Just keep running your laps, and he'll hire you back tomorrow.' So Barry says, 'He's out of his mind, right?' 'That's right, so get going,' I responded, serious as a gravedigger."

I didn't see Barry, so I asked the counselor, "How many laps had he done?"

"Close to thirty."

I was practically gibbering with fatigue, but I calculated the distance at about three miles. No way in hell was I going to stand there in the middle of the night waiting for a guy to run laps that were supposed to be a punishment for *him*. "Okay, tell him to take a fast swim and hit the sack." And I got out of there before I had to deal with anything else. These little incidents occurred from time to time, but were solved by even-handed retribution with a chance for redemption. It took a lot of our energy, but not maintaining a strict discipline code would have destroyed the camp. Once everyone became acclimated to our rules, things functioned more smoothly. Incidentally, later on that season, Barry was named the outstanding counselor for the camping session. The next year he became the assistant director reporting to Rich.

Another young man who made his mark at Kamp Olympik was the guy I've mentioned named Doug Kemble. A senior in high school, he lived just ten miles away and worked at the nursery his dad owned. When he heard that we were running a camp, he came and talked to me about becoming a counselor. "I've always wanted to work with kids, Mr. Bragg," he said. "I think I may want to go into teaching." He seemed like a nice, generous-spirited kid with his 6' 8" height supported by a slender but wiry frame. He was clearly an athlete and that, plus his desire to help kids, made him look like a natural for Kamp Olympik. So I gave him a chance. Two days later my new counselor buttonholed me outside the dining hall, and he was practically foaming at the mouth. "I don't know about these kids, Mr. Bragg. They must be deaf. They don't do a thing I tell 'em, just yell and carry on. Man, I think maybe I'll end up driving them way out and drop them off in the middle of the woods if they don't straighten up."

My ears pricked up, to say the least. "If you feel that way, then maybe you're just not cut out to be a counselor."

"How the hell do you expect me to go through the kind of shit these kids dish out on no sleep?"

"So you're not sleeping well?"

"Have you seen the bed I've got?" he squawked. His bed was standard issue but, yeah, with his height, he had a point. He continued to glare at me. "The only part of me that's got bed under it is my butt. And you know what? I can't take this nuthouse camp another damn second!" So Doug and I parted ways. Our relationship wasn't done, however. About a year later he started dropping by the camp to shoot baskets, but we both ignored each other, you know, looking the other way, kind of snooty.

He was going to college now, learning, growing up, and one day he said, "Hey, Mr. B. How 'bout a little basketball?" So I wrapped up what I was doing, and we had a game of one-on-one. It was a great icebreaker, and he soon became a fixture around camp. When he finished college, he assumed leadership of our educational program, and he was a genius at spotting jocks with smarts who'd fit right into our program. The thing about jocks was that the competitive gene had totally infiltrated their DNA. But Doug saw to it that this innate competitiveness went farther than Tarzanville or the basketball court. He instigated a competition that kept raising the bar on their teaching skills, and you could hear the buzz between the teachers about whose kids were the best at math or reading. One of the guys would say, "My kids aced the section on fractions. They're winners." Then somebody else would say, "Oh yeah? Well *my* kids finished the last grammar unit in four days. Eat my dust, Hot Shot."

At the beginning of the season, one of the teachers came into the dining hall all indignant. "One of my kids can't even read the title of the damn book. The *title*! They never taught him a damn thing in school!" Fast-forward one week. Same teacher struts into the dining hall. "Billy's reading up to his grade level. Hell, by the end of session I'll have him up to his academic level in both reading and math." He kind of looked around as if to say "Top that if you can!" And Doug would be sitting there with this big grin on his face. So though he was an utter misfit as a counselor, he was an intuitive and gifted teacher who knew how to motivate. He became a great friend. Friend, hell. We became almost like father and son.

That close relationship was made possible when the Bragg family moved from Trenton to live at the camp full-time. It was the greatest time of my life. Being outdoors in the Pinelands was a treat, especially after the nuthouse called Kamp Olympik closed for the season. There was peace and quiet and a sense of tranquility you can't get in any city; I don't care how many parks and duck ponds they've got. Theresa was terrific. She never complained, even though she had to drive over fifteen miles to get milk. Of course, the country driving was a breeze, with no real traffic, so it took no time at all to travel to and from the nearest town. One day I ran into a guy named Tony Bilazzio, a friend of mine who'd dropped out of Villanova. He ran a butcher shop in Egg Harbor, and he took pleasure in seeing that my campers got the very choicest cuts of meat. You don't get that degree of generosity from your run-of-the-mill city butcher.

So with the campers gone by the end of August, my family enjoyed the added bonus of the Pinelands' magnificent autumn, with nature reflecting the peaceful harmony of the forest. Our kids were in heaven since they had all the camp equipment to play on. Not only did they get to swim late into the season, they had a ball with the canoes, miniature motorcycles, and Tarzanville. On weekends they'd always bring kids home from school, and all the children enjoyed having their own private Disneyland.

During the season, it was fun seeing the little kids, my own and our campers, invent their own competitions, from who could walk a slippery log the fastest without busting their butt to who could cram the most green beans into one cheek. Problem with this last trick was that the competitors tended to start laughing before they swallowed, and the resultant geysers of semi-chewed beans became a regular hazard in the dining hall. I didn't come down too hard on the kids, because all jocks love to compete, and some of our grown-up contests weren't that much more sophisticated.

Competition. It's a way of proving yourself, of getting bragging rights, of keeping current, or of demonstrating—if only to yourself—that you can still strut with the finest tigers in the jungle. Arm wrestling was my weakness, and I was good at it. Even when I was in the hunt for an Olympic medal in pole-vaulting, I managed to make a name for myself as an arm wrestler.

Who creates these goals for us that become a necessity and a must?

—Don Bragg, "Games of Life"

So fast-forward ten years, and here I am feeling the itch to enter the gladiatorial ring one more time. I was primed for arm wrestling action when a guy named Neil—whom I'd known for some time—dropped by during the summer camping session. Now Neil was a promoter, and he never even scratched his nose without an ulterior motive. When he told me he'd just stopped by to say hi, I knew he was up to something.

He was.

First he gave my ego a thorough massage right in front of the dining hall, where he immediately attracted an audience. "Hey, Don! Running a camp must agree with you. I've never seen you in better shape." He looked me over admiringly. "Flat abs, great lookin' pecs, and biceps that won't quit. Damn. You getting in shape for the next Olympics?"

"You're full of it. I'll be forty before you know it, and my waistline's almost there right now."

"I'm telling you, you look terrific. Just as good as when you broke that guy's arm when you were arm wrestling several years ago." Then he shook his head sadly. "It's a real shame you're not arm wrestling any more. I know a guy—just a green kid, really—but he's pretty good."

"That's what they all say before they get beaten," I reminded him.

"You know Gorilla Monsoon?"

"The pro wrestler? Sure, I know who he is," I said. "So what?"

"This kid just beat him."

"Impressive." I agreed. "So what does all this have to do with anything?"

"See, the kid's gotten a little too sure of himself, and he needs to be brought back down to earth. Why don't I bring him by so you can teach him a lesson?"

With all the kids standing there saying, "Yeah, sure, Mr. Bragg's gonna kick his butt," I capitulated.

"Well, okay. Bring him around Saturday," I said. "We'll announce it to all the campers and possibly to some local papers."

With a wide, foxy grin, Neil slapped me on the shoulder. "Then we'll see you Saturday."

I really should've known better. The arm wrestling fraternity isn't known for its attention to the gentleman's code of conduct. So why didn't I back out right then? Because I was looking for another ego trip to Machoville.

We placed the table in the center of the basketball court and assembled the campers as well as quite a few locals. I took a look at my opponent, and nearly called off the match. He was fairly small, lightly boned: wiry, but without the bulging biceps I associated with champion arm wrestlers. For a moment I felt like I was taking advantage of a young kid, but he met my gaze and held it like somebody who really wanted to compete. So, with the campers hollering for Tarzan to beat the kid's butt, we settled down to our contest. I could feel hundreds of eyes watching, which really poured on the pressure.

Don arm wrestling as Dave referees.

So Neil says, "Ready, Don?"

Ready? I couldn't wait to get into it. "Yeah, let's do it." We gripped hands, each of us slipping into a position we hoped would bring us speedy victory. The ref gave the starting signal, and five seconds later, this kid I'd assumed was a rank amateur slammed me down. All was silence except for the sound of jaws dropping in awe. I could hear the buzz: that kid just beat Tarzan of Kamp Olympik! To salvage some self-respect and minister to my bruised ego, I said, "Could we go again? I wasn't ready." I mean I couldn't have been ready if he'd gotten me down that fast, right?

Wrong! I was sorry I'd opened my mouth. This kid popped me down for the second time in a row. I did manage to stave off the inevitable for a couple of minutes, but it was futile. Damn, I remembered being the victim of this unorthodox technique in the Middle East when I'd toured years before. Now here it was in the U.S.A., and still unbeatable: the technique would always trump strength, and therefore would always win. So much for a boost to my ego.

Once Tarzan played with the chimps, but after this match the counselors started calling me the chump—in a friendly way, of course. After all, I was still the boss, even if temporarily humbled by ol' Neil pulling a fast one. The counselors in fact owed me one. They'd wanted to bet in the beginning, and I said, "No, this sounds too easy; I'd be stealing money." That was the only good decision I made that day. Later the next year, Neil told me that someone in Philadelphia shot and killed the young man. He and his father were pulling a hustle for heavy money, and they got caught in the scam. And they paid heavily for it.

The one positive thing I took away from that embarrassing match was a resolve to learn how in hell this new technique worked, something that had eluded me so far.

In the interim, I made sure everybody at Kamp Olympik had the opportunity to do some high-end muscle building. Since my counselors tended to be jocks, I decided to incorporate a fairly elaborate weight-lifting setup, so I made space for it behind the arts and crafts building. Doug got involved with the weight setup right from the get-go, and we'd often work out together. Trouble was, the camp's weight-lifting arrangements wouldn't accommodate his 6' 8" frame, and he needed to build up his legs with squats. I sized up the problem and constructed a unique squat rack especially for him. Man, was he grateful! He'd tried the various health clubs, but because of his height, he couldn't use the equipment. Now, at that time, Doug had completed two years of junior college, and was trying to snag an athletic scholarship. Some college in Florida was his first choice, but there was a problem. "No way will they take me at this pitiful weight. I'll need to put on some muscle and at least twenty pounds. Can you help me?"

Could I? I sure was ready to try. I immediately put him on a protein mix and altered his workout program. We started to increase the weight he was lifting, though we used fewer reps so he'd bulk up. In no time, he'd gained seven or eight pounds of solid muscle, but, despite working his butt off, he didn't progress any further, and he had more than ten pounds more to gain.

He was frustrated as hell, and one day after a session with the weights he said, "Don, how about steroids?"

I had to reflect a minute. Steroids were new, and were supposed to be great for building muscle mass. I knew lifters who swore by them, but I'd also known guys who experienced some peculiar side effects, like breaking out in boils, experiencing accelerated hair growth, or wanting to fight the world every minute. I just didn't want Doug to become one of the athletes who depended too heavily on this new, supposedly miracle substance. "Okay, let's give steroids a try. Just don't get consumed by the stuff." Understand, this was during the earliest years of general steroid use, and they were still absolutely legal. Anyway, Doug went to a doctor who dealt with a lot of jocks and understood his plight. The doc started him out on a regimen of small doses, and after just one week Doug started to bulk up. He continued to work out heavy, and after six weeks he'd gained over twenty pounds.

Doug Kemble and Don after basketball challenge.

I didn't see him for nearly a week, then one day, while I was up on the dining hall roof doing some repairs, he comes flying into camp. He's standing there, his eyes bugging out of his head, waving his arms, and yelling up at me. I couldn't understand a word he was saying, so I climbed down the ladder, kind of irritated. "Now what in hell are you hollering about?"

"I've got it. Did you hear me, Mr. Bragg? I've got it!"

It almost sounded as if he were contagious. "What are you talking about?"

"The Florida scholarship. I went down for a visit, and the minute the basketball coach saw my size, he said, 'You're on the team.' Isn't that great? Boy, am I ever glad the steroids did the trick!"

I stopped and looked at him for a few seconds. He was a great kid, so full of his accomplishment, and I was truly delighted for him. I certainly hoped the steroids caused him no problems.

Doug continued to use steroids while he was in school, and at first he seemed okay. However, he soon reported that he kept picking stupid fights during basketball games as well as getting occasional nosebleeds while in class. "Then that's it for the steroids, Doug," I told him. "Stop them immediately." He followed my advice, and happily didn't fall into the pattern of most steroid users, thinking that more has to be better. Doug finally graduated and became the chief teacher at Kamp Olympik, relatively unscathed by his encounter with steroids.

While he was teaching at Kamp Olympik, we became very close. The rest of the camp would watch in awe when the two of us would have our vicious one-on-one basketball contests, but it never got personal. We traveled together whenever I had a banquet or speaking engagement, passing the time by philosophizing and arguing just like brothers. After he married and had two lovely children, he became quite the businessman, working in both construction and real estate. He never lost his love of teaching, though. He was still a young man when he lost his life in a fatal car accident, but I'll never forget his philosophy of life. He used to say, "Hey, Don, I didn't have to fight in Vietnam like a lot of guys did, I've got my health, a beautiful family, and no real major problems. So life is great."

He certainly was one of my best friends and I will miss him always.

As I said, the real enjoyment began for me and my family only after we'd wrapped up the camp season. It was fun to have family and friends visit and enjoy the overall atmosphere of the forest with us, but we also made new friends. It was a great day when Theresa and I met Walt and Virginia Priest and their large family. Walt had also grown up in our hometown of Penns Grove and was a distant cousin of my wife's Italian family. In fact, Theresa's dad Dominick had worked with Walt at the DuPont plant. As young men, Walt and his brothers would drive over from Penns Grove to hunt in the Pine Barrens, eventually building themselves a deer cabin. The Pines' lifestyle suited Walt's personality so well that he decided to make the Pines his permanent home. For a few years he ran a small store and gas station, and it became a focal point for the community, at least until it ran afoul of new state regulations.

He told me the story, which I found infuriating but, unfortunately, fairly typical. Some pipsqueak in a striped suit paid Walt a visit to inform him that the state had concocted a mind-boggling to-do list concerning the gas station's tanks. Walt was to conform to it, or else. Walt took a look at their demands and told Mr. Pinstripes what he could do with them. "Hell, Don," he told me. "They wanted me to dig up the old gas tanks, install some new-fandangled kind of tank, paint 'em pink—I don't know what all they had in mind. Compliance woulda cost more than the income from the whole damn business. Not surprised, though," he snorted. "Never did meet a government inspector type who had two brain cells to rub together. Don't they know they're supposed to be working for you and me?"

"So you closed down the store?"

"I did, and it was a damn shame. Local people and hunters and so on counted on me for gas and supplies and my wife's hoagies. Best damn hoagies in the state! Hell, the smell of those hoagies was what attracted so many deer to these woods."

"Helluva thing," I agreed.

As I remember it, Walt shrugged his shoulders and said. "Yeah, but the family's doing fine. Hell, in between fighting with the government and such, I went and built me a couple of houses, so I guess I won, huh?"

I really liked that man's style.

Having the jovial Priest clan as our neighbors gave our corner of the woods a family atmosphere and made us more comfortable living there. On weekends my older kids and I would jump on our little Honda cycles and head through the woods to the Priests' house. Theresa would follow more sedately on the main road in the station wagon with our younger children and several of her delectable Italian dishes to share. She didn't need to, of course: the Priests always laid out a feast that could've fed an army. On any given Sunday with just the Priest family alone there would be thirty to forty people. Kids would be bouncing off walls and nobody cared. It was family, and they were together, and that was all that mattered. Walt would prepare homemade pasta while Virginia marinated venison or baked fresh-caught fish. Great food topped off with some good Italian red wine and congenial company: my definition of the good old days.

Once the camping season wound down, we'd host some great parties in the camp dining hall. On Labor Day, birthdays, and on at least one anniversary, the Priests joined us Braggs, and fifty or more of us would have a ball. It was great for the kids, since they could run around and play safely, a collision with a tree being the biggest peril they'd face. But we all loved going to visit the Priests.

One day when I dropped by to visit Walt, his wife, Virginia, told me he was fishing down by the Mullica River. I took off for the bridge where he told me he fished, and found him without any trouble. There he was, crouching under the bridge, still as a stone, his eyes fixed on his fishing line. I said, "Hey Walt, what are you doing?" He put one finger to his mouth and shushed me. "Be quiet! One's just starting to nibble. Scare him off, and I'll feed *you* to the fishes!" He gave me an eloquent glare from under beetled brows. "So hush up!" Silently I crept over to his special spot, out of the sun and comfortable under the bridge. After a good five minutes, he goes for the line real slow, then, with a faster-than-lightning jerk, he sinks his hook into his striped bass. But he wasn't just setting a hook. No, I'd just witnessed the opening salvo of an epic battle that didn't end until Walt finally landed his fish about half an hour later. When I saw what he'd pulled in, I realized why. Flapping on the ground beside him was a thirty-two-pound striped bass. I felt my mouth begin to water. Are those ever delicious! With the practiced ease of the serious fisherman, he slipped the fish onto a chain dangling into the slow-moving water. I noticed there were two other fat stripers already secured there, each around twenty pounds. Selecting a fresh bloodworm with care, he baited his hook and cast it far out into the river.

I was enjoying the shaded peace of the river when I became aware of frantic hollering floating across the water. Sure enough, about 150 feet away, were several other fishermen watching Walt like hunting ospreys. "Hey, buddy! What kinda bait you using?" Walt didn't answer, just kept soft-talking the fish, but the other guys continue to scream, "What're you using to catch those fish?"

Walt answered "Yeh, uh-huh," as if he was talking to himself.

"Why in hell don't you answer?" I asked. "They're asking you about your bait."

"I know what they're doing," he whispered back to me out of the side of his mouth, "Boy, do you see anybody else on the river catching a damn thing? Nope, just me. Hell, I've changed my bait three times to find the right combination to snag these babies. Those bozos sit over there using the same nitwit plastic flies that didn't work two hours ago. Let 'em use a little imagination. Hell, their problem is they're just plain lazy."

So I'm sitting there grinning and listening to the guys across the river piss and moan. This is one slick old man, I said to myself. Here he is, making those fishermen think he's just a guileless old guy, when he's sharper than the whole bunch of 'em. Of course I also began wondering how many times he might have conned me with similar tactics.

There was a spot in Collins Cove near the bridge where Walt'd go in winter. He'd cut a hole in the ice and was fishing for perch. I wasn't impressed.

"C'mon, Walt," I said. "Those aren't even big enough to qualify as fish. Why bother to even pull them out of the water? Be less trouble—and it'd taste better—if you just bought fish sticks."

He gave me a pitying look. "Fish sticks, huh. Come by one of these nights for dinner, and I'll show you what good eating is." Three days later I took him up on his invitation, and boy, did I eat crow. Well, no, I ate perch, and those little suckers did make one of the best meals I'd ever eaten. Walt had shooed his wife out of the kitchen, and had prepared the meal himself. And why not? That was one hard-earned meal, and Walt didn't want to lose the essence by trusting the perch to anyone but the master.

Occasionally I would go to his place for conversation, and I'd find him down in his basement making homemade pasta. He had an original Italian spaghetti machine, and he worked the pasta dough into it at an even pace. Neither too fast nor too slow, just an even, steady motion. And each string of spaghetti was perfect. I offered to help him several times, but his eagle-eyed supervision of my efforts and his amused critique of my finished product were too much to take, so I'd just hang out and watch him.

I also loved to watch him prepare venison. He'd take some of the meat, mix in some fat to give it texture, and then grind it together to make the best damn meatballs and meatloaf I've ever eaten. Meatloaf! Some people carry on like meatloaf's a cross between Fermented Chicken-Feet Surprise and a fifty-year-old fruitcake. Walt's was gourmet fare. He could do it all, and he did it with incredible gusto.

One of those days I went to visit Walt, and Virginia said he was down at the swamp. "Oh, he's out there in his swamp skidding cedar logs. He'll probably be late for supper, and the hinges on that damn gate still ain't fixed."

I didn't want to let on I had no idea what in hell she was talking about, so I kind of grunted, "Oh, yeah, right," then headed for the swamp to find out. As I neared the area I saw Walt, maybe 145 pounds, tops, pushing these immense eight-foot-long logs of cedar around. He'd assembled several stacks about six feet tall by six feet wide, and I had no idea how he'd managed it! Understand, he was over seventy years old at the time, and it would've been a back-breaking task for a young man. I said, "Walt, what the hell are you doing? You're going to kill yourself!"

"No, I won't. It's just that you've gotta skin the bark off the trees, then you take the peeled logs and slide 'em with a pole for leverage. The idea is to stack 'em so the air can dry 'em out and help cure the lot of 'em."

So far as I could see he was assembling a Tinkertoy set for some behemoth. "Why go to all that trouble?"

"Because each stack should bring in over a hundred dollars, and that's pretty good money." Walt was one of those rarities who lived off the land by muskrat trapping, hunting, fishing, and by producing the best vegetable garden in the county. He'd also made a name for himself for catching and cooking snapping turtles, not a job for the fainthearted. One day a guy called him up from a nearby cranberry bog. "Walt, I got a crew digging here, and they ran into a great-granddaddy snapping turtle way down in this ditch. How 'bout you come on over and wrangle him for us?"

So Walt takes off and comes back an hour later with a snapping turtle that weighed in at over fifty pounds. "Look at this monster," he exulted as he prepared his catch for his famous snapping turtle soup. "It must have been down in that moat for twenty years."

When the Wading River worked into Mullica River and Great Bay, it met the surge of seawater coming in from the Atlantic. We'd catch eels in the brackish waters, and they were also great eating. A young guy was visiting once when Walt and I were talking about the good things to eat that were there for the taking in our corner of New Jersey—if you didn't mind getting bitten now and then. Finally, my visitor threw up his hands, totally exasperated. "Now wait just a doggone minute," he said. "You eat eels—you say they taste just like chicken."

"Uh-huh," nodded Walt. "What's your point?"

"And you eat rattlesnake," the guy continued. "Again, it tastes just like chicken?"

"That's true." Walt glanced at me with a just-perceptible wink.

"And you make snapping turtle soup. Tastes just like chicken."

"Exactly like chicken."

"I've been listening to all the close calls you've had catching eels, turtle, and snakes. If these creepy crawlies all taste just like chicken, why in hell don't you just eat the damn chicken in the first place?"

Walt slapped his knee and laughed like hell. He had that old-timer's wide-open sense of humor. In addition to providing food for his family and friends, he also managed— in the time I knew him—to build five houses for his wife and children. I learned a lot from this contemporary man of the wilderness about modern-day New Jersey.

If Walt took me in hand and showed me the ropes of wilderness living, I intro- duced Doug, my camp's young professor-in-residence, to life in the world of celebrity athletes. I'd take him to special events, and had to chuckle at his wide-eyed wonder at meeting the almost-mythic folks he'd read about in the sports sec- tion. At every special event he met quite a few famous jocks and reacted like a kid in a candy store, staring with his jaw practically on the floor. One time, while in New York at a *Sports Illustrated* cocktail hour, he was standing next to Cleveland's Hall of Fame run- ning back Jimmy Brown, basketball great Bob Cousy, and Johnny Unitas, the Baltimore Colts' fabled quarterback. Doug was so overwhelmed he was almost staggering.

And then he met Donna DeVerona.

Not only was she an Olympic swimmer who was making her mark in broadcasting, she was one beautiful woman. Doug's eyes just about popped out of his skull. He kept coming over to me, saying, "She's so pretty. And she's a jock, right?"

"Yes, she's competed all over the world, and she's been on TV." He continued to mutter how beautiful she was, and his eyes began to glaze over. Now this was way before Anna Kournikova hit the tennis court, and I realized what he'd been thinking. "Whoa, Doug," I said. "Don't compare all women athletes to the female jocks from Russia. Some of them are still staying in shape for the battle of Leningrad. Women like Donna, well, they don't think it's illegal to be pretty."

One May evening, I was asked to officiate at an arm-wrestling contest at a small col- lege gym in North Jersey. I'd arm wrestled quite a bit both in Greece and the Middle East as well as the United States and was hardly ever beaten until that new technique I've mentioned was introduced. This new way of arm wrestling wasn't a huge depar- ture from what we'd been doing, but it gave a competitor a tremendous advantage. Where we'd formerly extend our arms across a table with the elbow away from the body, the new style tucked the elbow in close to your side. This way you could use the impetus from both back and hip muscles to get your entire weight behind your attack. There was also more emphasis on overpowering your opponent's thumb, because then you'd control his hand. The new technique made sense, but I couldn't use it for the life of me. However, I understood it well enough to teach it to Doug. This technique, combined with the natural leverage of his 6' 8" frame, would certainly add up to a huge advantage for him. So Dave Miller, Barry Ross, Rich Cheung, Doug, and I crammed ourselves into the station wagon and took off for the arm-wrestling match. It was kind of neat: Doug and his Kamp Olympik entourage.

Doug tore through his early matches, and as the contest progressed, he emerged as a top contender. He was winning by overpowering his opponents with his leverage and quick, muscular slams, and he won every match. When he was coming down the home stretch, however, Doug's arm started to bother him, and he began complaining. The other counselors showed him no mercy. "Shut up with the pity party, already, Doug. Hey, Barry, go find some ice so we can cool down his poor little arm." Our would-be champion had good reason to worry about not being in top shape, however. There was a very strong contender from New York who was also winning his matches with ease.

When Doug came to me, he had a good case of the pre-competition jitters. I took him aside and talked basics to him. "Listen, you've got strength, leverage, and speed, and speed is your most important asset. Don't wait even an instant. I'll be the one to start the match, and when I say go, you damn well go. No hanging back. You got it?"

Doug took my words to heart. He took his position for the final match, and was primed for the attack, like a grenade with the pin pulled. When I said go, he surged from the top and jammed his arm down. His opponent caved before he even knew he was in a battle. Doug had performed magnificently, and became the state champ. Of course, the competition and his backers howled, "No fair that he won. We're from New York. We always win!" Since their only recourse was to petition the head judge, however, they were toast. I did mention I was the head judge, didn't I? Anyhow, I knew Doug had won by turning in a superior performance, and the judge's decision—my decision—was final. Damn straight!

The Kamp Olympik contingent got the hell out of the place as soon as possible, stifling our laughter until we were on our way home. Meanwhile, Doug was dividing his time between moaning about his arm and gloating about his victory. "Last time I arm wrestle. My arm feels like it's about to fall off." Then he'd grin, "But who cares as long as we have a three-foot trophy for Kamp Olympik." Then he'd catch himself. "Of course, you guys do know that this is *my* trophy. Right, guys? *Guys?*"

"Sure it's your trophy. Just make sure you have an extra one made for Kamp Olympik."

Chapter Six

Doug transferred from his Florida school and came to my college for his senior year. A fierce competitor, he was a standout as center on our basketball team and led the school to a winning season. This was quite an accomplishment for such a young school, and Doug was the hyped-up spark plug that made it happen. Barry and Dave were attending as well, and they brought some of the nuttiness from Kamp Olympik right along with them. As usual, 5' 8" Barry was constantly coming up with bizarre escapades, and Dave, towering over him at 6' 5", would nod vaguely and say, "Yeah, sure. Let's do it." The two of them would haul off and charge into some *Jackass*-worthy scenario a sane person wouldn't even consider. Hell, even *I* wouldn't have tried some of their exploits, like setting off firecrackers under the stands during the state basketball championships. Once they'd enrolled at my college, I damn near had a full-time job on my hands just keeping these two lunatics out of trouble. They'd do things like challenge the two best basketball players to a game of two-on-two, with the losers buying the winners a keg of beer. It was a damn close match, but Barry and Dave lost. For some reason, they chose not to pay up, and were constantly being pursued by members of the basketball team who wanted their keg of beer.

Now as it happened, my immediate boss at the college was a good guy, and we had an unusual rapport. If we hadn't, Barry and Dave wouldn't have made it through the year because of what happened one beautiful spring afternoon.

Now I wasn't there, but I sure heard about it. It was lunchtime, and the school cafeteria was packed. So here come a couple of guys—one tall, the other short—highly reminiscent of two noodleheads of my acquaintance. Both were wearing ski masks and nothing else as they streaked through the place at top speed. Talk about creating an uproar! With everybody dropping trays, the girls shrieking, and the cafeteria staff all outraged, it was the stuff of legends! The story hit the school papers, and was a big hit with the student body. Nobody talked about anything else for days—weeks. The idea that two of their fellow students had the audacity to stick it to authority and not get caught really appealed to the kids. Of course there was an inquiry into the prank, and of course it was unsuccessful. Some wiseass suggested that everybody attend class in the nude for a week so the dean could comparison shop for the guilty parties, but like most good suggestions, it was ignored. I finally began to breathe easy again, thinking the two screwballs had gotten away with their prank. No, I wasn't sure, but I had a pretty good idea.

Then my boss takes me aside and says, "Don, come down to my office later this afternoon."

I hadn't a clue as to what he had on his mind, but when I showed up at his office he said, "Let's go out and have a late lunch and a drink. The pastrami's great at Buckets of Blood." His face didn't give anything away, and his noncommittal calm was beginning to give me the creeps, like a scene from *The Godfather*. Well, we got our matinee social hour going, the drinks arrived, and then he faced me, saying, "You and I know who those streakers are."

I tried to appear as clueless as an incoming freshman. "We do?"

"Come on. Who else but your buddies Mutt and Jeff? They're always together, and from what I hear, the heights were about right. They're also the only students on campus who're crazy enough to pull a stunt like that, and I know that for a fact. So how about it?"

"It wasn't them," I said. "At 1:00 p.m. they were picking up equipment at the sporting goods store for the softball championship." At least I thought that's what they were supposed to be doing, but I didn't feel the need to mention that.

He gave me a long, knowing look. "Don, can I be assured that nothing like that will happen again? If so, let's have another drink and talk about something else. Just remember," he ended, "I *know*." We touched our glasses and said *"Salute."* Game over for now. After a session like that, it was a relief to get back to the usual insanity at Kamp Olympik when summer rolled around again.

Close to the camp was the little town of Sweetwater and a boys' private school, Greenway Academy. Their basketball team was first rate, but—big surprise—our counselors thought *they* were the greatest players ever to set sneakers on a court. It didn't take my counselors long to decide we should cook up a competition with the school's basketball team.

So, game time!

Halfway along the road to Sweetwater we had to cross a bridge that had a tower in the middle. It was a tall sucker—I made it to be at least forty feet high. Well, before the game started, our guys and the Greenway staff got in each other's faces about bragging rights to this and that. One of their counselors mentioned that the Greenway folks used to jump off the top of the bridge. "That's way higher than anything Kamp Olympik's got, right?"

It was, by four feet, but I wasn't going to concede anything with Kamp Olympik's macho license on the line. "A scosh higher," I said, "But it doesn't matter, 'cause on the way back home, we're all going off that baby. Right, guys?" I was feeling pretty good about having dared them all, but then I remembered there was a small matter of winning a basketball game to deal with first.

Well, the boys from Greenway Academy played as a team. Kamp Olympik had five guys on the court, each determined to outdo the others, the way they did in Tarzanville and on Kamp Olympik challenge nights. Greenway had a star, a slender Asian guy who was a terrific athlete. My counselors saw this right away, and they swarmed all over him, each one determined to keep the guy scoreless. They did a pretty good job of guarding him, but Greenway still won the game.

"How in hell did they do that, coach? We were in his face every second of that game."

"That's right," I agreed. "And you left the rest of his team wide open."

"But … "

"No, listen," I continued. "Basketball's about team effort, and it takes all five of the players to make it work. Every time you'd key in on the star, he'd pass off, and Greenway would score. When you had the ball, each of you charged for the basket like demons were on your tail, even if another of our guys was in a better position to score."

"Yeah, well …," they mumbled, but they got the message. We played much better after my little speech, but my guys' occasional practices never could produce the results that constant training did. Also, they never completely got into the habit of thinking like team players, rather than rugged individualists. And doing just that was a big part of what made the Greenway basketball team as good as it was.

Everybody was kind of subdued on the bus heading home, but then Barry pipes up, "Don't forget the bridge!"

Dave brightened up and added his two cents. "Yeah, I like bridges." And I was thinking, that's nice. Whatever floats your boat. We pulled over, and everybody piled out of the van, but only a few made the giant leap into the water. Understand that we had to leap far enough out—ten feet at least—to clear the road that ran below the bridge superstructure. Barry pulled out all the stops with some half-gainer somersault shit, and with my wildest Tarzan yell, I followed him in a graceful swan dive. About halfway down to the water it occurred to me that if our dives came up short, we'd be dead. You're brilliant, dumbass, I thought, but always a little after the fact.

We all made it, and stayed in the water playing tag over and under the bridge, only taking time-outs now and then to let boats pass by before their props cut us into little pieces. We'd been in the water a while when it occurred to me to check up on the guy who'd said he liked bridges. I looked up, then further up, and there was Dave parading around the trestle on the superstructure like he enjoyed heights. He was completely at ease. I was impressed: those steel beams up on top were slippery as hell, and you couldn't have paid me to climb up there and join him. Barry let me in on Dave's secret. He'd worked as a painter on the Commodore Barry Bridge on U.S. 322 that connected Jersey with Chester, and the guy absolutely loved scrambling around on the top. It was odd to see Dave showing off, since usually he was so quiet, but then I realized he was simply in his element and having a ball being there. Dave and my brother Georgie finally jumped off and joined our game of water tag. We returned to camp for Yolanda's special *prosciutto i piselli* pasta dinner as the conquering heroes despite the fact we had no victory to celebrate. Problem was, all the other counselors who hadn't been at the ball game wanted to go climbing up on the top of the bridge, but I nixed the idea. It was simply too dangerous.

"Too dangerous?" my wife chimed in. "Then how come all of you went and did it?"

"Because we're professionals, Honey, members of the Chance to Dare Club!"

Theresa raised her eyebrows, glanced at her mom, and then the two of them rolled their eyes and said simultaneously, *"Tu sei pazzo,"* then headed to the kitchen to get our un-victory cheesecake.

The Greenway basketball game and the bridge caper distracted me from an upcoming contest that was a camp favorite every summer: the watermelon bob. This was not a precursor to the SpongeBob craze of a few years back. It was the old Halloween favorite, bobbing for apples, only with watermelons. We didn't try to snag them with just our teeth, of course. It took all the arms, legs, teeth, and ingenuity the campers had to land the big green melons. And by the way, we didn't use any sissy tub of water; we used our entire swimming area on the Wading River.

It amazed me how the kids psyched up for any competition that promised rewards for the winners, even if they didn't win themselves. The littlest kids, the nonswimmers, couldn't really participate without half drowning themselves, so they stayed on the shallow side of the swim area and cheered their heads off for the ones battling it out for the prize. It was their way of competing, and it made the contest a helluva lot more fun.

As we usually did in our camp competitions, we set cabin against cabin, combining younger cabins with older ones for an even mix of kids, and these kids were feisty as they come. You would've thought the match was for gold the way they'd fight. Sometimes they'd make these pacts: we four will work together so we'll get that melon. They'd dunk and splash, and even upend each other, and if you had the melon under you, everybody'd jump on top of you, and the survivor would pop up looking like a sinking rat. The first year we tried this contest, we greased the melons, but not only was it messy, nobody could get a grip on the damn things. It was much worse than a greased pig. At least pigs have snouts and tails to hang on to.

The idea was to eat the melon after the battle, but they were so busted up, in halves or even smaller pieces, with disgusting-looking brown cedar water kind of oozing off them, that they were inedible. Disgusting or not, some kids tackled hunks of the fruit, gobbling them up right on the beach, seeds, rind, sand, and all. Eventually we filled large plastic pretzel barrels with water, and they were much more durable than the melons. It also left more melons for the kids to eat, which was the whole idea.

Once the kids were worn out, the counselor lifeguards would have their turn at melon suicide. These guys had no off switch on their competitive streaks, and once one of 'em secured a death grip on the melon, nobody was about to let go. So you'd have a dozen guys, all rassling and kicking and trying to drown each other over a watermelon. Sometimes the bunch of 'em would float out of the swimming area and down the river into the swamps, and the kids would be helpless with laughter. I mean, the counselors had been constantly lecturing the campers about sportsmanship and fair play. And here these same guys are floating downstream like a gang of rabid alligators, emitting blood-curdling shrieks while clawing and scrabbling all over each other. They'd disappear under the brown cedar water, then bounce to the surface, the cackles, oinks, and bellows getting fainter as they drifted away. We'd run after them with whistles to signal a time-out to bring the melon back to the swim area, the official battle ground. Problem was, we were laughing too hard to blow the damn whistles, and all we could get out of them was the sissy chirping of canaries. We couldn't have broken up a game of dodgeball at a Sunday school picnic.

The victors got the biggest slices of watermelon at dinner, but all the kids ate their fill. Where we consumed the melons was a bit problematical. We started out in the dining hall, but, hell, those kids would be cranked, and before long there were seeds and rinds and chunks of fruit flying all over the place. Then here comes Yolanda. "Will you look at this floor, and I just got it mopped! Out!" She had more to say in her native tongue, but the kids lit out for the safety of the pines without missing a beat. None of them was about to mess with Yolanda—not when her eyes flashed flames of fire and she spewed a torrent of maledictions—in any language. Besides, they knew there were innumerable pots and pans within her reach, a supply of missiles ready for launching.

Eventually we got the kids settled at picnic tables down by the beach, where they could be as messy as they liked. I wasn't aware that too many seeds or rinds got into the river itself, but I found proof that they did. One morning I was out walking along the Wading River downstream of the camp, and I saw these little green plants growing at the water's edge. That's right, they were watermelon plants. I doubt that they survived: the soil was probably way too acid for them. But wouldn't it be neat if some of them indeed bore fruit that some kid found one day, a fitting testimony to Kamp Olympik's watermelon bob contest?

Rich's two younger brothers, Mike—or Magoo, as everybody called him—and Andy had joined us by that time, and both were excellent staff members. Andy worked in the kitchen and even impressed Yolanda. "He's a good worker," she said, "as long as he has a challenge to keep his interest." Not a bad recommendation.

Magoo, the older of the two, was quiet but very aggressive, and he also had a keen analytical mind. Like their older brother, they both were students of martial arts and weaponry, not people to be taken lightly. One day some of the campers were out on the river in canoes, shepherded by a few counselors, including Magoo. They were on their way back to camp, enjoying themselves as they paddled under Godfrey's Bridge, when they found themselves bombarded with stones from above. Now the bridge traversed the Wading River, joining my property to the state campgrounds on the other side of the river. Hanging over its railing and heaving stones down on the kids were about a dozen of the park's overnight campers. Stones weren't the only thing they were hurling at our youngsters. Every other word from these assholes was a racial slur, and that scared the daylights out of my young campers. It wasn't that the kids had never heard those words before; they just were completely taken off guard by hearing them on a harmless canoe trip deep in the woods. Damn it all, and after we'd tried so hard to keep them feeling safe! Then these bloody rednecks—I don't know of a better name for them—started cannonballing off the bridge to overturn the canoes. Magoo got the canoes to shore and, leaving the other three counselors in charge of the kids, tore back to camp, a quarter-mile away.

When he got there, I was conducting the state inspectors on an obligatory tour, and couldn't even give Magoo two percent of my attention. From his breathless story, I knew there was bad trouble. "Go back and deal with it. Peacefully!" I said, and continued with the tour of the camp. Once I got the inspectors installed back in their car, I took off for the bridge like a scalded bear, getting madder by the second. I skidded to a stop before I came out of the woods, though, and eyeballed the situation from behind a screen of pine branches. A hulking, oafish-looking young man was jabbing his finger viciously into the air, damn near touching Magoo's chest. To his credit, Magoo backed up like a gentleman. But the redneck kept coming, poking away with his finger at Magoo. Finally Magoo must've figured being peaceful wasn't accomplishing a damn thing, so he assumed a defensive martial arts stance, and he looked dangerous. He was much smaller than the bully, but he never lost his cool.

Before any physical confrontation occurred, I burst out of the woods, hollering, "What's going on here?"

The head redneck wheeled toward me, his pouty Elvis-looking lips curled in what I think was supposed to be a sneer. "Who the hell wants to know?"

"The king of the jungle, that's who. Who are you?"

He came right for me, looking for trouble, his fist all clenched, and some really nasty words coming out of his mouth, so I assumed a solid stance. He didn't get the message, though. It was a little hard to take the guy's badass attitude seriously with his lips kind of quivering like he was about to barf. So here he comes with his finger, all set to do some poking at *me*. He pushed his finger solidly into my chest, and I sent him sprawling back against the rail of the bridge. Now he really has to prove his manhood or some such shit, and he comes at me like a bull. It took all my strength, but I forced him back. I guess he'd had enough, because his eyes got kind of panicky, and he tried to wriggle away.

"Nothin' doing, bigmouth," I informed him pleasantly as I forced him back into the rail, then pressed harder till he was bent backwards over the railing.

"You son of a …" he began, but I cut in.

"Just shut up and listen. If you ever bother my campers again, I'm coming back to your campsite and kick your ass till there's nothing left to kick." By this time he was squirming like a four-year-old who had to pee, but it was to no avail. When I thought I'd made my point, I turned him loose. That's when Mr. Tough Guy started mouthing off about suing me.

He said, "I'll get your ass for assault and battery!"

"Touch these kids or my counselors again, and I'll finish what I started."

It got back to me from a friend working for our municipal government that this guy rushed over and filed a complaint against me, but the dingbat filed it in the wrong township. Anyhow, I got over to the right township and filed against him first. So there.

The counselors who'd been involved in the Godfrey's Bridge incident were pretty unnerved by the attack on the kids. "We froze, Mr. Bragg. Hell, there were a dozen of them. Don't know what would've happened if Magoo hadn't been there. He wasn't scared at all!"

Reliability in a crisis—that was Magoo. Later on the following year Magoo received his Red Cross waterfront directors certification and became our aquatic director.

Now the counselors could all be officially licensed as lifeguards, which was a load off my mind.

Into the well of fire, into the cavern of the Minotaur.

—*Don Bragg, "Labyrinth"*

The Godfrey Bridge incident didn't come to court until several months later. Unfortunately, by that time my supportive witnesses were tied up with school or family, and they simply weren't available to testify. As I approached the courthouse, I noticed that my opponent, the head redneck, had a gang of his buddies hovering around him. They were glowering at me and trying to look evil, but I merely stepped around them, went inside, and notified the clerk of my presence. Although I kept telling myself not to worry, my attorney hadn't shown up yet. I was certain he'd be there, but once the judge entered the courtroom, I knew I was flying solo. Our case was first on the docket, and my old adversary and I both started to talk at once, each anxious to tell his side of the story. The judge held up his hands, and said, "Gentlemen, one at a time. I can't understand either one of you if you're testifying simultaneously. Mr. Bragg, you go first."

I had a hard time not giving that judge a big hug, because I just *knew* what was going to happen next.

"How come he gets to talk first?" snapped my opponent, getting red in the face. "I'm the one that brought this lawsuit."

"Well, no," said the judge. "Actually, Mr. Bragg filed his lawsuit first."

I raised my hand, like a nice meek citizen, "Actually your honor, he did file first. Of course, it was in the wrong township." I really wanted to get that part into the court record.

"No, Mr. Bragg, you just go ahead and tell your side of this matter."

But the opposition had to dig his grave just a tad deeper. "No way will I accept him talking first."

"*What* did you say?!" I could tell the judge thought the other guy was way out of line by the way His Honor's eyebrows had disappeared into his receding hairline.

Now this idiot—I'm sorry—now my worthy opponent, who was missing one of his shirt buttons, decided to cut himself off at the knees, juridically speaking. "What the hell's going on here?" he demanded, glaring from the judge to me with his squinty little eyes. "I wasn't born yesterday, so don't think you city slickers are gonna get away with shafting me."

The sound of the gavel cut him off, and the judge said in a stern voice, "I've never met this gentleman before in my life. I don't know him. If you continue in this manner, I'll dismiss the case."

Some people don't know when God is telling them to shut up. This guy got real belligerent, and started saying things you just don't even admit to thinking, not in a courtroom.

The judge's gavel thundered. "Case dismissed," he snapped. "And if there's one more word out of you, I'll hold you in contempt of court."

The guy kind of made some gagging noises, but shut up. I felt like buying his blabbing mouth a beer. Because of it I didn't have to deal with a fine or with jail time. I walked out of the court and noticed my attorney scurrying across the street. The redneck bully, however, had to get in my face one last time. He said, "I know a friend of yours, you know, Mr. America. He said if I had a physical confrontation with you, I wouldn't be talking about it. I'd be in the hospital for some time."

"That's certainly a possibility," I said, trying to sidestep any further trouble.

In the middle of all this, my attorney starts tapping me on the shoulder. "Come on, Don. It's about to start."

"No," I said evenly, "it's all over, and I'm not paying you for sightseeing!" He laughed, slapped me on the shoulder, and we retired to the best steakhouse in the county for cocktails and a victory lunch. Kamp Olympik wins again!

Just a few days after the bridge incident, however, I had another opportunity to note the consistency of Magoo's strength and character. My counselors were always up for any competition, and they decided it was time to put their skill in the canoes to the test. As soon as Magoo and Andy got wind of the proposed canoe race, they started practicing during free period in the evening. Magoo, sitting in the back, would be hollering at Andy as they worked on synchronizing their paddling. Andy's big problem was remembering to lift his paddle out of the water on the bends in the river. When the river curved, it was all about steering to perfection, and if you screwed up, your canoe would get slammed against the far shore by the current. So every evening the woods would echo as Magoo yelled, "Dammit, stop paddling and let me steer!"

To make things interesting, anytime they competed, each counselor would ante up a little cash and it'd go into the pot. I'd sweeten that pot by matching whatever the counselors had collected. Now this particular canoe race was to start upriver at Hawkins Bridge, then would follow the river trail that traversed the forest until it reached Kamp Olympik's beach. The beach would be the finish line of the seven-mile serpentine course. This was normally a three-hour trip, and it was an excellent test of a canoer's stamina and focus.

Magoo and Andy started off with the other competitors on that muggy, overcast afternoon, and they were paddling like the devil, determined to win the prize. They were stroking with their paddles in a synchronized rhythm except on the bends in the river, when Magoo, steering in the back of the canoe, took over. Once they negotiated the turn, they were right back to full cadence, aggressively pursuing the river's path to victory. However, just before they reached the Kamp Olympik beach, the canoes had to paddle under Godfrey's Bridge, where the redneck confrontation had taken place only days before. I wondered if that might be a factor in the race. Of course, all the campers crowded onto our beach so they could cheer for their favorite, but I moseyed on over to the bridge and watched the contestants paddle under it. There were four canoes in close contention, all pushing hard, making incredible time. Magoo's boat was in the lead, but he couldn't afford to let up or the competition would be on him. I watched closely as he approached the bridge. His neck and shoulders tensed, as if the memory of that other day—and the danger the kids had been in—rose up out of the shadow of the bridge. I was pretty sure he was close to losing his concentration, but he hung on, paddling even stronger. His canoe swept under the bridge and, several minutes later, right up on to the beach. His time was one hour and twenty-two minutes, which was phenomenal. He was the winner, all right, in more ways than one, and it was an honor to hand him the prize.

Like I said, Magoo was an invaluable addition to Kamp Olympik. Andy had another opinion of his brother, however. As they beached their canoe, Andy jumped out of it and flopped down on the beach. "That's the last time I get in a canoe with that psycho, and I don't care if he is related to me. He's a bloody slave driver."

"Well, you guys did win," I began.

"Yeah, but only because he wouldn't let me take even a ten-second break from paddling. Look at my arms, will you. My knuckles are dragging on the ground 'cause every damn muscle in my arm is wasted."

"You're also sprawled on the beach—that might have something to do with where your knuckles are." He just gave me a dirty look and staggered off to the mess hall, since his shift as Yolanda's go-to guy was about to start. I thought that was that until Yolanda buttonholed me later that evening.

"What did you do to Andy? He came wobbling in to help with dinner prep, and he wasn't worth two cents."

"Why?" I asked. "What did he do?"

"Nothing," she trumpeted. "Not a doggone thing. I asked him to go get me some parsley, and I found him standing in front of the open walk-in, staring at a pound of parsley. 'Just hand me the parsley, for heaven's sake,' I told him. And he looks at me with these sad cow eyes and kind of moos, 'I can't. My arm muscles are all in the river.'" Now Yolanda's glaring at me as if I had something to do with Andy's condition. "Just keep my kitchen helpers away from your crazy stunts," she said. "I don't think he'll even be ready for work tomorrow."

"Where is he?" I asked.

"In his cabin, moaning and groaning like a sick calf." Her eyes narrowed and she gave me a look just one step away from the evil eye. "Whatever you did to him, don't do it again," she commanded, and hustled back to her pasta machine.

If I fire her, I'd have to do the cooking, I told myself, so I bit my tongue and exited before I got myself into worse trouble.

But there was another aspect to the race I need to mention. Not long after the race started, a bunch of little campers came to me all indignant. "Hey, Mr. Braggs, we saw a couple of counselors slinkin' away, and we saw them hide a canoe in the weeds upriver, just past Godfrey's Bridge. It looked to us like they were up to something sneaky!"

Oh, out of the mouths of babes! I told Barry Ross what the kids had told me, and just like I had done, he figured out exactly what these two jackasses were up to. "Those buzzards are gonna launch their canoe a quarter mile from camp and make out like they just paddled their way to victory down the entire course."

"How do you think we should handle it?" I asked, wondering if Barry's ingenuity and mischievous streak would save the day.

"Just leave it to me," he said with an evil grin, and headed back to camp.

Well, what he did was this. He got a few other counselors together, and they moved upriver with a good deal of laughing and high-fiving. Nearly two hours after the race started, the two jackasses evidently dragged their canoe out of its hiding place, got it into the water, and started paddling toward the beach. Before the two of them got to the finish line, however, they had to paddle by the diving tower and the surprise that was waiting for them. They didn't realize that the race had already been won, and as they came in view of the beach, they began punching the air and making out like winners. They were just gliding past the diving platform when Barry and his cohorts began cannonballing them. The canoe capsized, and our two great pretenders were treated to an unforgettable demonstration of why trying to cheat at Kamp Olympik was always a bad plan. The drubbing their buddies gave them was a perfect end to a great day!

A fter several years of living at the camp, Theresa and I were delighted when her sister-in-law and her two sons, Craig and Marc, moved to the Pines. The boys immediately became playmates for the little Bragg kids, Mark, Renée, Tracey, and Jeff. Off-season, the entire camp was their playground, and they used it to the utmost. Craig and Jeff were inseparable, just like brothers. They even had their first day of school together, in a little one-room schoolhouse out in the Pines. Except for the Priest family, Theresa and I and the kids never did quite fit into the local social scene, and so the children had a strong camaraderie with one another. Adding to the family accommodations, Yolanda and Dominick bought a sixty-foot trailer that they situated just beyond our cabin. It was large, an incredible grandkid magnet, and it provided all the extra space our extended family needed. Once all the facilities were connected, it was self-contained and very comfortable.

Now I have to hand it to Theresa. We stayed in the uninsulated cabin for three years after we started living at the camp year-round, and she was an incredibly good sport about it, even though I'll have to admit she really didn't have a choice. Of course, the kids and I loved it. What could be better than living rent-free in the middle of the magnificent state forest surrounded by nature? There was a hookup for electricity, and we had access to all

Bragg's family cabin at camp.

the water we could use, also free of charge. While there was no insulation, the cabin interior was paneled, which helped retain the warmth cranked out by our primitive heating system. That was a cast-iron Ben Franklin stove fueled by propane gas logs. Of course, some heat did escape through the chimney flue, but I installed a cookie sheet to redirect the heat back into the room. The cabin was not impossibly large to heat, to say the least. The main room was about twenty by thirty feet, with an additional eight-foot-square room for the kids. I could tell the outside temperature by how high the frost had mounted up on the interior wall. One foot of frost meant that it was fifteen degrees outside—way too cold to venture out.

We had television, too, which helped preserve the family's sanity during the shut-in days of winter. Luckily, I'd made a TV commercial years before, and they'd given me the fiberglass pole I used as a souvenir of the shooting. Once I clamped it to the roof with two brackets, it made a great TV antenna. Since it was made of nonconductive fiberglass, it worked well even during lightning storms. The only problem was that the wind would twist the antenna away from our reception of Philadelphia broadcasts. So during football games we'd have to go outside and boost my son Mark up on the roof so he could start twisting the antenna. I'd run inside and monitor the TV, and when the picture sharpened up, I'd holler to my wife, who'd holler to Mark, "Hold it right there; we got it." Some especially cold and windy nights we never finished our shows, because somebody would've had to stay up on the roof holding the antenna in a death grip to keep the reception steady. It was easier to turn off the set. At bedtime our kids wore sweat suits over their pajamas, and they stayed nice and warm. Several times a night I'd check the temperature in their room, and on occasion it dipped close to freezing. Being kids, they didn't mind the cold except for when they had to climb out of bed in the morning. They still loved living in the cabin because it was like camping out all the time.

The cabin had an attic, just like the cabin Uncle Joe had used, and when we started hearing noises up there, I was concerned that a battalion of bats was beginning maneuvers. One evening I handed Mark a flashlight and boosted him up into the attic to reconnoiter. I heard him scrambling around, then a bunch of "*Ooooh!*"s.

"You okay up there?" I shouted, suddenly anxious.

Mark's head popped down through the access vent. "It's not bats, Dad, just a bunch of cute little chipmunks."

I acquired a small ladder to access the attic from the living room. It wasn't unusual for us to come home and find the ladder in place and our children nowhere to be seen. "Are you kids up there again? What in heck are you doing?" I'd holler.

My daughters' little voices would respond, "We're just feeding the chipmunks, Daddy. It's winter, and they can't get any food. And they are *so* cold."

Needless to say, nobody raised a hand against these adorable furballs, even though they kept us awake nights with their scratching at our ceiling and having what sounded like late-night bowling tournaments right over our heads. We finally adjusted to the racket, and why not? After all, we were in their territory.

But although my wife didn't make a fuss, our living arrangements really got to her mom.

"When are you getting these kids a proper house?" Yolanda would say.

"As soon as I get enough money saved up for the house Theresa and I really want." I wasn't just trying to put Yolanda off, either. It was the absolute truth. When I was growing up, mom and dad had trouble making ends meet, but I'd always had definite ideas of the kind of house I wanted for my own some day. I also knew damn well what I didn't want: some cookie-cutter three-and-two tract house that fell off the assembly line. Whatever it cost, I wanted my dream home to be magnificent: nonconventional, but with a woodsy look that would fit in with the natural beauty of the Pinelands. My wife wanted the house to be elegant—she loves having people over and sharing her home with them. If ever any woman possessed the hospitality gene, it was Theresa. We also both wanted a house where our kids would have plenty of room just to be kids, to have friends over, whatever.

It wasn't long before I was on the prowl for another piece of property. One day old Fred Brown happened by, and I mentioned that I was looking to buy some more land. "You don't happen to know of a nice parcel of land with a lake and maybe a little high ground, do you?"

"Y'already got the one lake. You expectin' a lot more campers next season?"

"It's not for the camp," I explained. "I want to build a new home for me and my family."

He thought a minute. "There is one nice spot just down the road that's on a lake. And I do believe there's high ground enough to suit you."

He took me to a spot about six miles from camp and pointed up through the trees toward a lake framed by the fragrant pine forest. "That what you had in mind?"

It was perfect. Even from the road, I could picture my house set back in the woods next to the lake. "How much are they asking for it?"

"I don't rightly know," Fred responded. "Don't even know that it's for sale."

"Then why in hell did you show it to me?" I exploded.

"Hell, son. Sooner or later, everything's for sale. It's just a matter of price."

"Okay," I said, "then who owns it?"

"Don't know that either." The old man watched me with amusement as I climbed aboard my emotional roller coaster again, then added, "We can go the tax office and find out, quick enough." Again, an old-timer had made the young man look foolish.

Well, I bought that piece of property: 350 acres of timberland with its flooded cranberry bog that had become a permanent lake. It was home to waterfowl and game fish alike. I had truly found my Golden Pond in the forest environment, and it was a dream come true for the whole family. My sons tried their hands at hunting, and though deer eluded them for a year, Mark regularly swaggered home with a brace of geese or ducks for supper. Jeff,

Bragg's Dream Home on the lake.

on the other hand, quickly became an accomplished hunter of deer, duck, and geese. In the summer we had a private swimming lake, which was transformed in winter to our own skating and ice hockey rink. The acreage was also crisscrossed by trails that we used for biking and for our own motorcycle course. God had smiled on our family through the success of Kamp Olympik, and we thought ourselves the luckiest family in the land, and probably were. And once we had the land, the Bragg estate began to take form.

Maybe it was the work ethic common to all serious athletes that helped me keep our dream in focus. And, yeah, all tough-talking, hard-as-nails jocks are dreamers at heart. Taking that championship, breaking the world's record, winning your Olympic gold medal, maybe we don't talk about it until we've hit the big time, but that dream occupies an important corner of our souls from the get-go. It has to. We believe that if you're willing to sacrifice for that dream, persevere, keep it in focus, and keep your nose to the damn grindstone to *make* it happen, then it will become a reality.

I worked with our architect, poring for long hours over the blueprints, determined to make the house nothing less than what I'd visualized in my mind's eye for years. I was a horrible client, in some ways. The poor architect would tell me, "Mr. Bragg, you can't eliminate that wall; it just won't work." I'd do it anyway and everything worked just fine, despite his gloomy predictions. Of course, the realization of my dream house would've been less excruciating if I'd had all the know-how, to say nothing of the obligatory professional licenses, needed to complete the job with only my family to help me. Once I actually started building, I discovered that my older son Mark knew more about what doing a job meant than some of the dingbats I foolishly employed. Take the mason I hired, and I wish you had. He came out to lay the foundation and the first floor, and stood staring glumly at the building site. "They say this here place is too marshy for building. They say, four, five year, and the foundation's gonna sink. You sure you wanna do this?"

"Yes. How 'bout getting started?"

He continued to stare at the dirt as if he were reading his own obituary. "Four or five year. That's what they say."

By "they" he meant the old-time Pineys who'd been living in the area for generations, and they could be a grim lot. Whatever you were trying to do, they'd tell you it was doomed to failure and would either kill you or so impoverish you that you'd be selling pencils at bus stations with a tin cup in hand … if you were lucky. Cheerful little rays of sunshine, those Pineys.

"Hear you were up at the farmers' market buyin' fresh cranberries," one of the Pineys said to me one gorgeous autumn day.

"That's right. We're making cranberry sauce for our Thanksgiving dinner."

"Heard people died a few years back from eating cranberries they bought from right around here. Those berries were full of cancer, and that's not something you'd want to be serving up at your Thanksgiving dinner. Surprised you haven't heard about that. It was in all the papers."

What the hell do you say to something like that? Yeah, I'd heard about the carcinogens from the DDT or whatever, but that had been years ago. And this mason I hired was a Piney, through and through. Even after I convinced him I expected him to do the job we'd agreed upon, he still dragged his feet. I'd come by the site on a fine morning to find him gone after having laid his two bricks for the day. I should've been grateful he showed up at all. One day when he didn't, I went looking for him at his office: the local pub in Tuckerton.

"Oh, he's gone fishing," his buddies told me.

"Where?" I demanded, imagining the evasive scoundrel hip-deep in some flooded berry bog, whipping the shallows for pickerel.

"Hell, he took off for some place in Maine. Don't imagine he'll be back in a hurry."

Maine? For one of the few times in my life, I was speechless. There was no way I could find to light an effective fire under this mason of mine, and so, when he'd stalled for the umpteenth time, I fired his sorry behind and found somebody else. This new guy was terrific, and finished the job with dispatch. He also brought along this fragile-looking old fellow to install the living room fireplace, and this guy was an even greater gift.

The fireplace was to measure ten by fifteen feet. Faced with stone, it would reflect strength of family and of nature, and would form a unity with the forest. We'd be able to see the forest, too, through five-by-ten windows. I told the elderly stonemason what I had in mind, and he got busy. He was a cool guy. He didn't talk much, just squatted there, sipping rum and doing magic with the stone. When he'd raised the stonework to a height of about one foot, he asked for my opinion. "Is this what you had in mind?"

"Not quite. Think of the jagged rocks you see around a waterfall. You've got the surfaces way too smooth."

"Gotcha," he said, and went on to create a masterpiece of rugged stone, exactly what I'd visualized. I didn't need an additional career as a full-time woodcutter, so I installed four-foot gas logs in the fireplace, as well as fans that would blow heat into the living room.

Another local who kept an eye on my interests where the new house was concerned was Frankie Dougherty, from Wilmington. He was a good friend who'd absorbed what I was trying to do with the house. Evidently the painting crew that came in to do the tongue-and-groove ceiling was a bit on the officious side, and blew off Frankie's opinion as to the stain they were using. "Bragg'll never go for that," Frankie opined.

"What do you know about it, Frankie?" the others said. "Hell, our manager said this color stain's all the rage."

"That may be true, but I've known Mr. Bragg for years, and I'm telling you he won't like it." When I got in and saw they'd turned my beautiful ceiling into something that'd escaped from the circus, all manner of shit hit the fan. They'd used this godawful shade of brassy orange, and I made 'em do it over. Frankie didn't rub it in, just gave the painters an "I told you so" grin while he sat there sipping his beer.

The living room was built with family in mind. There was nothing dark and dingy about it, since I'd put in those incredible windows plus a twelve-sided skylight that corresponded to the shape of the room itself. The living room was forty-eight feet across, just what the laird of the manor had in mind. Theresa's eyes lit up when she saw the finished space with its twenty-four-foot-high peaked ceiling. It was as if she already imagined the crowds of kids and the daylong parties that would fill the room. And the room would never be chilly in winter. I made sure of that by installing double-paned windows. After all the frigid days in our cabin, I wanted my family to be warm when the weather wasn't.

Don with Jeff, Mark, and Renée outside home.

Now those mammoth windows looked out onto a wraparound deck so we'd have a great view of our lake, only twenty feet away. Being a humble soul, I named it Lake Bragg, and it was well worth looking at. We could watch the otters frolicking in the water, raising Cain with the flocks of Canada geese that called the lake home during the winter months. Now and then a half-dozen or so swans would swoop down and visit for a few weeks. I loved watching them taking off: power and grace in one beautiful package. In the warmer months, we'd have an eagle and some ospreys for company. Sitting by the windows nursing a martini and observing all the comings and goings on the lake was a fantastic way to spend time.

And here's where Theresa and I had our first serious disagreement about our new home. I saw her bustling around with a tape measure, and I asked her what she was up to. "I'm measuring for curtains. The windows look naked without them."

"I paid top dollar for those naked windows. Do you know what it cost to get that much glass tinted?"

"Yes, honey, but we really do need to get some curtains up. The windows face west, and curtains will cut the glare. They'll be lovely, you'll see."

Lovely, my ass! "The whole point of the tinted glass was so we could enjoy watching the sunsets together without getting blinded by the sun. How're we gonna do that if you cover the windows with a bunch of dimity or some such shit?" She gave me the pitying look women have been giving men for centuries when the guys are making perfect sense, but somehow violate the buttons-and-bows concept of style. The windows stayed bare as God intended, and Theresa forgave me for acting like such a—pardon the expression—man where decor was concerned.

When it came to installing my patient wife's kitchen, I made sure that everything was top of the line all the way. The appliances were all built-ins and included a Jenn-Air with grill, and we installed a copper hood over the cooking area. Well, let's say we *eventually* managed to have it installed. Both Theresa and I described in detail what we wanted, a graceful copper hood that would flare out and sort of melt into the ceiling. We both had spoken plain English and used simple, descriptive phrases like "not boxy" and "use curving lines" when we'd told the guy what we wanted, but maybe we should have stuck to words of one syllable. You wouldn't believe what they carted into our kitchen. My first warning that something was amiss was a yelp of alarm from my wife. She was standing in the middle of our kitchen, pointing at an ugly, undersized copper bread box that determined men were hell-bent on attaching to our ceiling.

"What in hell is that?!" I roared. "Didn't anybody at your company read the design specs? It looks like something Fred Brown designed to catch rats in his shack."

"You don't like it?"

"Do *you*?" The man had the decency not to answer, so I didn't need to damage his skull. I began to doubt the sanity of everyone in the building trade, however. Why in hell don't they listen to their clients? Because it would make sense, that's why.

Slowly Theresa's dream kitchen took shape. We installed an oversize sink, an extra-large fridge that matched the kitchen paneling, and a ten-foot-long counter with six captain's chairs at dining-table height. No perching on tippy stools for us Braggs. If you can't be comfortable eating breakfast with your family, when can you be? We usually did eat in the kitchen except for Sunday dinner and parties and such. That's when we used our twenty-foot-square dining area, which was just off the kitchen and elevated above the level of the living room. While we ate there, we could look across the living room to the lake, visible through the large living room windows. Eating Theresa's lasagna with my family, while looking out over the lake—that's what all the work was about, and it was sure worthwhile.

I made a few additions with my own comfort in mind, too. I put in a ten-by-forty wine cellar; I built our sauna and lined it with sweet-smelling white Jersey cedar; and

I installed a six-jet whirlpool myself. It was perfect for overstressed muscles. The room was dark, and I'd go in there and hang out in this womblike space, just like William Hurt did in *Altered States*. Only I did it ten years earlier.

We used board-and-batten construction on the outside of the house, and I stipulated two-by-fours for the battens so they wouldn't be dwarfed by the size of the house. I mean, could you imagine gingerbread-house-looking shit on any place I'd live in?

Theresa: *Talk about multitasking! With Don working at the college, it fell largely to me to supervise our workers as they clumped about our gonna-be house, each with his own aesthetic and agenda. Since I had to tear between the camp and the house several times per day, my nerves' split ends soon developed into a full-fledged frazzle. One of the workers had decided he'd like to occupy one of the capacious bedrooms permanently, a notion hotly contested by Don's brother Georgie. One morning I heard Georgie threatening to kick the friend's butt and, as usual, I dashed out to play peacemaker. Before I could calm the two of them down, however, a combination of exhaustion and tooth-grinding frustration caught up with me and I fainted. Of course, Georgie forgot his quarrel and rushed me to the hospital.*

I was not a very good patient. Despite the doctor's stern orders that I rest, I fretted constantly about the house, wondering what well-intentioned mischief our volunteer crew of helpers might wreak upon our undefended dream home. And then, finally, I was coming in our front door on Don's arm, absolutely stunned by the transformation before my eyes. In my absence, my parents had moved into the house, tidying it and setting everything in place. What a transformation! It was like an Extreme Makeover television show. I'd left a house clad only in carpet, but I returned to a home with our furniture in place and every cabinet and closet tidily filled. What a gift that was!

The new house was six miles away from camp, enough to give us some separation between our work and our home life. As a reward for some special achievement, I'd bring a few campers over, now and then, and they'd sleep in the large rec room, cozy in their sleeping bags. I think the big attraction for the campers was that it made them feel like they were a part of the family. Which, of course, in large part they were.

We continued to live in our old cabin when camp was in session, since being even six miles away from all the action created some absentee management problems. I guess people on the camp staff just weren't able to function away from the sound of my resonant bellow telling 'em what was what. But though the cabin was pleasant enough during summer, it felt just grand to retreat to our real home on Lake Bragg.

O ne of the things I'd sometimes miss during the winter months was the campfire we'd have every night at Kamp Olympik. It was a restful climax to a day crammed with physical activities, and I'd say everybody looked forward to it. Each cabin had their assigned day for campfire responsibility, which entailed combing the forest for firewood. It was understood that fallen trees were to be the prime source of wood for the bonfires, but our enterprising campers may have occasionally helped a tree get fallen.

Now, since I owned land inside the state park, there was always a conflict brewing with the forest rangers, mainly because on my land I did things pretty much the way I wanted. Boy, did they resent the fact that we did not have to abide by their rules. Why are people like that? It's always puzzled me. But whatever the reason, anytime they had an opportunity to oversee our activities, they jumped at the chance with their great big booted feet. So one day some campers were out collecting firewood and, not knowing that green wood doesn't burn, they chopped down a live tree. The tree in question was on state property, and the rangers immediately grabbed the kids and hauled them back to camp. It scared the hell out of the kids, too. The rangers said I was responsible for their actions and that I had to pay a fine. We argued that it was their action, not ours, and we'd told all the campers to keep their hands off wood that wasn't lying on the ground. Conversation with these rugged men of the law was futile. It wasn't paying the fine that bugged me, but rather the principle of the situation. It would've been more constructive if they'd had the kids work off a penalty. That way the campers would've truly had to take responsibility for what they'd done. And they might've listened the next time somebody told them "No!" So the incident really got my fur ruffled, and marked me as a bad apple in the eyes of the rangers.

But back to the campfire.

We'd always have various forms of entertainment during ceremonial sessions of the campfire. Some cabins would present skits or tell stories and jokes. There'd always be a series of tricks played on new campers, and the tale of the Jersey Devil would be retold to set the campers' flesh crawling. Most of the time there would be challenges for boxing between the cabins, and of course I couldn't keep the counselors out of that. They were always up for fisticuffs and the bragging rights that would be granted with a victory. But the campers' acts took the cake. It constantly amazed me how creative some of them were, especially the skits. But they couldn't match the major effort that fueled the talent night we'd hold in the dining hall at the end of each session—but more of that later.

Everyone in camp rallied to any challenge that came his way, and both campers and counselors would fight to the bitter end to come out on top. We assigned individual cabins the duty of preparing the campfire, and every night the kids from one cabin went scuttling through the woods picking up sticks and branches and pinecones, enthusiastic as hell. Unfortunately, it was that enthusiasm that got things galloping out of control. It was fantastic when the "let's build the biggest fire in the world" idea caught on, but it damn near closed down the camp. Once we set their mountain of kindling alight, I was really pleased. Then I realized that this innocent fire was enormous, and when I noticed that the tops of pine trees at least fifty feet away were getting singed, I became concerned.

I wasn't the only one who noticed.

A frantic call came in from a friend of mine in the fire watchtower ten miles away. "What in hell's going on over there, Don? There's smoke pouring out of your area."

"Not to worry, we're just getting ready to roast marshmallows."

"Marshmallows! From the amount of smoke you're generating, they must weigh 400 pounds each. Where'd you get 'em, the Fee, Fie, Fo, Fum Food Mart?"

"Yeah, well, we'll be careful."

"You do that. Hell, I thought there was a forest fire. Damn near called in an alarm."

"The fires aren't really that big," I said, trying to allay his fears. "They may have thrown a little extra wood on the fire; you know how kids will do."

"That's not a little extra wood, my friend. Less wood than that fuels a blast furnace."

From that time on we had strict limits on the size of our campfires, but we certainly couldn't eliminate them. The kids loved the camaraderie of sitting around a crackling blaze while we told ghost stories, including the tale of the Jersey Devil, again and again. After the bonfires would subside, we'd shoo all the campers off into the woods for an energetic jog so they'd burn off some of their energy. If we didn't, they'd be bouncing 'til after midnight. As they ran through the woods after hearing all the harrowing campfire stories, however, they were certain that the Jersey Devil was only two steps behind them, so we never had any stragglers. Damn, but those kids sure could run. Some nights we'd cook hot dogs and roast marshmallows. The marshmallows often became airborne as the kids started lobbing them at each other, or stuffing them down the shirt of an unsuspecting camper. And those marshmallows were still hot from the fire. So we had our share of lively interpersonal confrontations.

When the kids showed up for breakfast the next day, most of them had bits of toasted marshmallow stuck in their hair and eyebrows, and the sticky decorations stayed there till swim period. At least once a session some counselor would emerge out of the dark forest dressed as a weird Piney and scare the hell out of the kids. We had to stop these charades, as some kids became so afraid that they wouldn't sleep for hours. Nobody needed a nightlight at Kamp Olympik, however. From the cabins, which circled the fire, every kid could watch the campfire slowly subside as darkness enveloped the camp. A mysterious tranquility, haunting yet peaceful, settled in as the day was laid to rest.

Chapter Seven

It would be impossible to relate all the tricks we played on each other. It was simply a case of an ongoing challenge, and we all learned that it was never safe to lower our guard. One evening I returned to camp after dark and took my customary tour of the facilities. As I approached the director's cabin, I heard sounds of muffled exuberance coming from behind it. There was clapping, and voices were cheering someone on with a rhythmic "Go, go, go," but then they'd quiet down, as another voice urged them to shut up. It was clearly some sort of athletic contest, but as I crept closer to check it out, a foul odor assailed my nostrils. I glanced around, mystified, because the johns were a good fifty yards away. When I was finally able to make out what was happening, I didn't know whether to laugh, barf, or head for the sanity of a nuthouse. Yes, there was a certain amount of physical effort going on, but it was the straining associated with peristalsis under duress. That's right, these idiots had been cheering on their colleague's successful attempt to produce a steaming pile of excrement that he was catching in a paper bag.

Now I didn't immediately assume these guys had lost their minds. The counselors were pretty tight with one another, and new hires always had trouble breaking into their clique. The newbies sort of hung around in limbo until the established counselors thought up a fiendish initiation to put them through. Then they were accepted. So I had a pretty good idea where this particular bowel movement and its attendant paper bag were heading. I stayed hidden in the wooded darkness watching to see this incredible scenario play out before deciding how to handle it. Also, it was so patently off-the-wall, I just had to see the outcome. The defecator finished filling his paper bag, although most of his comrades had backed away due to the truly revolting aroma.

"Okay, your destination is Cabin 11. The cigarette lighter's right over there on the fence rail. Now get going." So this guy goes creeping away with the reeking paper bag, and he's trying to be stealthy. Stealth was a waste of time, believe me. He could've been invisible, and a corpse with a head cold would have smelled him coming. So he takes his odoriferous parcel and places it about ten feet from the door of Cabin 11. He sets fire to the bag, and it's immediately engulfed in flames. If there had been brush or anything combustible anywhere near the blaze, I'd have intervened immediately … but there wasn't, so I didn't. Meanwhile, the perpetrator scuttled off behind a tree to watch the fun.

The first sounds of life from the cabin were sleepy grunts followed by irritated grumbling. Evidently the smell of smoke finally penetrated the counselor's sleep-drugged brain, and he flung open the cabin door. With a yell of alarm, he leaped through the doorway, dashed into the clearing, and immediately began stomping out the fire. Only after he got the flames under control did he realize that, one, something was sticking to his shoes, and two, it stank worse than a stopped-up public toilet at high tide. When it finally dawned on him that he was getting up close and real personal with somebody else's excrement, he went charging to the lake and jumped in, clothes and all. He flung his shoes into the river as howls of laughter emanated from the shadows around the beach. The counselor who'd been the butt of the joke thus became a part of the gang, but what a price he paid! Of course, I was bent double in the bushes nearly strangling on the laughter I was barely suppressing. It took me a while to get a straight face in place, but eventually I made my appearance and acted as if I were completely ignorant of the hilarious initiation ceremony I'd just witnessed. This atmosphere of a prank at any price permeated the camp throughout the season, but it didn't really bother me. It certainly was a lot more wholesome than drugs or alcohol.

With a campful of kids to worry about, I had to stay vigilant in case booze or weed—or worse—in fact made an appearance. On one occasion, I thought something very illegal had slipped past my vigilance. It was another warm night, and I was taking my customary stroll through the cabin area. The campfire had long since died down, and with it the pervading aroma of wood smoke. A sweetly woodsy scent was blowing through the forest, and I decided there must be honeysuckle or jasmine growing not far from camp. Then a sharp, jarring odor struck my nose, and with the size of my nose, it would've been impossible for me to miss it. Like any experienced parent, I started sniffing, hard. The breeze was still blowing, and the acrid smell would vanish for a moment then reappear. It took a lot of willpower to stifle my growing anger, but I knew I couldn't release it quite yet. On quiet feet I padded through the somnolent silence of the camp, turning my head from side to side, sniffing experimentally, checking my bearings, until at last my nose brought me right to Cabin 2.

Realizing who Cabin 2's counselor was made the matter worse. I knew this kid's dad, and he'd told me that his son, Sol, really wanted the experience of working with kids. The boy was into saving the world, finding himself, that sort of thing. In other words, he was fifteen. "He's a cerebral kid," his dad had said. "He's different; he might not fit in too readily, but he'll do a good job for you."

So Sol had made the trip up from Baltimore and joined my staff. Outside of never changing his clothes, he was an excellent counselor. Of course, none of the other guys were that fastidious about changing their duds either, but Sol took it to extremes I hadn't thought possible. Otherwise, he was a good kid. He worked hard; he really cared about the campers; and he'd done a first-rate job. And now here he was smoking dope? I felt as if I'd been had. Without ceremony, I jerked open the door.

"Oh, Mr. Bragg! Hi," he said, as wide-eyed as a startled lamb as I barged into the cabin.

I think it was the innocent act that really made me lose it. "Don't you dare Mr. Bragg me," I shouted, seizing the astonished counselor by his neck and heaving him at the closing door. He just about went through the screen, but it bounced open, and he tumbled into the clearing outside the cabin.

"How the hell could you do this?" I charged back outside and stood over him, mad as hell. "All this talk of yours about teaching impressionable kids, and you're smoking God only knows what?"

"But Mr. Bragg, I didn't … "

"Don't give me that." I tapped my nose meaningfully. "Nobody's amputated this baby—I could smell it halfway across camp. What is it, pot?"

So here's this kid, down on his hands and knees, looking up at me, all pitiful. "But Mr. Bragg," he sputtered. "I didn't … it wasn't … " but I wasn't having any. Hell, I'd trusted this kid, and I shouldn't have, and the knowledge infuriated me. "Please, Mr. Bragg, I'd never do that!"

"Right. Just get up. You're going to call your parents and tell them to come get you."

Just then Barry, our assistant director, came running over. "Sol told me he's into another eastern religion, Mr. B., and he has to burn incense while he chants."

I glanced at my wristwatch. "He's in there chanting at nearly one in the morning?"

"Well, he's got the youngest cabin, and there are at least four bed wetters. You know what that smells like?"

"Yeah, and what you do is scrub out the bunks."

"He does that every morning," continued Barry in this earnest, intense voice he has. "But he could still smell urine, so he leaves the incense burning. That's all it was."

The incense also might've helped cover up the odor of Sol's reeking clothes, but I didn't mention that.

Of course I apologized to Sol, and he laughed about the incident, but I wasn't sorry it had occurred. As a result of it, my reputation as a supernarc soared. Nobody in camp dared fire up anything even vaguely illegal from then on. They knew there was a canny old bloodhound who roamed the camp in the wee hours of the night, ready to bust anybody for any shenanigans that violated the rules or code of conduct of Kamp Olympik.

O n dark nights an otherworldly atmosphere descended on the camp, and the most mundane noises would send shivers of fear down the spines of those who walked in the shadow of the woods. In other words, everybody had the living daylights scared out of them at least once a session by yelping coyotes, screech owls, or raccoons breaking into the trash cans behind the dining hall.

Rich, my camp director, came to me one night with a story that contained a touch of the macabre, and it had some of the counselors spooked for days. Every counselor had to take a turn doing cabin duty, usually just once per session. That meant they'd have to monitor the cabin area for fights, fires, upset stomachs, or any other emergencies. It was a pain in the butt, but not really a big deal. This one particular evening, though, as the campers were finally settling down, somebody started crying in Cabin 2. The cabin monitor immediately investigated and found that one of the kids had fallen out of bed and scraped his knee. The kid was taken to the dining hall for immediate treatment. Then the duty counselor hears more commotion in Cabin 9, and discovered that yet another camper had fallen out of bed and scraped his knee. Off he goes to the dining hall to have the cut tended to. So far nothing out of the ordinary.

"But then," Rich said, "I glanced over the first aid log and was aware of an icy sensation running over my spine."

"How so?"

"The last names of the two kids were the same. Each child had a small laceration on the left knee. And each incident happened at almost the exact same time."

"You're kidding," I said, definitely impressed.

"So we asked both boys for an explanation."

"And?"

"They just shrugged it off. 'We're brothers, that's all. Things like this happen all the time. Sometimes Mom says we're like twins born three years apart.' But here's the problem. The guy on cabin duty lit out from the dining hall, muttering, 'No more cabin duty for me, thanks. This is beyond weird.'"

"So who's next in line?" I asked.

Rich just continued to look at me with this enigmatic half smile he had. "Not me, Boss."

I conceded his position had merit and took up guard duty for the rest of the night, making my rounds with stolid regularity. And I was a mess. You'd have thought a horde of chain saw-wielding masked assailants had sent word they'd be joining us for the night. Every little noise, every crack of a twig, every sneeze made me jump. I was sure evil things were lurking behind each tree. Around midnight I smelled something odd that my thoroughly spooked brain told me had to be the nauseating stench of the Jersey Devil himself. It's a wonder I didn't dislocate something from the wild gyrations I performed by constantly leaping into defensive stances to confront things that weren't there. It was maybe 1:30 when I passed the director's cabin and poked my head in the door to inform Rich all was well.

I guess he didn't realize it was just me, because his entire body shot three feet up in the air, then promptly crashed onto the floor. "Hey, Rich," I couldn't resist saying. "You didn't happen to scrape your left knee, did you?" I left his cabin laughing, really pleased that I'd discombobulated our imperturbable camp director. But then, on my way back to my cabin, I heard a soft noise, a kind of echoing, scraping sound. That really motivated me, and I lit out for home, constantly glancing over my shoulder, ready to fend off some ghoulish attack.

Possibly because of some saintly facet of my personality, I've always seemed to attract pranksters in need of redemption via immediate and fearsome retribution for their dirty work. Especially during the early years at Kamp Olympik, it seemed I was driving out to the camp every weekend to expand or improve something. If I wasn't paneling the dining hall or adding cedar-shake sides to it, I'd be repairing the roof, rescreening broken doors and windows, or refurbishing the cabins. Steve Farber came one weekend off-season and helped me with the cedar shakes; he was a terrific help. But it was lonely work, and I was happy to take along whoever was available for company. Perhaps I should've drawn the line at Mike, a friend who thought he'd shrivel up and die if he wasn't planning a trick to spring on somebody. That guy had the beadiest eyes I've ever seen. They'd get this mischievous glint, and you just knew he was conjuring up some wild intrigue. Whenever I became a target, I'd retaliate immediately, only with bigger guns. For instance, one Christmas morning in Trenton, I opened my door and found a shoebox sitting on the stoop, and inside was a dead bird. Knowing Mike's calling card, I returned the favor with a dead rat wrapped in festive Christmas paper and red ribbon. This shows the sophisticated, urbane level of our exchanges.

> **At night, death comes to me alone, it whispers and beckons,**
>
> **but I'm not at home.**
>
> —*Don Bragg, "Death Tempter"*

It was about 10:30 one Saturday night, when I returned from the camp to find the house completely dark, so I moved quietly, assuming everybody was tucked in for the night. I'd just stepped inside the door when I heard a noise from upstairs. Aren't those kids asleep yet? I mused as I locked the front door. Then I saw a sheet of paper lying on the hall table. It was a note from Theresa telling me that our friend Gene Kilroy had given her and the kids tickets for the Ice Capades in Philadelphia. She'd be home after the show, probably a little after 11. I stiffened. If Theresa and the children were away, who'd just made that shuffling sound upstairs? Someone else was in the house, and I wasn't just being paranoid, either. A string of burglaries had plagued our neighborhood in recent months, so I knew I had to search the house thoroughly before my family returned.

Systematically I moved through the empty downstairs rooms, but as I approached the stairs, I felt my apprehension growing. Was the intruder armed? Desperate? I'd just put my foot on the lowest step when I heard a suspicion of noise close to the top of the stairs. It's my imagination, I told myself firmly, but I was pretty sure it wasn't. Forcing myself to move more deliberately, I checked out the upstairs bedrooms. They were all empty, but I looked under every bed, steeling myself for a confrontation. I began to breathe easier when my examination of the second-floor rooms didn't turn up any burglars. I laughed a little at my overactive imagination. Suddenly there was another noise, this time on the steps leading to the third floor. The door to the stairwell was closed, and I began to sweat lightly as I prepared to open it. Get it over with, I commanded myself, and I yanked the door open. There in the darkened stairwell, a grotesque creature stood. Its face was twisted, its eyes were fire-red, and its hair stuck out all over like frozen flames. Its face seemed to be oozing something repellent. At first its mouth was opened in a wordless snarl, but then a hoarse gurgle began emanating from it. Slowly extending its arms, its fingers curved into talons. It wasn't human; it didn't even look like a respectable alien, but whatever it was, it wasn't going to stay in my house. "I'm gonna have to kill you," I gasped, ramming its head with all the strength in my right arm. With the damnest cackling noise I'd ever heard, it lunged at me. I proceeded to pummel that ugly head, noting in passing that it was the hardest damn head I'd ever come up against. Hell, the blows from my fists were actually glancing off it and hitting the stairwell wall. My fists were pulsating with pain, but I didn't stop trying to beat it into submission, not with Theresa and the kids on their way home.

Then the thing started to talk in this weird turkey-gobbler voice. It was gibberish, nothing that belonged on this planet. I thought, so that's what Martian sounds like. Then I realized it was saying something almost intelligible. "Don," it gasped. "It's me."

I was sure it was, but I saw no reason to stop my onslaught. It might know my name, but it was an intruder, and I wanted it outta there. Then the words, "Please, Don. It's me, Mike!" penetrated my red-hot fog of protective anger. The alien form vanished, and Mike, battered and bloody, was swaying in front of me, sounding like he was dying. I came to my senses. I stood there, pain shooting up my arms, knuckles bleeding, staring at my good friend.

"Mike! What in hell are you doing? I thought you were some kind of cockamamie space invader. I damn near killed you!"

"No shit," he replied. "Your front door was unlocked so I let myself in. After I read Theresa's note, I realized I had a fantastic opportunity to get you good. I've been waiting more than an hour to do it."

"Yeah, but look at you!"

He started to laugh, but the laugh turned into a groan, and he grabbed his jaw as if it were about to fall off. "I rubbed your menthol shaving cream into my hair so it would stick straight up. Then I smeared it all over my face—good and spooky, I thought. But the menthol made my face sting, and I kind of scratched at it, so some got into my eyes. Man, but that burned. I was trying to wash it all off, when I heard a car drive up. So I applied more shaving cream, and found a place to hide."

"It was spectacular," I admitted. "The eyes especially—they're really devilish."

"That's nice to know, but damn it all, Don, I can hardly see."

That got us both laughing. We laughed all the way downstairs, and all the way through a half-gallon jug of wine. Then Theresa and the kids came home. She just stood looking at us both for a minute and then asked, "Mike, what the hell happened to you?"

Using the alien's weird gurgling speech, he replied, "I was attacked by an interplanetary space protector." Then he burst out laughing again. Theresa just sighed, and went off to get the kids into bed.

Mike and I laughed some more, but I knew somebody I absolutely *had* to lure up into the lair of the Jersey Devil for a taste of his own medicine.

Several months later I got my chance. A bunch of us, Mike, Steve, Herbie, and I, were playing basketball at the park in Trenton. It was quite a workout. At 6′ 3″, Steve was my height, a little stocky, but well coordinated and fast for his weight. Herbie's build was lighter, and an inch shorter. Mike was a scrappy 5′ 11″. I really had to hustle to keep these guys, all in their early twenties, from trouncing my middle-aged butt.

After our game I casually inquired if anybody felt like taking a ride down to my camp and giving me a hand with a few little things that needed doing. "I'll pick up some burgers at McDonald's on the way down," I said, knowing exactly the bait that would tempt this bunch of scavengers. Of course they bit, and the hook was set. Mike was my primary goal, but the others could help sell this spoof.

"Just how far away is this camp of yours?" Herbie demanded as they piled into the station wagon.

"About twenty minutes below Trenton. Give or take." Well, half an hour later, they began to inquire about the time. "Just a few minutes more," I answered, the way you'd address a carful of squirmy five-year-olds.

Once it became dark they became a little more adamant. "Just exactly where is this McDonald's?"

"McDonald's?" I said, offhandedly, like I'd been thinking of far loftier subjects. "There aren't any stores this deep inside the state forest. But not to worry; we'll stop on the way back." Without any moon, it soon became very dark, and the darkness became impenetrable as we ventured deep into the heart of the Pine Barrens. And it was panic time. Forget about five-year-olds. With all their complaining, my passengers might as well have been two and overdue for their naps. "Just a few more minutes," I assured them. A moment later I turned onto the dirt road leading into the camp.

Herbie peered out the window and whispered to Steve, "Where the hell are we? This looks like something out of *Deliverance*."

"That was a great movie," I commented. "Wasn't it?"

My passengers greeted my film critique with appalled silence.

Mike kind of leaned forward, and I could feel his beady eyes on the back of my head. I think he knew something was up, but he only said calmly, "This is a truly historic area, guys. You'll be seeing nature at her finest. At least you would if you could see a damn thing out there."

Steve kind of growled, "Who gives half a shit?" but by that time we'd arrived in camp. I slowly drove by the first cabin, the oldest one in the complex. It almost seemed to float in the moonless night, all awash in the fog that was creeping off the river. Steve continued to complain, "This is the spookiest place I ever saw. What in hell are we doing here?"

"When do the monsters with the laser-ray eyes show up?" Herbie wanted to know as I parked near the dining hall.

"Take it easy. They never show up until well after midnight." I got out of the car, with Mike on my heels, but I turned to Herbie and Steve and said, "I'll be right out as soon as I turn on the camp electricity."

"Electricity is good," Steve said, huddling in the back with Herbie. "But we're locking the damn doors till you get back. This is one scary place."

So Mike and I went on in, I flipped the switch in question, and then we each had a soda and made small talk for a few minutes before heading back to the car. I made sure we approached the vehicle from the rear, and gave a healthy rap to the back door. You've never heard such a ruckus. It was as if the car had a dozen girls inside. You know, those big-eyed, not-too-bright little blondes they raise especially to scream in horror movies. The shrieking and carrying on really did my heart good, but Mike was laughing, too, and he was my principal target for the evening.

"Okay, guys. Time to go to work." I slipped behind the wheel and drove down to the old cabin next to Uncle Joe's Bat Cabin and stopped. "Out of the car, I really could use a hand here."

Steve surveyed the cabin. "It looks just fine the way it is."

"Nonsense. Get out of the car, will you, or do you want me to haul you out?"

Muttering unhappily, they exited the wagon. I just stood there enjoying the way they were twitching as they tried to scope for demons while maintaining their exterior cool. They had me chuckling in no time. I unlocked the cabin, and the three of them clumped in behind me. I had them help me pull down the ceiling ladder. "If you guys will climb upstairs and close all four windows, I'll go out back and repair the water pump. Okay?"

They all yelled "No way in hell," with Mike leading the chorus.

I merely shrugged and went out and fussed with the pump. As I recall, there wasn't anything really wrong with it, but when I came back in, the guys were still standing on top of each other looking terrified. "What is this? I thought you agreed to help me out? We aren't leaving until you go on up and close the windows." I surveyed their faces. "Don't tell me you guys are scared of a little darkness?"

"Absolutely, we're scared—right out of our minds."

"Then you'd better take this," I said, handing them the flashlight. From the looks on their faces, you'd have thought they were climbing into the city morgue at midnight. I had to chuckle: as if it were going to be that easy for them!

It took forever, but finally I saw the last of their feet disappear into the attic opening. With a last chuckle, I slid the ladder back into the ceiling, and latched it shut. Who says revenge is a dish best served cold? I had the bunch of them corralled, and it felt absolutely marvelous, since I'd left them no avenue of escape that I could see. The sounds floating down through the ceiling could've come from a score of bison demolishing several barns rather than from three guys in tennis shoes merely getting nervous. Through the cacophony of howling and screeching about the Jersey Devil, I heard my name mentioned in conjunction with some pretty creative genealogy, but

I didn't mind one bit. I slammed the outside cabin door, and as I locked it, I heard somebody scream that their mothers would be worried sick if they didn't get home soon. Hearing this from three guys who didn't have the word *curfew* in their vocabulary really broke me up.

I started the car, and started to drive away very slowly, hollering "Good night guys, sweet dreams."

"Don't leave us here," Steve and Herbie yelled, their voices shaking. "It's inhuman."

Mike was more explicit. "Let us out, Turdbird, or I'll get even if it's the last thing I ever do!"

My response was to gun the motor and laugh maniacally, which evidently got to Mike. I glanced back, savoring my revenge, and saw the window screen in the attic pop out. A flashlight pinwheeled out of the darkened window, followed by what looked like a large yet flabby beach ball. This shapeless sphere, which appeared to be powered by some otherworldly force, came bouncing wildly toward the car. The shrieking from the attic was now even more strident, more outraged, and higher pitched, as if a gang of elderly nuns had suddenly spotted some naked rats fornicating in their cloister. Next thing I knew, here comes Mike galloping alongside my car. I forgot to lock the doors, so he opened his side and flopped halfway in the door. Scrabbling his feet along the ground, he finally got a foothold and managed to pull himself inside, huffing and puffing. Gasping for air, he finally found the words to express his innermost feelings, as I braked to a halt. "Bragg, you buzzard crotch! You baboon butt-face, you eat elephant dung!"

But I cut his fun short. "Mike, after what you did to me, you can't think the score's anywhere *near* settled yet."

"But what did the other guys ever do to you? They're back there scared shitless."

This was true, and I had a feeling both Herbie and Steve would be getting me in their payback cross-hairs, which was okay, because it would keep life interesting. "It'll be good for their character." I said. "But they haven't complained." I'd spoken too soon, however. What was clearly a mastodon bellowed in agony from the dark attic, and an instant later the whole car jerked as a definite tremor rippled across the road. An earthquake? In New Jersey? For a moment I felt disoriented, but as a hulking figure limped into view, I realized it had only been Earthquake Steve. He kind of collapsed into the car.

"What the hell happened to you?" Mike and I asked together.

Steve gave me one long, reproachful look. "After Mike sailed out the window, I thought I could kind of ease myself over the window frame, hang onto the sill with my fingertips, and then drop to the ground with not much trouble. I was halfway out, then decided it wouldn't work. But a couple of bats chose that moment to try to fly down

Herbie's shirt, and he starts yelling bloody murder. I let go, and numbskull Herbie comes down on top of me just as I land. I think I broke my damn ankle."

"You may have broken an ankle, but you still made better time than Herbie. Where the hell did he get to?"

We retrieved Herbie from the hole he was burrowing into under a clump of bushes, and we started home. I noted with amusement that each of the guys had a death grip on their door handles. If somebody tried pulling them out of the car, those doors would've gone right along with them.

We were no sooner out of the camp than they began to laugh, though I suspected some of their merriment was old-fashioned hysteria.

Herbie said, "We wouldn't help you again, Bragg, even if you were dangling off a cliff. We'd rather see you dead."

The ride home got pretty hilarious, with each of them giving his interpretation of the entire event. As we neared the city they became even braver. "Hell, we weren't really that scared."

"I know I wasn't," said Steve, "but when those two bats flew into your face, you looked like you dropped a load in your pants."

Herbie just kept looking out the window. "Oh, really? I'm not the one who broke my ankle getting the hell outta there."

In an aggrieved voice, Mike joined in. "Aw, hell. Check my new sneaks, will you? They're almost worn out from getting dragging alongside the car."

At that very opportune moment I spied a familiar eatery just ahead. "Hey, guys, here's the McDonald's! You want fries with those burgers?"

"Screw the burgers! Just get us back to the city so we can get our cars and go home."

When we finally stopped beside the deserted basketball court in the park, the trio exited the car, swaggering a little, calling me every bad name in the book. As Steve limped out of sight, I yelled to him, "Hey, Steve, do you still have my flashlight? You'll have to pay me for it if you lost it back at the camp?"

His final words floated back to me on the night breeze. "Screw you, Bragg!"

Needless to say, word of my ingenious reprisal spread throughout Trenton. People would barely talk to me, let alone get into a car with me. Yeah, it was sort of a shame that Herb and Steve had to suffer along with Mike, but I got Mike good, and we both knew it. So Kamp Olympik became a great venue for pranks both during and after camping season.

Although the entire family enjoyed life at the camp, getting from one end of it to the other could be a time-consuming ordeal. Before I invested in our little fleet of motorcycles, I decided that my wife, Theresa, needed some means of transportation to use within the camp. I found a nice used Cushman cart—that's the golf cart job they use for mail delivery—and bought it at a good price. Luckily, it featured a compact cabin enclosure for the driver with a small truck bucket on the back, which made it especially useful for camp travel—when it was available, that is.

Problem was my kids took an immediate shine to the Cushman. As soon as they realized they could drive it around, the cart's job description changed from camp maintenance to playground duty, and that was often inconvenient as hell. For instance, we had to fog the camp for mosquitoes every evening or the entire camp would morph into one immense, red, itchy welt. As second eldest, Renée was the

Jeff, cousin Craig after wild ride on Cushman cart.

supervising operator, and she thought herself the queen of the camp as she piloted the Cushman on its rounds. My other kids or assorted nephews sat in the small truck bed controlling the sprayer. They were making a sizeable contribution to camp operations, but they thought the chore was fun, not work.

There was one major bug in the ointment, however. The campers would start chasing the vehicle the second they heard its telltale *putter-put-put*, so we made a strict rule prohibiting Cushman tailgating and enforced it with both vigilance and lung power. But that Cushman cart paid for itself a hundred times over.

It was fascinating to hear some of the motor horror stories that came to light once their statute of limitation had expired. Jeff was nearly twenty when I heard about his exploits that occurred just after his seventh birthday. He'd been given a small cycle, and we practically had to pry him off the damn thing at bedtime.

Well, unbeknownst to me—although all the campers were in on it—Jeff developed the habit of bird-dogging the cart, cutting in and around it on his cycle, scaring the daylights out of his sister and his cousins. One day when they were going to Mick's Country Store to gas up the Cushman, Jeff climbed on the bike, sneaked out of camp, and followed them. When they'd reached a particularly narrow section of dirt road, he decided he'd pass the cart and terrify his sister. So he goes charging out from behind the cart, and starts to streak out in front. Unfortunately, a bread truck was

CHAPTER SEVEN **113**

tearing toward camp making a late delivery, and it damn near turned my son into a grease-streaked pancake. The deliveryman gave a blast on his horn, and Jeff veered off, bounced over a culvert, and ended up in the cedar swamp. The cycle immediately sank, buried in the mud, taking Jeff partway down with it. Renée stopped the cart, and she and her cousins raced over to where they'd seen Jeff's cycle go down.

The cedar water still roiled around a little heap of mud. Renée told me that at first she thought her brother was dead, but then the mud heap started heaving. Man, he was a mess! His helmet was twisted nearly front to back, as if *The Exorcist*'s demons had been repositioning his head. It was also caked with mud inside and out, but so was Jeff. The bedraggled mud monster held out an arm, and eager hands pulled him to safety. It was a miracle that his bones and teeth were all intact, this time, at least. But there was still the problem of the cycle.

No way was Jeff going to ask his dad to pull the bike out of the marsh. Hell, if he had, he'd *still* be grounded. Uncle Joe, on the other hand, could be counted on to lend a helping hand and keep his mouth shut about Jeff's transgressions. So Jeff asked Uncle Joe to bring his truck, haul his cycle out of the swamp, and take it someplace inconspicuous for repairs.

I never did find out about the accident then, although I seem to recall that his bike was out of action at about that time. When I inquired about the bike, I think Jeff said, "Uncle Joe's giving it a tune-up, Dad. Something about the motor getting flooded." Which under the circumstances was a perfectly reasonable explanation, although it was more like a major overhaul.

Did Jeff learn his lesson? Hell no! A daredevil at heart, he's continued flirting with suicide. He's been helicoptered out of cliffs and ravines; he's ended up in the hospital a few times—you know, guy stuff. Even now, Jeff occasionally comes to California to compete in tough motocross events. So much for the theory that making insane mistakes as a kid necessarily guarantees a sane life thereafter. Each close call with disaster seemed to whet his appetite for even more dangerous challenges. I really can't understand that strange tendency. It must come from his mother's side of the family.

Although the kids all loved using the Cushman cart, it nearly got put off-limits when it ran afoul of Yolanda. One evening, Renée drove the cart a little too close to the dining hall while she was fogging. Evidently, Yolanda looked up to see an opaque cloud of insecticide rolling toward the dining room. "That man!" she exploded. "Just look what he's done now!" According to Andy, Yolanda flung dish towels over everything edible and began delivering a rapid-fire Italian malediction that sounded like the curse of the mummy even to his untutored ears. Some things transcend language, after all. He figured my name was mud, and ran over and got me out of a mini-meeting I was having with three of the teachers. "She's mad as hell, and you're on her hit list!" Andy informed me.

"What for? Did the insecticide actually flood the dining hall?"

"Not really, but it was thinking about it. That's enough for her."

Wearily, I jogged up the dining hall steps. "I hear you had a problem this evening, Yolanda."

"Yes, and it just got here," she snapped, giving me a disapproving stare.

Feeling persecuted, I said, "Hell, not that much of the bug spray blew in here, did it?"

She waved my objection away with an imperious hand. "You need to hire a fogger from Trenton. Then there'd be no more of these close calls!"

I was in no mood for this. "Fine with me," I said. "We'll simply take the expense of a pro fogger out of your food budget. But it'll be okay. The kids will do fine on canned creamed corn and Chef What's-his-name's canned spaghetti. It's pretty good stuff, y'know," I said, unable to resist throwing just a little more kerosene on the flames.

"You touch one penny of my budget, and your butt will be in this kitchen cooking!"

"Fine, your budget's safe. But forget the professional fogger," I said. "Deal?"

She gave me a grudging smile. "You and your deals. Just go away and let me put this kitchen back together." Holding up an admonishing finger, she added, "Just see it doesn't happen again."

I took Renée aside and gently laid down the law. "Listen, honey, here's a map with the new route for fogging for mosquitoes. You absolutely must stick to it, no matter what. Do you understand why it's so important?"

"Uh-huh," she nodded. "Grandma's mad at you again, and if I mess up, you'll get it."

My daughter was right on. Nobody in their right mind messes with somebody as feisty as Yolanda.

There were a million improvements I wanted to make at camp, so finding new ways to put a few extra dollars in my wallet was imperative. I took advantage of the off-season to rent out the recreational equipment: minibikes and canoes and, occasionally, our clean, shaded picnic tables. It was only a short segue from that to organizing a modest RV campground on a remote area in the front of our property. With a small bathhouse in the center, it consisted of approximately twenty-five campsites with electric and water hookups. The following year, I added some sites with sewer connections as well, incrementally adding more sites with the triple hookups in place. One small geological fact made this all possible. The big well near the dining hall that supplied the entire camp was a hundred feet deep and had been drilled professionally. But in the Pines, good water was there for the asking once you drilled even a fairly shallow well. At the onset, I hadn't a clue as to how to go about drilling one, but I was primed to find out. I was out in the woods, trying this and that, hoping I was making progress, when Walt Priest happened along.

"What in hell are you doing, Bragg?" he bawled at me.

"I'm digging a well."

"You won't get yourself a well by beating on the ground with a hammer."

Gathering my wounded pride in one hand, I displayed my pipe wrench with the other. "I wasn't," I said, with dignity.

Chuckling, Walt climbed out of his truck. "You think a pipe wrench's better than a hammer? Son, just you let me show you how it's done." Hands on his hips, he scanned the area with a judicious eye. "First you gotta build you a teepee."

"Uh-huh," I said, picking up the wrench once more. "Then I'll run home and get my Davy Crockett coonskin hat, and we'll play cowboys and Indians." Then I realized from the look on his face that I shouldn't be talkin' shit to this old man.

He paused, stared, and said, "I'm saying you'll need three six-inch cedar posts ten foot long, and you'll tie 'em together teepee style, you know, where the poles cross."

"Like a tripod," I said, finally visualizing what he was talking about.

"Okay, city boy. Like a tripod. You'll want to buy some good-quality pipe, say an inch an' a half wide."

"I know what you mean. It comes in four-foot sections."

"Right. Now you'll have to rig a rope pulley on your teepee."

Suddenly I wondered if Walt knew exactly what I wanted to do. Did he think I was going to lower a tiny bucket for the water?

It was as if the old fox had read my mind. "You're gonna need an iron well-point rod with a brass or steel-mesh screen, then you'll put a cap on the first one of those pipe sections and drive it in good."

I nudged the iron bar on the ground with my foot. "I'm way ahead of you."

"And you'll be using the pulley to pull the iron rod driver up, so when you drop it, you get maximum impact." He looked a little startled as I walked away from him, headed for my truck. "Where in hell you goin'?" he demanded.

"To get some cedar posts," I laughed. "Some smart old codger just convinced me I gotta build me a teepee."

Even with Walt's instructions, however, driving a thirty-foot well was slow going. It was back-breaking work to drive in the rod, and it only advanced a quarter-inch at a time. If you hit a heavy section of gravel, then it hardly seemed to move at all. Now and then, you'd hit a stratified layer, and then you'd get an inch of penetration at a time.

Once the pipe was installed to the desired depth, I had to screw a hand water pump on top, pour down a bucket of water for suction, and get cranking, hoping like the devil that I'd actually tapped into an aquifer. The pump, by the way, used elbow grease, not gas, and my back was already hollering for mercy after driving in the pipe.

Then the procedure became devastatingly simple. It was a matter of grind your teeth and keep going. Even though your arms start knotting up, you couldn't stop, not for an instant. If you did strike water, then you hooked up a motor to the pipe and kept it going till the water cleared of all the drilling debris and surrounding dirty sand. What you were doing was creating a pocket where clear water could pool; then you could pump it on up. You'd sample the final product until the water tasted good, then you had your well.

There were six of these thirty-foot suckers on the property, and when I was done, I had the biceps and shoulders of a Greek god—much better results than with weight lifting. Mr. Universe, eat your heart out.

I'd like to say that was the last of my water-witching, but you see, I have this wife. My beloved Theresa had a unique habit: she didn't wear clothes out, she washed them out. I couldn't step out of a pair of fresh-laundered jeans to take a shower and find them again after I'd toweled off. Hell, no! They'd be in the laundry along with the shorts I'd worn for maybe an hour.

I tried to reason with Theresa. "Honey, we're camping out in the woods. I don't need to change into clean underwear every fifteen minutes."

"What if you were in an accident? I don't want those nice nurses at the hospital to think you don't have a pair of clean undershorts to your name."

"Fine. I'll get a little card and keep it in my wallet. It'll say: Theresa Fiore Bragg is in no way responsible for the condition of this patient's underwear. Okay?"

She simply walked away and started another load of laundry. So I did what any red-blooded American male would do. I went out and dug another well right behind our cabin, which really wasn't too big of a deal, since Walt had taught me how. Living with a washing machine that never slept did raise hell with the drainage, however, so I ran a good-sized pipe out back, where it'd empty onto the sandy soil and drain away in no time.

Then here comes Theresa again, with a full wash basket. "There's something wrong with our water. Nothing is getting really clean. Feel this sock. It's all slick."

"That's your imagination," I said. "We have the cleanest clothes on the East Coast." Yet I had to admit, our water'd had an odd taste lately, like we'd bought it at a flea market or someplace unsavory. So I went to chew over the problem with Walt. He came over, scrutinized our cabin area, and then pointed to my drain pipe. "Here's your problem," he said. "All that detergent from your washer is overflowing right onto the ground."

"Yeah," I said. "So?"

"Just look at it, dummy. It's got a downhill path from your drainpipe to this wellhead right here. Hell, you can see the soapsuds."

"It's just old-fashioned soap," I argued.

"Maybe so, but you're cooking with polluted water. Drinking it, too."

"So that's why every time I drink a glass of water I start burping bubbles? What in hell do I do about it?"

"Just run your drainage pipe at least fifty feet in the other direction, where it's downhill of the well. That should do you. Run your pump a few hours to clean the soap outta the pipes and well, and you're done."

"I should've seen this coming," I said.

"Not at all," Walt shot back. "Happens occasionally in the deer club cabins when they place their field drains too close to the well. Another thing, if you begin losing suction, it could be that the iron pipe's head is corroding at the bottom."

"Then I have to drill a new well?" I asked resignedly.

"Hell, no! You want to uncap the pipe, then take your shotgun, point it down the pipe, and let fly. That should clear out any accumulated crap." He gave me a wicked grin as he climbed into his pickup. "Course you *could* dig a new well, if you've got your heart set on it. Shotgun's a hell of a lot easier is all."

"You know, Walt, we've got great natural water, and yet we go and do things that screw it up. Hell, we create our own pollution. Man is really a mess, isn't he?"

"That's the truth, and no mistake," he replied with regret in his voice as his truck crunched away on the dirt-and-gravel road. "Well, I'm going deer hunting. Stop by tonight for a venison dinner, why don't you? I guarantee it'll be cooked in clean water."

Once I solved my family's water problem, I had to direct my attention back to the RV campground's wells. They were providing an unending supply of crystalline water, my bathhouse was in operation, and I rented out campsites for the hunters for a nice off-season income. I wasn't hurting for customers, either. Hunters swarmed into the Pines during hunting season, since the pine woods sheltered a plentiful supply of waterfowl and game. However, that meant I needed to keep my nonwinterized bathhouse open from late September to November. Therein lay the difficulty. When the weather started to freeze, the bathhouse pipes began bursting as if they were made of Dresden china rather than workhorse iron. Paying off the stratospheric cost of plumbing repairs in addition to laying out more cash for new pipework ate into our profits considerably. Although the RV camp continued to attract customers for the remainder of the hunting season, I couldn't call the undertaking an unqualified success.

I did a brisk business renting canoes from my river entrance, but between the cost of replacing lost paddles and life jackets and the utterly insane demands of the customers, I was more than ready to throw in the towel at the end of October. One broad-beamed quartet really got my goat. "Hey, these canoes aren't wide enough. Couldja get us the next larger size?" I just stood there and stared, waiting for the punch line of the joke, but these guys were dead serious. Evidently they spent way too much time browsing the Hammacher Schlemmer super-posh catalog.

Then there were the folks who asked what kind of picnic lunches I could provide. I had to tell them that the Cucumber Sandwich and Petits Fours Department was closed for the year. "But you can pick up sandwich fixings at Mick's Country Store," I told them, trying to be helpful. "It's just down the road, and there's a special on lunch meats."

"Oh. We just assumed this was a full-service recreation center."

"We've got canoes, paddles, life vests, and the canoes don't leak. Around here, that *is* full service."

"Well, we're not from around here."

"No shit!"

Did this guy actually expect me to call up my mother-in-law and say, "Oh, Yolanda. Hustle over and whip up a few picnic lunches for the L.L. Bean crowd, will you?" She'd have scalped me with a grapefruit knife! But now that I think of it, maybe I should've sent them over to Yolanda's trailer and let *her* inform them where the sun really rises. No, that would've been cruel and inhumane punishment, even though it would've been fun to watch.

A few hunters acted as if I was their carpool mommy for the day. One guy unrolled a serious-looking map. "We'll canoe downriver and into the bay. Friends will be picking us up about here." He tapped a spot that looked to be four miles out in the ocean. "So plan to collect the canoes in a couple of hours."

"I beg your pardon?"

"We'll hardly feel like paddling back upriver. We're meeting people for lunch, you see."

"Then your best bet would be to drive around the bay, park your car, and go eat."

"No, we're going by canoe."

"Not in my canoes, you're not!"

It also occurred to me that another source of off-season income could be cultivated if I rented out our mini-motorcycles. I didn't think there'd be a problem, since my campers had done so well on them. Besides, the woods were intersected by a maze of deer paths. You couldn't ask for a more perfect system of bike trails.

Talk about an excruciatingly bad idea! I still wake up yelling after I revisit the cycle experiment in nightmares. The bottom line, however, was that rental income never quite covered the cost of repairs, to say nothing of the gargantuan insurance rates I paid.

Now please understand that every person who took out a cycle swore he was an expert cyclist. When *I* say expert cyclist, I'm thinking of somebody in my son Jeff's league: somebody who knows how to handle a bike and how to handle himself. Oddly enough, other people seem to think the fact that they've watched five minutes of an Evel Knievel stunt video qualifies them for motocross.

There was also another phenomenon involved that I'd been unaware of. There are people who, when they swing a leg over a cycle, experience a kind of brain drain: their brains melt and drip out their ears. You wouldn't believe the dumb stunts they pulled.

Take steering the bike, for instance—it's not that hard. I must've watched hundreds of kids negotiate those trails, and even the youngest of them had the smarts to steer around obstacles like boulders and trees. Some of my adult customers had no grasp of that concept. I remember seeing one steering his cycle toward a fairly large tree about thirty yards away. The guy wouldn't turn to the left; he wouldn't turn to the right. No, he chose to open the throttle and charge right into the damn tree at full speed. So I run up to see if he's hurt, and he's sitting on the ground beside the cycle, which is in several pieces.

He points at the bike, and he says, "Oh, look! It broke. Get me another one, will ya, buddy?"

Grrrrrr!

Then there were the wanderers. They'd take a bike out, and do something dumb, like getting off it right beside a ditch with the kickstand only halfway down. When the cycle tumbled into the ditch, they'd leave it there, and go to get help. Not back to camp, mind you. They'd strike out into the wilderness, certain there'd be a ranger station just around the next clump of trees. More than once, I received a phone call from some irate Piney. "Bragg!" they'd holler. "I just found one of your idiots trampling through my vegetable garden, yappin' about how his cycle got drowned. Will you come take him off my hands before the wife invites him to supper?"

When I'd finally get a hold of this nitwit, I'd say, "The closest ranger station is six miles away. Why in hell didn't you just retrace your steps back to the camp if you needed help?" And the guy would just stand staring at me as if I were speaking Urdu.

Man, things like that drove me crazy. Then Theresa and I had a talk.

"Don, this RV camp is taking too much out of you, and you don't seem to be enjoying it at all. We really do need a breather after the boys' camp shuts down."

I knew she was right. Running Kamp Olympik itself was arduous, but I enjoyed it to the hilt. "Yeah, but I want to get a little more money in the bank."

"Aren't you the one who's always saying a person should stick with what works? Expand in your successful pew. Aren't you always telling me that?"

"Well, yes," I admitted.

"And how *is* Kamp Olympik doing?" she prodded.

"Great! It's growing by leaps and bounds, and I don't see any end in sight." I thought a minute and looked down into my petite wife's earnest blue eyes. "You're right, Honey. Kamp Olympik has to be my main focus. The rest is just incidental pocket change."

I didn't dump the RV park, but I did discontinue the recreational rentals. As a result, the extra bucks from my entrepreneurial efforts with the campground provided us with a midwinter vacation in Florida. So the remaining hassles at least produced some benefits in the off-season.

Chapter Eight

Perhaps only a few people remember the innocent era when the worst insult you could hurl at a guy was the epithet *chicken*. It implied the designee was a coward, a sissy, a mamma's boy, or all three rolled up in one disgraceful ball. Jocks took particular exception to being called chicken, and that included the guys at Kamp Olympik. I remember one day down by our waterfront, somebody dreamed up one wicked challenge. The idea was to climb up a tree near the bulkhead and dive into seven feet of water, the measured depth at that spot. And the tree in question wasn't your full-limbed spreading chestnut, either. This cedar was thin at the top, and it swayed back and forth whenever the wind was blowing, which was usually. Something else that upped the scare quotient was the fact that cedar trees have been known to snap just below their top third if the wind got heavy enough. And then there was the unvarnished fact that if you were going to clear both the bank and the bulkhead, you needed to leap out at least ten feet into seven feet of water.

Of course Tarzan had to go first, so up the tree I climbed. I hadn't imagined the degree of difficulty either: the branch that was the takeoff spot was shaking like the devil with the DTs. Okay, I thought, I'll make this work for me. Willing my heart to stop pounding in my ears, I waited for the wind to plow into the tree again, pushing my branch forward toward the bulkhead. When the branch swung out, giving me a crucial couple of feet of wiggle room, I lunged out with as much extension as possible to clear the bulkhead. It was a blissful relief to feel the water enclose my body. Better that than mother earth. But I couldn't float on my laurels. Immediately I turned my body sideways, so that my shoulder rather than my head would hit bottom. I barely scraped the bottom, and when I emerged from the water I remembered to remove any trace of relief from my facial expression, and to swagger a bit, as if it were nothing.

"See?" an exuberant eight-year-old camper crowed. "Didn't I tell you he's really Tarzan?" I graciously accepted the accolades, and then with the authority of the king of the jungle, I suggested nobody else try the dive. It was way too hairy, and a miscalculation could initiate disaster. "So just you all forget about this particular stunt," I said. "The climb's tough, balancing at the top is way too dangerous, and the launch over the bulkhead is more of a challenge than anybody in his right mind needs."

Well, my choice of words turned out to be all wrong. I'd used one c-word and intimated another. Assistant Director Barry Ross was on it in an instant and said to the other counselors, "Don't you get what he just said? This stunt is way too challenging for anybody but Tarzan here. So if we don't try it, we're *chicken*."

"Now wait a second. I said no such thing," I retorted, getting a little hot. "Diving off that unstable branch is tricky, and I strongly suggest that none of you commit to that dive."

But Barry was already sizing up the tree, looking for footholds. I couldn't believe anybody could be that stubborn. I mean it wasn't as if he were related to me or anything. "Fine," I said. "Go ahead and break your neck. I won't pay for the funeral, though."

"You know, there are hardly any branches till you get a third of the way up," one of the counselors said, looking a little dubious as he peered up at the swaying cedar.

"Then how 'bout a ladder," suggested Barry. They decided this was fair, and two CITs were sent in search of the requisite ladder. They reappeared five minutes later, two solemn, pint-sized pallbearers with the world's weirdest coffin suspended between them. It looked like part of a circus clown act.

Barry went first. He too made use of the forward movement of the branch to propel his body past the bulkhead. It was a much-chastened assistant camp director who climbed out of the water, however. "Geez," he muttered to me as I gave him a hand up onto the bank. "Why the hell didn't you tell me what a close call that'd be?"

"If you mean I didn't stuff you in a burlap bag and have the CITs drag you back to your cabin, yeah, maybe I didn't give you enough of a warning," I snapped back. "You're okay, though, right?"

"Yeah, I just took a little off the bottom as I turned."

Rich Cheung, who weighed in at close to 300 pounds, was next.

"God help us," I groaned under my breath. "This is a truly bad idea." The problem was, Rich, being the camp director, seemed to feel he had to prove his courage. I went over to him as he checked the steadiness of the ladder. "Are you sure you want to do this?"

"Want to? Of course not. But I'm going to do it." And up the ladder he went.

With a leadership ethic that approached that of a military man, Rich climbed the ladder and got a purchase on the first tree limb above it. He gave the appearance of a rotund mini-tank, resolutely advancing up this vertical plane. Branches were breaking under his weight and showering down on us, but he kept climbing. He made the dive, but he didn't quite catch the limb's forward thrust as Barry and I had done. In fact, when he leaped, the tree limb swung in the opposite direction, away from the water because of his weight. I held my breath as he barely cleared the bank, his body almost seeming to graze it. He sank like a boulder, appearing to go straight down. A moment later, a fat divot of mud and leaves bubbled to the surface, and we stared at it in amazement. Had the river mud in fact swallowed Rich? Then the mini-island began to disintegrate, and revealed itself to be Rich's head. The other counselors hauled him out of the water, but my mind was busy elsewhere.

Mud. The Wading River was notorious for having a treacherously uneven bottom: perhaps this challenge was more menacing than even I'd suspected. I started to yell a command to the next diver, one of the counselors, but he was already sailing down from the treetop, and I could see the dive was a little off to the right.

He knifed into the water, and then we were treated to an incredible show. Out of a torrent of hippopotamus-worthy splashing, a foot appeared briefly, followed by an elbow which made mysterious circular motions. Next came an algae-bedecked face clearly gasping for breath. "Stuck," the apparition managed to sputter, and the rest of us jumped in and hauled him out of the submerged mudbank. Every orifice on the poor guy's body was stuffed with the debris from the mucky river bottom, but he was otherwise unharmed.

"No!" I roared as another counselor started up the ladder. "I'd say that we've just about used up our daily ration of good luck. Somebody pull down that ladder and put it back. Game's over."

So, having acknowledged that we'd had our fingers smacked by Mother Nature, I thought she was done with us, but I was wrong. We were just putting the ladder away when a lady drove into camp, crying her eyes out. Naturally we all gathered around to see what was wrong.

"It's my youngest son, Bobby," she sobbed. "He took off on his surfboard from Evans Bridge, and I was supposed to pick him up downstream at Beaver Branch."

"When was that?" I immediately asked.

"It's been four hours, and he hasn't shown up yet," she said.

Now that's a two-hour canoe trip, and on the lighter-weight surfboard, the kid should've made better time. No wonder the mother was on the verge of hysteria. "Relax if you can," I said. "With our campers running into the forest every so often, we've become experts at finding people who've gotten lost in the woods." Theresa hurried up just then and led the distraught mother and her other son, Hank, over to the dining hall, while I started organizing our rescue mission.

With the late afternoon light already fading, I realized that time was indeed of the essence. Twelve counselors helped me load four canoes into two trucks, and then we piled into the vehicles and took off for Evans Bridge.

When we arrived at the bridge, I made certain everyone had his flashlight, because darkness was only a few hours away. "We'll meet downstream at the Munion Field campsite," I told them. Feeling more anxious than I wanted to admit, I sent two canoes paddling downstream after the boy, one starting at the bridge itself and the other dropping in about halfway to the Beaver Branch site. Backtracking upriver, I dispatched the third canoe with instructions to paddle upstream from the Beaver Branch site. It would be a tough paddle for them against the current, but they'd probably have to cover less of a distance. Then my son Mark and I headed into the Piney trails following the deer paths alongside the river. After a half hour's hard going, we hadn't found one trace of the boy, and there'd been no response from anyone else. I was almost certain we'd be heading back to the Harrisville Lake rendezvous empty-handed. It seemed certain to me that the young man would be spending the night in the woods, and the Pines' voracious insects would eat him alive. If he were injured, he'd have an even rougher time of it. Suddenly I said to Mark, "You know how there're a few channels that veer inland off the main course of the river?"

"Right. Sometimes they double back," he said.

"And sometimes they don't. The kid just might have pulled off into a dead-end stream."

"And have gotten stuck there," Mark shouted exultantly. "Where do we start looking?"

"I think we should try the cattle crossing." Putting a strain on the truck's shocks, we tore down the rutted old path, now in a race with nightfall. Once we were there, I began to beep my horn and flash my lights. We hopped out of the truck and ran to the slow-running stream, hollering his name. "Bobby, Bobby," we yelled until we were hoarse. Five minutes of this, and I was ready to try another location, but Mark waded into the shallow water, and began to move upstream, still calling into the darkened forest.

Then he froze. "Dad, I think I heard somebody."

I strained, trying to sift through the night sounds of the forest for the unmistakable quality of the human voice. Then I heard it too, but since sound has a way of bouncing off water, I couldn't home in on where it was coming from.

As we felt our way through the water, ducking tree limbs and skidding against the slippery banks, we finally heard the voice in the distance become clearer and stronger, echoing through the night. It was Bobby. He was shivering one direction and shaking in another, and was barely able to hold on to his cute little red surfboard. We bundled him up in a blanket, and I carried him back to the truck. As soon as I got the heater going, I asked him, "What the hell happened?"

"Well, it was so beautiful out on the river with the gold sunlight coming through the trees that I stretched out on the board to enjoy it. I guess I fell asleep."

"What happened when you woke up?" asked Mark.

"I woke up shaking with cold, and the river was real narrow and overgrown. And the light wasn't gold anymore; it'd turned kind of dark and spooky. I figured I must've drifted off the main course, so I paddled till I couldn't go any farther. Then I just lay on the board and thought about dying." He wriggled his little cocoon of a blanket closer to me. "Did you ever hear any stories about the Jersey Devil?" he asked, and his voice was trembling.

"Don't worry about him. He's not going to get you," I told him. Next I radioed the other truck to pick up our scouts, hoping they hadn't gotten themselves lost, too.

When we got back to the dining hall, his mom was a wreck, even though Yolanda had poured her a couple of glasses of red wine, an Italian remedy for every emergency. She was laughing and crying when she finally left with both her sons. But that wasn't the last I saw of them. Bobby and Hank returned to the camp the following year as counselors, which I thought was kind of nice.

After my wild day, I was more than ready to hit the sack, but Theresa headed me off. "Where do you think you're going?" she demanded.

"Bed. I'm bushed, Honey."

"And miss campfire? The kids would never settle down." So the camp shifted back into play mode, and the campfire ceremonies gently returned me to business as usual, surrounded by the safe environment of Fortress Kamp Olympik.

There was a magnificent loneliness about the Pines, which could be utterly exhilarating, but if you weren't born and bred a Piney, it could sometimes be just plain lonely. When we first started living permanently at the camp, we didn't have many real friends. One exception was Tom Marshal, who'd married Walt Priest's youngest daughter. He first visited the area as a hunter and met Walt when the head of the Priest clan was still running his store. Walt can spin a yarn with the best of them, and Tom loved to hear all about Walt's hunting experiences.

Tom was a bit of a rarity: he was a great listener. Thus he learned all he could from Walt's trove of wood lore, like where to put your deer stand and how to bait your hook for trophy-sized striped bass. Walt even introduced Tom to the mysteries of when to fish where, something I never quite grasped. Tommy made Walt's shared skills his own, although he never picked up Walt's ability to trap anything on four legs. By the time I got to know him, Tommy was known all over the Pines as a formidable outdoorsman.

He also liked to try his hand at just about anything of a competitive nature. We were having a picnic the day he first visited my camp, and a lavish spread it was. There was the usual picnic fare of hot dogs and burgers, with the addition of Yolanda's perfectly roasted chickens. Dominick and Walt saw that we had a constant supply of Jersey corn, tomatoes, and juicy melons. There was always homemade pasta with peppers and sausage, and everybody's favorite, buckets of clams and blue pincer crabs served with yet more pasta. It was a feast fit for any clan, but while Theresa, Yolanda, and Virginia Priest were putting the finishing touches on our repast, Tom and I got into a bit of friendly competition. We swam, dove, played tag in Tarzanville, and did a little one-on-one basketball, and he acknowledged me king of the hill. Then we tried our hand at shot put. Boy, did I meet my match. I could maybe throw past his first effort, but he'd always come back with a better throw. There was no way I could beat him, so I finally conceded—also, it was time for chow.

Like I said, Tommy had a competitive streak that wouldn't give up, and I loved that about him—not that I shared that same quality, of course. One year we went to a New Year's Eve party held at a local Piney tavern close to our homes. It was bitterly cold, one of those still winter nights when a thin sheet of ice would form on the river. As we were driving to the party, I glanced at the river, noting how frigid it looked with its glittering coverlet of ice. So it was great to take refuge in a warm, friendly place full of conviviality and good humor. During the party, we got to talking about weight lifting, and Tommy threw me a challenge. "Let's do some bicep curls and see who can lift the most weight." That sounded like a plan, so we grabbed Barry Ross and my son Mark, since neither of them had been imbibing and, with some of Tom's younger friends, drove over to his house. At Tom's house we had our competition, which I won, at 185 pounds. I have to admit, though, when I was done, my biceps felt like they were about to burst through my skin. Still, that wasn't too shabby for a guy well under the influence of Captain Morgan's truth serum. Tom surpassed me in the bench press, so game over? Not quite. I'd just remembered the ice-covered river, and how cold it looked. "Y'know, Tommy," I said. "We've been thoughtless. Look at these other guys here. They didn't get a chance to get in on our challenge."

"And?" he replied with a gleam in his eye.

"What we need is a challenge everybody can share. Let's drive over to the camp. I just had a brilliant idea."

Booze influenced their decision—obviously none made a concession.

—*Don Bragg, "The Leap"*

As the lunatic-in-charge, I decided we had to make use of the ice-covered river I'd noticed earlier in the evening. "We'll all climb the diving tower and go into that water headfirst. How 'bout it?" My fellow imbeciles agreed with enthusiasm, so we drove into camp and trooped over to the swim area. Once we dumped our clothes and stepped into the water, I had second thoughts, and my buddies were right there with me. I mean we had sheets of ice sloshing against our ankles, and I could feel icicles swinging from body parts that were trying to climb back into my body.

"Y'know, Don, if we go off that tower, into this water …," said Barry.

"Yeah. We could die!" somebody else agreed.

So we made a unified concession to reality. "Okay," I said, "then let's say you've gotta go in over your head to qualify for the honorary stupid team." As if the fact of standing around naked, freezing our butts off in the middle of a January night hadn't already qualified us for a padded cell.

I led the way into the water, up to my knees, my waist, my shoulders. I kind of asked myself as pieces of ice bobbed against my jaw, *Bragg, are you out of your mind?* Of course, I replied, and ducked my head under the water.

Let's just say I fully grasped the word *excruciating*. Needles of piercing cold shot through my ears, into my eyes, even assaulting my brain, and then I exploded back to the surface. I don't know what the record is for getting out of nearly six feet of water, but if it's over two seconds, seven guys, including my son Mark, broke it that night.

Once out of the water, we seven polar bears extended no mercy to the two who'd blown it. They had to answer to "Hey, Chicken" for days afterwards.

Once we got back to the Lower Bank Tavern, Walt, who'd stayed to keep the women company, let out a whoop of laughter. "You went and did it, didn't you? I was telling Theresa I had a pretty good idea what you hooligans were up to, and I was right." He took a closer look at us. "Lord, you guys are turning blue. You come on home with me: I've got just the thing to warm you up." The party broke up, and we all headed to Walt's house, where we completed thawing out with mugs of good coffee with just a touch of anisette.

As I've mentioned before, Rich Cheung was an invaluable part of the Kamp Olympik staff, one of the most disciplined individuals I've ever known. He loved martial arts as well as all other things of a military nature. He brought his *sensei*—teachers—to the camp to teach the kids in addition to giving incredible exhibitions. They broke cement blocks and boards with everything they had, hands, feet, and even their heads. And then there were the ingenious displays of dexterity with immensely long, curved Japanese swords. Well, of course the kids ate all this up. The only problem was that for days after these exhibitions everyone paraded around camp pretending to be Bruce Lee. Not that there was any fighting, just kids making exaggerated high kicks at nothing at all—and often ending up on their behinds. They also constantly indulged in peculiar hand gestures, like a thoroughly snockered sorcerer's apprentice attempting to cast a spell, accompanied by—and this was what really drove me nuts—the cooing hoots of amateurs trying to sound like badass ninja warriors. You couldn't get away from the sound unless you got your head underwater and kept it there. None of it bothered Rich, however, who was delighted that the classes and demonstrations he'd been instrumental in coordinating had made such an impression on the kids. But his warrior soul soon made an even more invaluable contribution to Kamp Olympik.

One weekend we heard that a motorcycle group from Philadelphia called the Demons was having a massive campout in the state forest, and I'm talking about hundreds of cyclists. I felt some trepidation, and intended to keep clear of these known troublemakers. Well, as we often did, Barry and I cycled out to Mick's Gas Station on our little Honda 90s to gas the bikes up. And guess who was waiting for us? A dozen Demons refueling their big bad hogs. I could see Barry tensing up as we approached the group, so I thought I should break the ice.

"Hi, guys!" I called over to them. "Wanna race?" At first they didn't answer and just stared, glancing from our little bikes to their own powerful choppers. Barry said nothing, but he was giving me an eloquent look: are you out of your frickin' mind? I couldn't really argue with him, because the bikers just continued to stare, and the silence had grown heavy and menacing. I figured I really put my foot in my mouth this time, and wondered if Barry and I were about to get stomped real good. Suddenly the Demons burst out laughing, saying, "Hey, man, that's pretty cool." Barry and I got the hell out of there; I don't recall that we did in fact buy any gas. But we were grateful to have extricated ourselves from a sticky situation.

To further complicate matters, I was still working in the governor's office as a recreational and youth advisor, which took me to Trenton four days a week. I tended to my health club after work, so I didn't get back to the camp until late. The idea of leaving the camp unguarded with the nearby woods teeming with Demons was unsettling, to say the least.

As I left for work one day during the so-called motorcycle jamboree, I told Rich to be alert at all times, but to be especially vigilant once the sun went down. Since I wouldn't be able to relieve him until late at night, I instructed him to call Tom Marshall and the Priest family if it looked like serious trouble was brewing. "They'll be here in five minutes with their hunting arsenal. They'll make West Virginia's hillbilly sharpshooters look like kids with popguns."

I swung by the state ranger headquarters to get some assurance that they were on top of the situation.

Ha!

"Please understand, Mr. Bragg," the stiffly correct ranger assured me, "this group has obtained the required permits, and has not violated any park regulations. Until we have evidence to the contrary, it's just another group of law-abiding guests."

"Are you out of your mind?" I retorted, "Doesn't the name Demons suggest what they probably have in mind?" Realizing that Jack the Ripper could come use the campground next to my camp if he filled out the correct paperwork, I tried another tack. "How 'bout checking some of these Demons for warrants? You could do that, right?"

"Actually, Mr. Bragg, I'd have no warrant to do that." He started snickering, so I assumed he thought he'd made a joke, but I wasn't laughing.

"Then at least beef up your patrols around my camp while the Demons are here," I said, concerned for the campers, my staff, and my family.

"Unfortunately, we haven't the manpower or the funds to do that."

That's when I just about lost it. "Then how 'bout monitoring this motorcycle gang as strictly as you monitor me and my campers?"

Well, he didn't like that, and ended our enlightening discussion.

We heard that the Demons had camped upriver at Hawkins Bridge, and the first night we saw the glow of a roaring campfire. I was surprised. I hadn't thought the bikers had the woodsman's skills necessary to gather sufficient wood to produce a fire that size. The next day I learned the entire story. No, the Demons lacked the foresight to collect firewood during the day, all right, and they hadn't chopped any wood either. How could they, since these upstanding citizens hadn't brought one damn ax to their campout? What they'd done was to strip wood off the bridge as well as from every outhouse toilet in the vicinity and burn *that*!

I got on the line with the state troopers. "Did the fire threaten your property?" they wanted to know.

"No. But they tore the outhouses apart, and denuded the bridge of every scrap of wood. The campsite won't be fit for anybody to use this season. What are you going to do about that?"

"We have them contained, Mr. Bragg."

"*Contained?* The forest rangers gave us a summons for accidentally chopping down one small tree. I suggest you get off your butts and get in there and do something, dammit! Why won't you?"

"Because, Don," the trooper continued in an urgent voice, "it would take at least a hundred troopers if we resorted to physical force, and we'd probably have a riot on our hands. So we're just going to keep an eye on them."

"That's crazy!"

"And how could we carry out mass arrests? The state doesn't have enough buses to transport them out of the forest. You do see my point?"

"But what about our camp?"

"I understand, but the best we can do is to make sure that next time they don't receive permits for a repeat situation," he said cheerily.

He hung up and left me staring at the phone in disbelief. Next time? So we were on our own.

Back at Kamp Olympik, the situation had deteriorated, and the entire camp was restless. Every so often some Demons would roar up to the camp and stop at the entrance. They'd assumed it was their campsite, and weren't pleased when they realized it wasn't. They'd sit there, revving their motors and cursing, and they kept this racket up all through the night. I grew angrier—and more worried—with every passing day.

One night I got home quite late and immediately started a walk-through of the entire camp. I was pausing by the front entrance, slowly scoping for any sign of intruders, when I heard a disembodied voice.

"Halt! Who goes there?" it said.

"Who in hell is that?" I began, but I shut up when I heard a click, as of a gun being cocked. What in hell was this? "I know you're behind that big pine tree," I shouted. "Come out so I can see you."

The only answer I got was a command delivered in a soulless monotone. "Advance and be recognized." I took two steps forward, and had the delightful experience of being blinded by a flashlight. Then the impersonal voice morphed into that of my camp director. "Is that you, Mr. Bragg?"

I said, "Yeah, Rich, you dumbass! What the hell do you think you're doing?" As he moved into a more brightly lit area I was treated to an apparition that kept me laughing the rest of the night. Deciding I needed a coffee, I jogged over to the dining hall, as always the nerve center of the camp. Yolanda and Dominick had already gotten started on breakfast prep for the next morning. Theresa was there, as well as several counselors, due to the nerve-wracking night we were experiencing.

As I sipped my coffee, I related my experience when I'd just entered camp. My audience was surveying me as if they thought I were hallucinating, and then, just in time to give credence to my tale, in marches Rich. He was dressed in a karate outfit with a samurai sword; strapped to his waist was the companion *katana* sword. The belt contained grenades, and they weren't just for show. His bandolier of bullets was impressive as hell. Hanging across his shoulder was a set of nunchakus, lethal cylinders connected by a chain, and he held a rifle with a live clip in his hands, ready to go. He topped off his improbable outfit with a World War II–era German helmet, complete with swastika. Our homegrown Rambo was ready for action.

Everyone stared at him in stunned silence, and then dissolved into howls of raucous laughter. Our amusement didn't touch Rich, however. With quiet dignity he turned and retraced his steps. It was time for him to continue patrolling. Nobody was going to attack our camp on his watch.

Barry was on the floor. "And you wanted us to call the Priests if we ran into trouble? By the time they showed up, there wouldn't be any Demons standing."

"Right," I agreed. "They'd either be dead or laughing themselves silly."

For days afterward, I kept picturing Rich in his updated samurai attire, and I couldn't stop laughing. But even though it was funny, it struck me that his watchfulness was certainly performing above and beyond the call of duty. At the end of the summer session we awarded him a fake silver star. He accepted it with a big grin, knowing we all appreciated having him as our de facto guardian angel against the Demons.

Another sometime visitor to the camp was my sister Diane, or Dietzie, as we nicknamed her. Not only had she trapped muskrats with my brother and me when we were kids, she'd also been one hell of an athlete in high school. She'd also been the bow and arrow champion of the state of New Jersey several times. This was in addition to being pretty handy with firearms, you understand. During one autumn visit to Kamp Olympik, she began agitating for the two of us to go hunting in the woods. Now we both loved trapping, but shooting a gun was not my cup of tea, and my baby sister knew it. Dietzie, however, was nothing if not persistent. So off into the woods we went one overcast day to find a propitious spot for spying a deer or two. She selected a small creek off the main river just a stone's throw away from where a deer path crossed it. As we settled down behind a screen of cedar and withered weeds, Dietzie gave me a sly look. "You won't shoot a doggone thing, you know. You're so softhearted, you'll get buck fever and won't get off even one shot."

Me, softhearted? "Oh really? If one deer shows up, I assure you it's gonna get nailed right between its big brown eyes."

We crouched in our blind, silent as the cedar tree beside us, and after an hour's vigil we were rewarded with a faint rustling. Dietzie tensed and motioned for me to be quiet. After another half hour, a beautiful deer slipped out from the trees, right in front of us. Softly, as if it were walking on thin ice, it cautiously stepped forward. With a jerk of her head, Dietzie gave me the go-ahead to fire. My finger tightened on the trigger, but I hesitated, absorbed by the beauty of this lovely innocent creature. It isn't hurting anything and I'm supposed to separate it from nature, from its family, by taking its life? For an instant I felt like an executioner, but then I noticed the knowing smile on Dietzie's face.

Well, all right. Buck fever might be assailing my sensitive soul, but I could damn well put meat on the family table. I pulled the trigger, and the deer toppled into the creek. Seized by an adrenaline rush beyond my experience, I leaped to my feet and dashed into the creek, sinking up to my neck in freezing water. I nearly went under, but I felt the muddy bank reassert itself beneath my feet. Enter Bragg: Primal Man. With a triumphant screech, I grabbed the prey and slung it over my shoulder like a wigged-out Neanderthal and waded back across the stream. Half running, I carried it all the way back to camp, and when I got there I couldn't wait to shout, "We eat tonight!"

Then I heard Dietzie laughing, and that sobered me immediately.

"That's it, Dietzie," I told her. "I'll never kill one of those beautiful creatures again."

"You didn't have to kill this one, you know."

"The hell I didn't. You challenged me when you said I wouldn't shoot, so I was committed. But never again!"

A sometime friend of mine named Frank had also just arrived at camp for the weekend, and when he saw my deer, he began regaling us with his exploits as a great white hunter. "Yeah," he began, "I've hunted grizzly bears, mule deer, and polar bears."

"Grizzlies?" I asked. "And you're still in one piece?"

"Only because I'm one helluva shot. Me and another guy, we'd been out stalking grizzlies this one time, and hadn't seen so much as a bear whisker. We were dead beat by the time we got back to our camp, and guess what?"

"No idea," I said, wishing he'd just tell the damn story.

"We'd just come in sight of the camp, when I sensed something was wrong."

"Wait a minute," I cut in. "If you were in sight of the camp, you could see what was going on, right?"

"Well, yes, but the point is a couple of grizzlies were tearing into our supplies."

"Must've been smart bears to have torn down your tree cache."

"My what?" Then he laughed. "Oh, yeah, that bit with the two ropes tied way up between two trees. Nah, we didn't go to all that trouble. The thing is, while we were out hunting bears, they'd been stalking us."

"Stalking your bacon and Velveeta, you mean."

"Whatever, but they didn't have any right to our stuff. So, keeping a safe distance between us and the bears, we pulled out our rifles and opened fire." Then Frank started laughing.

"What's funny?" I really didn't see the joke.

"Well, the bear doesn't die right away. It goes plain crazy and starts destroying everything. Shredded the sleeping bags, tore up the tents—hell, the damn bear tore up the entire campsite." He took a swig of his coffee. "You've never seen such a mess!"

So this "helluva shot" wounded a grizzly bear. Wonderful. "What happened?"

"The other bear rears up on its hind legs, looking for all the world like a human being scoping the area for its prey. It almost made eye contact, and I got a little worried. You know how fast those suckers can charge."

"But you guys still had your rifles," I said, with some regret.

"Right, but we didn't need 'em. The damn bear finally decided to scram and took off. But we got some great steaks off that other bear." He drained his coffee cup. "Yeah, hunting is my real vocation," he said. "Y'know, back in Albania in the old days, if the lord of the estate wanted venison, it was the gamekeeper's job to bring in a deer. My great-great-grandfather was a gamekeeper for some baron or duke, and he had a helluva reputation as a hunter. So it's in my blood."

I just sat there thinking, then God help us all.

Next this guy goes to his car trunk and pulls out a pump-action 12-gauge shotgun and wanders back to me as he starts to load. "Okay to get in some target practice? I like to keep my eye sharp."

"Sure," I said, "but stay away from the kids. Try down by the river."

What a mistake! Once he started shooting, any bird that moved was blown from the sky. Nothing, from sparrows to crows, was safe. He blasted away at every tree or bush with a touch of color, as well as at the buoys I had floating on the lake to separate the shallows from the deeper water. Of course, my kids and Frank's two gathered 'round to watch, and from their admiring "ooohs" and "aaahs," they must've thought he was Deadeye Dick in the flesh. Finally, he had the kids throw an old basketball in the water, and he began unloading on the pathetic, aging ball, bouncing it around the river with every shot.

Finally, I said, "Frank, enough already! I'll have nothing left. You've killed all the trees, birds, buoys, and balls in sight. Save some ammunition for some real prey if it shows up." The shot-riddled remains of the ancient basketball washed up at our feet. I hauled the handful of tattered rubber out of the water. "Unless you want to try cooking *this*?"

"Yeah, okay. That's pretty good thinking. But man, I'd love to get me a deer like what you just brought in."

We all had fresh venison except for Theresa and our daughter Renée. The two of them weren't about to eat Bambi, but that didn't bother me at all. It just left more for the rest of us.

After our feast, we started setting up for our family campfire, a camp tradition we continued long after camping season was over. The campfire was a time to relax with family and friends and tell stories while we roasted marshmallows and hot dogs. We never started the fire until well after dark, but we wanted to have everything ready to go.

Suddenly Frank comes running in. "Hey, you got Honda 90s out there."

"You ride?" I asked.

"Aw, hell, yes. Helluva rider, too. Had a cycle myself, years ago, but of course it was much bigger than the little ones you have. What say we go for a little ride before campfire?"

"I don't know, Frank. It'll be dark before too long."

"Nah, we'll be fine. Hell, the bikes have lights on 'em, don't they? C'mon, guys," he called, rallying Dietzie, Barry, Dave Miller, Mike, and my son Mark. "Let's all of us just follow Don and have us a little ride in the woods."

"Y'know, these woods aren't all that orderly," I began, but he cut me off.

"Hey, buddy, I don't know about you guys, but I've never met a tree I couldn't handle." He went charging outside to saddle up so fast that he didn't catch the looks the other guys were giving each other.

"Is this guy for real?" somebody asked.

"Not sure," I answered, heading out the door. "Let's go find out."

Okay, so we got the cycles up and running, except for Frank, who was having trouble with his. He fiddled with the choke, which didn't improve his steering skills, and the engine kept cutting off on him.

Then Frank said, "Your cycle'd do me better, Don. How's about we swap?"

"They're both Honda 90s," I replied.

"No, yours is put together a little different." I think what he meant was that I was able to make mine go where I wanted, a mysterious feature on some very special Honda 90s. But what the hell, I let him have my bike, and he settled himself with the guttural grunts and growls of the true biker.

"Yeah, much better. Now let's get the lead out, guys."

The trouble was Frank still couldn't make the damn bike behave, so I asked him, "You sure you know what you're doing?"

He got kind of ruffled and indignant. "Certainly," he responded. "I'm a professional."

Barry leaned over toward me and whispered, "Yeah, but a professional what?"

"You got that right," I chuckled back to him. So off we go towards Godfrey's Bridge, which crossed over to the state property. I saw a forest ranger patrolling the area so we hung back till he'd passed through. Then, following the winding deer paths and crisscrossing dirt tracks, we took off. It was a beautiful evening, and with night settling over the forest, the air was bracing, so of course we had a great ride. But it was getting pretty dark, so I said, "Okay, let's head home for campfire."

"What the hell!" Frank complained. "I'm finally getting the hang of these half-pint bikes of yours. Let's stay out a little longer."

"Look around, Frank," I said. "It's getting too dark to see, and the lights on these bikes don't produce sufficient light for negotiating these trails at night."

"You're forgetting I have the night eyes of a hunter," he said. "Anyhow, all we have to do is follow the damn path."

"You win," I conceded. "We'll go a little farther." So we continued along the main river path, with its branching foot tracks that would swoop down to the river itself. These little paths formed breaches in the surrounding trees and let in both light and the wind off the river. They made the ride especially pleasant. But it was getting hard even for me to see where I was going, and I knew we were done. With a sharp U-turn, I got us headed back to camp.

We stopped at Godfrey's Bridge and waited for everybody to catch up. Eventually we saw a dim light flickering through the trees as it approached. "That must be Dietzie and Frank," I said. "They must've taken a wrong turn."

"Wrong, Don," came Dietzie's voice from a few yards away. "I'm right here."

"Hey," Barry called, "where'd that light get to?"

The dim light we'd been watching had in fact flickered out, but slightly upriver, we heard an odd gurgling slosh followed by frantic splashing. We peered into the dark, not quite able to make out the source of the commotion in the shallows.

"What the hell is that, a boat?"

"It looks like a kayak. Wait, it's sinking!"

"I think we just found Frank," said Dietzie, as a familiar voice began yelling for help.

So our guest with the night eyes of a hunter had gone and driven his cycle right into the river, and evidently planned to stay there until we came and fished both him and it out.

We finally dragged the cycle out of four feet of water, having found it by Braille, diving and groping around in the mud. The cycle was unrideable, of course, but we left it on the bank so we could pick it up in the truck. Frank was another matter. We made him walk the 200 or so yards into camp since nobody was about to ride double with this guy.

We arrived back at camp in plenty of time for campfire, and Frank made the most of story time to give his version of the bike ride. I have no doubt that his embroidering of his part in the ride was helped along by the prodigious amount of beer he'd imbibed. He clearly planned to make himself out as the hero of the evening, but I doubt if even the youngest among us was taken in by it. The fact that his fellow cyclists would explode with laughter every time he added another embellishment didn't help his cause, either.

"So here I am, tearing through the darkened woods, when I see someone go in the water," Frank said in an awestruck voice. "I thought it was your kid sister, Don."

Dietzie responded with a juicy, resonant Bronx cheer, but Frank continued undeterred. "No, honestly. I was trying to save her."

"There was nobody else in the river, Frank," laughed Magoo. "Just who in hell did you think you were saving?"

"It was probably just a reflection from the water; with those dinky little lights you've got on the bikes, who could tell? Didn't I say those lights were too weak for a night drive?"

"No!" all of us bellowed back at him in unison.

Then Dietzie spoke up. "Frank, you are so full of shit. After we turned around and looped back, you kept wandering on and off the trail. I'd been keeping an eye on you, but I wanted to catch up to Don and the others. When I passed you, you looked scared out of your mind, which is okay. What is not okay, you jackass, is that you reached out, grabbed me, and pulled me off my cycle, then charged on ahead."

Frank looked mildly surprised. "Oh, was that you? I thought I'd hit a deer!"

When the shout of derision at his alibi had died down, Dietzie caught his eye and held it. "No, you didn't, you buzzard!" she said with a rasp in her voice. "You pulled me off my bike so you could pass me, 'cause you couldn't stand being the last one in line out there in the dark. Admit it, Chicken Shit!"

Everybody laughed again, and then somebody else started telling a story. But I have to give Frank credit. He proved to me he was in fact the superb outdoorsman he claimed to be by the way he emulated weasel behavior in sidestepping any responsibility for the chaotic ride. He was like a great big wet dog that you couldn't stay mad at, however. But that cycle ride taught me we had to limit risky fun-time activities, and soaring insurance premiums were only a part of the reason. Hell, I had little kids to worry about; I didn't need another full-time job monitoring incompetent grown-ups who were a menace not only to themselves but to the forest as well. If another one of them screwed up, Mother Nature would probably find some awful way to get even.

With the camp so close to the river, I often had people ask, "Aren't you afraid of floods?" The river did in fact flood its banks maybe four times during our entire stint at Kamp Olympik, so we simply learned to adjust: no big deal. The dining hall and the cabins were on a slight ridge, so we kept dry where it counted, but the first year we confronted a deluge that would've overwhelmed Noah. River water crept a hundred yards into the surrounding forest, putting our bathhouse and septic tanks underwater and out of commission. The little creek that cut through camp also burst its banks, adding to the general hilarity of what should have merely been a disaster. But we had to improvise someplace to go, and fast. Calling on my vast experience shoveling stuff, I ramrodded a ditch-digging crew. After some hard labor, we prepared a serviceable trench on higher ground, with a log for squatting suspended between two trees for the users' convenience. At night we'd shovel in enough dirt to cover the noisome contributions on the bottom, and start fresh, so to speak, the next day. The following year, I ordered four port-o-johns and installed them around the camp, keeping them locked until another emergency threatened. Much more civilized. I also built a bathhouse on higher ground a few seasons later, which was even better.

Not that any of this bothered the campers much. Most of them treated flooding like an exciting adventure. They seemed to like the improvised schedule, which redesigned the camp program for a day or two. It almost never took much

River flooding during summer storm at camp.

longer than that for the floodwaters to abate due to the sandy, porous soil in the area. That soil never created the sort of muddy mires that defied all manner of vehicles, so truck deliveries to the camp could continue uninterrupted.

Watching the kids slosh through the water in their flip-flops as they headed for chow was always fun. I'm pretty sure their active imaginations had them wading up unexplored rivers or moving like seasoned assault troops onto hostile beaches. And all it took to release this kind of mind adventure was a little rain. The kids who only had sneakers would usually hop a canoe to cross the creek to the dining hall, but that was exciting in its own right.

In fact, setting foot outside after any flooding could be downright hair-raising. Snakes and all kinds of varmints from rats to possums and skunks went shimmying or paddling through the standing water. Counselors had to make the rounds to escort the littlest campers to the johns, but the critters just went about their business and ignored all of us. Nature-loving Tracey really had a field day, and she enthusiastically called the campers' attention to every species she set eyes on. That a girl could be so at ease around the four-footed and no-footed invasion made it all less frightening to the younger campers. That was a terrific help.

Contrary to what happened to the original Noah's Ark, ours ran into trouble when the heavens opened. The flood lifted our boat off its pedestal-like structure and swept it away. Downstream of the camp it had gotten wedged between two stumps, filled with water, and sank up to the gunwales. With hundreds of volunteers eager to join in the salvage operation, however, I was sure we'd shortly have *Noah's Ark* back home.

Armed with whatever camp equipment I thought would come in handy, we made our way to the stricken craft. With buckets and a hand pump we emptied the vessel of as much water as we could. Without its cargo of water, the boat wobbled to the surface. Next we tied one end of the sturdy camp tug-of-war rope to the boat's prow cleat and the other to a semi-submerged—but well-rooted—oak. Then the assembled campers and counselors all pulled as one, and slowly the boat floated toward the bank. When we had our ark well under control, we unhitched it from the tree and began to pull it upstream to the Port of Kamp Olympik. The counselors started chanting, which got the whole mob pulling in unison. It kind of gave me chills to watch, since that same scenario had been enacted millennia ago on the banks of the Nile by fishermen. It was also great to see everyone band together as brothers and attack the task at hand.

A couple of times we transported our campers to baseball fields in nearby towns until the floodwaters receded. Almost immediately the townspeople flooded the camp with complaints. The fields were there for their use, not the use of out-of-towners. The fact that they weren't using them—when we were—didn't matter.

Since I like to choose my battles, I decided we'd just have to try to create some memorable challenges by taking advantage of our dilemma. Hell, everybody loved water games. So why not invent a few ingenious ones? Like running the river in our canoes: it would be almost as exciting as white-water rafting, and a treat for our water-logged campers. Rich's brother Magoo, our waterfront director, and I brainstormed over every detail of our diversions, and since the meticulous Magoo was involved, we paid the utmost attention to safety. If you're around water, though, there will be some risk, especially with the river running at about five miles per hour. That's why I reserved the adventure for campers who'd passed their Junior Lifesaving test. The kids' eyes were all sparkling as they envisioned a ripsnorting trip down to Evans Bridge, which normally took a few minutes shy of an hour by canoe.

As the first twelve canoes set out from the beach I heard somebody yell, "We're gonna get there in half an hour." There was entirely too much cockiness aboard, despite the life jackets. Because Magoo, in charge of the final canoe, was the safety net for the expedition, I squelched my misgivings and walked back to camp.

Since Evans Bridge was only a fifteen-minute drive away, we didn't rush off. But when we finally pulled up in sight of the bridge, several of the counselors were already on the span, waving frantically. Running onto the bridge, I glanced down. A couple of life jackets and a paddle were bobbing against the bank. Then they told me the bad news. Where the river had widened, some of the canoes foundered on submerged tree stumps, and at present we were missing four counselors and eight of the older campers. Dashing for the bus, I was staving off panic in order to initiate a search party when I saw ten figures in the distance running down the road. When I realized it was Magoo followed by a handful of dripping water rats, I was weak with relief.

Magoo was apologetic. "I'm sorry we lost some equipment, but between the low-hanging tree branches, the tree stumps, and the current, it was impossible to keep the canoes upright. I had my hands full just getting everybody to safety. We collected as much equipment as we could, then tried walking back through the flooded forest, but it took forever without any visible trail to follow. Sorry, Boss."

I didn't say anything: I was just too grateful everybody was safe to say a word.

It took a couple of days to retrieve the canoes. One we never found, one was split in half, and the others were jammed between trees, one barely visible above the river water.

Of course the campers who hadn't been on the ill-fated canoe trip were insanely jealous. So the next day, we arranged for a few of them to free-float down the river while wearing their life jackets. They were to start at Godfrey's Bridge, just a couple of hundred yards upstream. With our most adept canoers accompanying them, I stationed Magoo and other counselors armed with poles—as well as rescue rings on ropes—all along their river route. This particular challenge concluded without a hitch, and the kids had a great time.

But I didn't.

The minute the river expedition pushed off, every possible freak accident that could occur flashed before my eyes. And when they were five minutes later than my estimate of what their outing should take, I was flipping out. When Magoo finally paddled back all by himself into the canal that fed our swim area, I yelled, "Where in hell are the kids?"

"They're already back up at Tarzanville."

"But that's all flooded." I objected. "Don't tell me they took their life jackets off."

"They're wearing their jackets. But they're swinging around on the ropes, skimming along on the water with their feet. Damnest thing you ever saw. I didn't know we offered water skiing, Boss."

So I shouted, "That's it! Get 'em out of there. It's over." As other counselors joined us, I roared, "No more crazy river excursions! I don't care if we have to play water polo on the basketball court or if the kids have to swim to first base on the softball field. If all there is to do is play in the mud puddles and make mud pies, that's what we'll do. Everybody understand? Now move it!"

From then on, even when it rained, we stuck to our normal routine, which was full of enough craziness in its own right. I just thank God we never had rain that lasted for forty days and forty nights. If Noah had been at Kamp Olympik, he couldn't have handled it either.

But rain or shine, spring or winter, it was never a question of "out of sight, out of mind" where Kamp Olympik was concerned. Before we took up permanent residence at the camp, I'd spent many an off-season weekend tending to maintenance and repairs. Our kids loved to come with me, and while I worked, they'd play in the dining hall or run around outside. As they grew older, they became my helpers, and often saved me a whole workload of time by fetching me things when I was up on a ladder.

During winter I took care of the indoor improvements, and my kids still kept me company. After I was done with my work, we'd head back to Trenton, but we'd stop and get our sleds out of the trunk and go sledding on the frozen cranberry bogs. That was always a treat: one good push from me would give the kids a ride of several hundred yards.

When I started paneling the inside of the chow hall, the children loved to jump out of the rafters into the "Cloud 9," the inflatable pit I was given for promoting its use for the pole-vault landing. Its design was truly ingenious. It had a fan, which kept it inflated until something landed on it. Then it slowly released its stored air, absorbing the g-forces and providing a softer landing pit than the old bone-jarring sawdust. Jeffrey passed the time by riding his cycle around the dining hall in first gear, all decked out in his helmet and goggles. That's just who he was. A Piney drove up one day and heard the kids shrieking with delight as they flung themselves into this inflatable pit. "Those youngsters of yours are pretty wound up, huh? Sounds like they're bouncing off the ceiling." I just smiled and sent him on his way. Some things you just don't try to explain to a Piney.

Once I finished paneling the dining hall, I decided to shingle the outside to maintain a rustic look and give some cold weather protection. Then I moved on to doing something about the cabins. They'd been constructed of cedar tongue-and-groove board, but the knotty cedar wood had dried out, and the knots had dropped out of the boards. As a result, all the cabins looked like they'd been built of Swiss cheese and weren't long for this world. As Mark pointed out, the holes were great for air conditioning but did nothing to keep the bugs out, especially the Jersey mosquito, which had a talent for biting you where you didn't want to be seen scratching in public. The only sensible solution was to cedar-

Barry shingling campers' cabin.

shake all the cabins to cover the rapidly increasing number of holes. Barry was going to help, but this was a major undertaking, so I also hired some of the teenage boys from the Priest family. Working every weekend, we finished the job in just over a month, and the completed cabins looked great.

Since my Priest family connection allowed me to tap into a cheap, reliable workforce, I decided on another major project. I'd painted several of the cabins red, but though they looked pretty spiffy, they stuck out like large, inflamed thumbs from the rest of the unpainted cabins. Why not paint all the cabins red and establish a cheerful uniformity?

Little did I know what I was in for as I negotiated a good price on the paint and—no, I wasn't drunk at the time—bought a compressor to spray paint the cabins. After several days, a third of the cabins were finished, and the camp began to take on a uniform, cohesive appearance. Then things began to unravel just enough to worry me. First, the compressor went prima donna on us, jamming with incomprehensible frequency. Then it languished there gasping until we disassembled the damn thing and gave it a thorough cleaning. Then rain came and went and came again, which not only delayed the work but teased us with clearing skies that darkened as soon as we set up to paint. So there was a lot of frustrated energy lurking around the camp.

I made a quick run to Mick's Country Store for bread, salami, and fruit, but when I drove back into the campgrounds, I slammed on the brake in alarm. The whole place was dripping red paint, as if it had just experienced a gigantic hemorrhage, and I am not exaggerating. The trees, the ground, the cabins, and the screens all pulsed with scarlet, and I got out of the station wagon wondering what the hell happened. Then the grinning culprits came out from behind one of the cabins, and they too were covered in red paint. Yeah, bored with inaction, the Priest boys decided to have a spraying contest, and you might say things got out of hand. I couldn't help laughing, but I needed to clean up my workforce before I sent them home to Virginia Priest.

Since I'd chosen a water-based paint, I decided that it wouldn't harm the environment if they washed off in the river, so in they went. The autumn had turned chilly, so that water was cold. The boys jumped in anyhow and got human-looking again, though I wondered what folks downriver would make of the gory-looking stain drifting from Kamp Olympik. The kids at their school were merciless, razzing the Priest boys about their bee-yoo-tee-ful red hair, and the boys wouldn't go anywhere they didn't have to until they stopped being redheads, so as a result I lost my labor brigade. Still, I guess we all got off light.

Chapter Nine

Doing necessary maintenance around the camp was a year-round job. The lavatories and bathhouses needed to be kept in good working order for the sake of cleanliness, health, and keeping them sewer-legal so far as state regulations were concerned. The major contributor to the plumbing problems was sabotage by rambunctious kids playing "I dare you to!" with mind-boggling contributions to our plumbing system: little things like whole rolls of toilet paper and shoes (plus, I have my suspicions of where a few missing baseballs ended up). The bigger and more unlikely the object, the more time and cunning the kids were eager to expend in seeing it disappear down the tube. In addition to performing shoe-ectomies on the sewer lines, I was also kept busy constantly tweaking the drainage system to keep the septic tank happy.

But what I really loved doing in the off-season was putting in improvements that made the camp better for the kids. When I realized that one group of our campers was being left out in the cold, I had to do something about it. Though the majority of the campers loved Tarzanville, some younger campers were simply too small to use it. So I designed a pint-sized Tarzanville and named it Fort Bragg.

It was a tree fort situated in a cluster of five trees. Only eight feet

Reneé, Tracey, Jeff, and Mark in front of Fort Bragg.

high and accessed by a ladder, it even had an additional lookout tower another four feet higher where the little ones could look out over the entire camp. To keep the kids from falling off, I surrounded all above-ground structures with a picket fence. There was a little gate on the platform, and the little ones had a ball swinging it shut then hollering triumphantly that they'd captured the fort.

There were a few ropes installed under the fort, so the youngsters could swing like the big kids, and I put in two sliding boards for a safe return from the fort's platform. It was fun to build and, even better, my sons gave me a hand in its construction. Mark was around eight years old, and not only was he a dependable gofer, he also just loved to bang nails. Did a good job, too. Jeff would be unbelievably enthusiastic for about an hour, but then he'd wander off, for a glass of water, he'd say, but before long I'd hear his little cycle putting around camp. I could've chased him around, reprimanded him, but then I wouldn't have gotten a damn thing done. So I more or less said screw it—and let him ride. I mean, he was only five years old. So much for my slave labor! But though Jeff hadn't helped too much in its construction, he was one of Fort Bragg's most frequent visitors. It was great to see the really little kids get such a kick out of their private preserve.

Theresa: *I also had kids sharing the wonder of Pinelands and the exhilarating smell of the outdoors with me. The confiding little hand clasped in mine, the trusting big eyes, sure that I'd explain everything to him—how wonderful was that? Once one of them asked, "Hey, Missy Bragg. Back home, an awful lot of stuff smells really bad. How come it smells so nice and clean down here?" I reached up and twisted a handful of pine needles from an overhanging branch, crumpled them in my hand, then held them under the little one's nose. "That's it? That nice smell comes from squashed pine needles?"*

"No, Sweetie," I replied. "But when the wind blows, it brushes against all the pine trees and spreads their fragrance through the whole woods."

"Do you gotta wash the trees?" he asked.

"That's one of the things the rain does," I said, smiling at him. With an awestruck look, he turned away, then wheeled back to me. "Is Mother Nature doin' all that work?"

"Uh-huh, with some help from God."

A knowing look spread over the boy's face. "Like how my dad helps my mom?" I nodded. He nodded back, saying, "So Mother Nature does all the work while God watches baseball. I didn't know that!"

Theresa wasn't alone in spreading unintended bits of lore. Sometimes the counselors would come to me wild-eyed, demanding answers to the most implausible questions. "Hey, Mr. Bragg," Dave called out to me after he'd chased me halfway across the camp. "Where in hell does the mist come from?"

I was in a hurry, so I said, "From the dew fairy, when she starts sweating."

"No, really, a bunch of my kids are into what causes the mist in the morning. So where does it come from?" I told him about condensation and temperature differentiation, and his eyes glazed. "I think I'll stick with the sweating dew fairy," he said. "And why does the water sparkle even though it's all brown?"

"The water's clean, but there's a lot of iron in it. And it picks up some coloration from flowing in and around cedar."

"Water brown, but clean. Clean water sparkles." He thought for a minute. "Yup, that should do it." And he trotted off with his questionable explanation to educate the curious minds in his charge.

There wasn't any guaranteed downtime for the Kamp Olympik staff. Things calmed down in the evenings, but one hour after supper during free period we'd ring the bell for canteen time, and havoc reigned. I'd stand in amazement watching a spot-on re-enactment of Pavlov's theory of stimulus response. At the very first sound of the bell the salivary glands of the camp shifted into high gear. Drooling campers queued up in the dining hall for their choice of candy bars, Popsicles, or chips, leaving little puddles of spit in their wake. Most counselors considered candy-time duty as worthy of combat pay and usually dreaded being assigned to it. At least it started that way.

All of a sudden I have counselors volunteering for the candy detail. What a nice attitude—trying to make a real contribution to camp operation. That's what I thought for about two minutes, and then I began sniffing around to find out what they were up to. I took a good look at how our system worked. We kept a list of the kids' names, and we checked them off as they picked up their treat. Now goodies were at the top of most campers' want list, but not everybody's. The kids had to sign up for canoes and sometimes had to wait for a couple of days to get their turn. When they finally got their canoe, a few weren't ready to lose it so they could snag a piece of candy. Or sometimes campers were so engrossed in Tarzanville they didn't hear the bell.

This meant a few kids didn't turn up for canteen time. And that was the basis for the chocolate collusion that was going on. After all the kids had grabbed their chocolate or sugar fix, there'd be extra candy left over. So the beady-eyed counselors in charge would simply cross off names of the kids who hadn't showed up, and pocket the dozen pieces of candy for their own use.

"What the hell were you thinking? Stealing supplies—I can't believe it," I told the culprits. The candy was far more than a sweet treat. It was the common currency of the camp. Some kids would pick up their candy, then race down to the beach to exchange it for a canoe for roaming-free period or to boost themselves up the line waiting for the basketball court. My enterprising counselors had an answer.

"Yeah, well, Yolanda gives kitchen helpers cake or cookies. They get milk, too, and that's just for cleanup details. "

"What about the way Uncle Joe gives candy to anybody who helps with trash pickup? Why not a few candy bars for us counselors on canteen duty?"

That sounded reasonable, so I finally consented. "But no more than six per night of canteen duty. Just don't eat yourselves sick."

"Eat? Are you crazy? Candy bars are way too valuable."

They were right. Kamp Olympik had returned to the barter system, and a Snickers bar was the gold standard. But my counselors weren't the only ones up to a little skull-duggery. After getting their candy, some kids would hide their loot, run around the dining hall, and then sneak back in line for a second hit. Unless their counselor was on candy duty, they were rarely caught. I saw kids race back to their cabins with their candy, only to reappear wearing different T-shirts and line up for seconds.

In the end, I had Rich take over the canteen, since he knew more different faces around the camp than anyone else, so end of problem.

Or so I thought.

One day I needed Rich, so I went to his cabin. Calling his name, I walked in, and there in plain sight were several boxes of candy bars.

"Sure, Boss. I bought them for snacks. Running around this place takes energy."

Uh-huh. I told Barry to keep an eye on our rotund director, but then I thought, hell, and who'd keep an eye on Barry? So sanity prevailed before I engineered a "let's you watch this guy" network to rival anything hatched by the KGB.

Pretty much everyone had his share of candy except the cookie boys, who were shut out of the canteen treats. This was pure retaliation because, as Yolanda's helpers, they got all the leftover snacks, yet failed to share them with the counselors. It's odd to consider what becomes important in a closed environment, even if it's a fun-time camp. It's not that far removed from what goes on in a prison. I guess it's all relative, but at least KO campers were amateurs, and the only repercussions of their bartering were a few stretched rules and maybe a need to brush their teeth a little harder.

My daughters Renée and Tracey didn't draw canteen duty, but they kept busy. Renée handled all the arts and crafts activities, and Tracey quickly graduated from merely being Renée's aide to running our nature program herself. She not only loved taking the campers on nature hikes, she had a genuine talent for it. Tracey quickly became an expert on the local flora and fauna so she could explain to the kids what had just hopped across the trail and what it had been eating. If you couldn't find Tracey, she was probably crawling around on the riverbank taking plaster prints of the footprints animals had left. Hormones were stirring among the older campers, however.

"I don't know, Daddy," Tracey said one time. "It was so fantastic—on the nature hike this morning we saw a doe with two fawns! But half the boys were looking at me, not at the animals. What's wrong with boys?"

"Nothing, Honey," I told her. But some of our adolescent campers, clearly smitten with puppy love, were following her around like moonstruck calves. That's when Theresa and I decided that she shouldn't take the older groups deep into the woods anymore. The younger groups were fine, since they had the sense to be fascinated by bunnies and quail, not by our daughter!

Located immediately adjacent to the basketball court, the arts and crafts cabin contained an old well with a creaky hand pump. We didn't plan to use it, since we had an ample supply of water from our other wells, and so we never had the damn thing inspected. I posted a NO DRINKING sign, and every time I went into the cabin I'd say, "Don't drink water from this well." I assumed everybody would take the hint.

Then one day Theresa asked me, "Aren't an awful lot of kids going in and out of the arts and crafts cabin?"

Hmmm. I went over to size up the situation, and sure enough, a steady stream of campers was moving in and out of the cabin where Renée and Tracey were working. Had the entire camp developed a king-sized crush on our daughters?

Wrong. Kids were coming off the basketball court after a game in the blistering heat, and headed over to the arts and crafts cabin for a long drink of the forbidden waters of the old well.

"What the hell are you doing?" I demanded, pointing to the sign on the well. "Doesn't that sign say not to take a drink here?"

The culprits were apologetic but unrepentant. "Yes, but that water tastes much better than the other stuff," meaning the certified, inspected water from the other camp wells. "And it's twice as cold. Geez, Mr. Bragg, do you know what city water tastes like?"

I gave the well water a taste, and I had to admit the kids were right. But I still had to tell them not to drink that water. Maybe the fact that it was forbidden was what made the water so desirable. It seemed to be true of blueberries. Naturally, the kids all adored blueberries and would pounce on them whenever they found them in the woods. Then one day they came running into the dining hall to tell me that they'd found this huge field not far away, and it was full of juicy blueberries. Problem was that Mick, who ran the little grocery and gas station, owned the property next to mine, and he raised those blueberries to sell. We'd tell the campers to lay off Mick's blueberries, but the kids only took that as a suggestion.

Then campers began coming down with mysterious stomachaches. "Did you eat anything out in the woods?" I asked anxiously.

"Nothing in the woods," they wailed in reply. "Ooooh, my belly hurts bad." One glance inside their mouths pretty much let the cat out of the bag: their teeth and tongues were stained bright blue.

"You've been into Mick's blueberries." I said. "What else have you been eating?" But the kids stoutly maintained that all they'd ingested were those luscious berries. I didn't see the connection to the bellyaches, though, until I ran into Mick.

"I haven't seen those campers of yours in my berry patch lately," he told me with a big grin on his face.

"That's right. Something's been giving the kids bellyaches, and they're afraid to eat any food that Yolanda doesn't give them."

He slapped his knee and laughed outright. "I knew it would work. Those kids are worse than a plague of locusts, so I bought me a little locust insurance."

"How so?" I asked, wondering what he'd been up to.

"I sprayed all the berry bushes on the outside of the patch with insecticide. I figured that'd keep the pests off."

I was mad as hell that he hadn't informed me before, but they were his bushes, and the campers had been sampling them regularly. When I broke the news at camp, my family was indignant. "That's a dirty trick," said Tracey.

"At least we know where those stomachaches were coming from," was all Theresa said, but I knew she was pretty steamed. But at least that was the end of the belly-aches. I was proud of the discipline even the littlest campers showed in staying away from the forbidden fruit. I'd really expected some attempts to circumvent the embargo on the blueberries, but none came.

Years later, I learned the reason for the campers' fortitude. "Oh, I'd take the kids in for blueberries every other day or so," Tracey smiled up at me. "They just adored those berries."

"But the insecticide," I began, but my daughter waved away my objection.

"We all knew about that; we just worked our way into the center of the patch. That's where the biggest blueberries were anyhow. Besides, we were careful not to break any branches; we just worked our way in and delicately gorged ourselves on those luscious berries."

"And I never had a clue!" I marveled.

"Of course not. I had them wash their mouths out at the bathhouse on the way back."

"You did?" I finally managed to say. I couldn't believe the cool criminal cunning of my younger daughter.

"Sure. Otherwise you'd have been really pissed off. But the berries were just irresistible," she continued, closing her eyes in the recalled pleasure of contraband berries. "Besides, the campers said they didn't ever do any blueberry picking in the city."

"Maybe that's because they don't grow *anything* in the city. Thank God you didn't help them stage a raid on Walt Priest's tasty garden delights while you were at it, you wouldn't have gotten out alive," I reminded her, but she just gave me that cutesy casual comment, the way daughters do.

"Oh, Daddy, don't be silly."

Renée also had a few blueberry confessions. I was talking to her just the other day, and we were trying to place the time of some incident at camp, and she said, "I'm not sure, Dad. It was around the time Mark got shot."

"Mark got *what?*"

"Shot. He was in the blueberry field, and one of Mick's guys winged him with rock salt from a shotgun. I guess we never told you."

"I guess not. So come on, tell me now."

"He was in the berry field gathering blueberries for Aunt Ruth, you know, Uncle Joe's wife?"

"Yes, we've met. He's my uncle, not yours. I do know him and his wife. Go on."

"Well, she'd tell us that if we'd bring her eight cups of blueberries she'd make us a pie. We just had to get those blueberries, or we'd miss out on some fantastic pie."

"Get to the part where Mark gets shot," I said, not about to be drawn into a philosophical plane where blueberry pie was the categorical imperative.

"He came running into camp holding his butt, which was all black and blue, and he told me what'd happened."

"My butt's burning like hell," he said. "Dad's going to have to take me to the doctor."

"Are you crazy, Mark?" I said. "Your butt may hurt bad now, but Dad'd absolutely kill you if he knew you were into Mick's berry patch. You'd never sit on a motorcycle again."

I could see her logic. Why should the campers abide by rules my kids ignored? I had to insist on compliance from my own family.

"Anyhow," she finished with a little sigh, "Mark cooled his butt off in the lake, and that was that."

"So that was the end of your blueberry poaching, right?"

She gave me an enigmatic smile. "Sure, Dad."

So I not only had rebellious campers evading camp rules, my own kin—from grand-motherly pie bakers to sweet little daughters—were investing long hours to finding ways of bucking the system.

But back when her sister was leading forays into Mick's blueberry patch, Renée, in charge of the arts and crafts cabin, was in her element. "Dad," she said. "You know how the kids drop everything and take off like lightning when the canteen bell rings? Some of my kids in here are so preoccupied with their craft projects, they don't even budge. It is so neat!"

They were especially big on pot holders: every kid in camp wanted to make one to bring home to mom. I think we could've carpeted several counties with the colorful yarn squares the campers turned out. They also loved pouring the plaster to make little figurines and such that they could paint themselves, but the most impressive outlet for their creativity became the making of lanyards. You know what they are: braided cords made from strands of plastic. Multicolored, they could slip around your neck or your wrist and you could attach keys, whistles, or penknives. Every session, Renée would start teaching the campers lanyard techniques, but before long the campers would start improvising and trying out different approaches. They'd end up sharing new stitches and designs with their teacher. It was as if the kids' creativity was getting its first real outlet. I hope three weeks of camp wasn't the only chance they got to use it.

One thing that never got old for me was the arrival of the new campers every session. Unlike some of the green counselors, I wasn't put off by the brass knuckles and knives we routinely confiscated. These kids were still in survival mode, learned the hard way on mean city streets. They also took immense pride in their neighborhood gang affiliations, the gangs being another essen-tial means of survival. The bus from Bergen County, for instance, contained members of the Garfield Rangers and the Lodi Warriors, and each kid would shout out their gang ties, proud as Scotsmen affirming their clans. I really enjoyed strolling among them getting them registered, which often took a little cunning on my part, since kids would get their nicknames tangled up with their last names. If we'd only compared the names the kids gave us with the official rec department roster, we'd never know who in hell was attending camp. I remember asking one first-time camper what his name was, and he stood there regarding me solemnly with big thoughtful eyes before responding, "Oha Bougah."

I paused a moment, curious. "Is that an old family name?" I really wasn't sure how to spell it.

The youngster stuck out his chest and answered with tremendous dignity, "That's a Swahili name. It's an old African name, cause, see, my great-great-grandpa and his great-great-grandpa were tribal chieftains."

Smiling at his pride in his people, I approximated the spelling of his name the best I could, and Oha Bougah walked off with his counselor to his assigned cabin. Okay, so I moved on to the next kid who seemed to be highly amused at something. He gave me his name, and we chatted a minute, but then he kept standing there, smiling up at me.

"Mr. Director," he finally said. "That boy there, he's in my class at school, and he didn't get his name from no Swahili chieftains."

"Oh? Then please tell us where he did get it."

"Gee, Mr. Director, all day in class he's pickin' his nose. All day long. Every day, always diggin' away and talkin' 'bout what he finds. Whenever he hits pay dirt he shouts, 'Oh! A booger. And it's nice and big and ripe.' So we call him Oh-a-booger. Ain't nothing Swahili 'bout it." While this kid is giving me the low down on Oha Bougah, the counselors standing beside me began retching and gagging delicately.

"And that ain't all. When he hits a score in his nose, he looks around, and if nobody's watching, he shoves it into his mouth and eats it up like it was candy."

Magoo, who has turned green while listening to this recital, says, "Just don't assign him to my cabin. Please!"

So I'm chuckling at Oh-a-booger as I go on registering campers. A few kids later I came to a short little guy who looked like an anvil fell from the sky and squashed him into his compact but muscular body. He had a great smile, and it lit up when I asked him his name.

"Me? They call me the Duke, 'cause I look and act like John Wayne. 'Course some of the kids call me Dukie, but I can handle that." The Duke picked up his bag and followed his counselor to his cabin. Then I noticed a kid giggling behind his hands.

"What's so funny?" I asked, after I got his name.

"That kid there," he snickered.

"Who? Dukie?"

"Hey, man, I'm in his class at school," the kid shot back with a cocky little swagger. "And the kids don't call him Dukie—they call him Doodie Drawers."

"Is that a fact?" said one of the counselors, coming closer. "How 'bout you tell us how he came by that name."

"Nuthin' to it. He used to mess himself somethin' bad. We'd be sittin' there in the classroom and all of a sudden here comes a real bad smell. Teacher knew what to do about it. She'd say, 'Doodie Drawers, you get your sweet self to the bathroom and clean up real good before you dare show your face in this classroom again.'" The boy was in hysterics by this time, and was barely able to say, "And then she says, 'And this time, use plenty of soap.'"

"Doodie Drawers," said the counselor. "That's just wonderful."

"Mmm," said the boy, as he continued. "Nobody would hang with him. I don't know why he thinks anybody'd mix him up with John Wayne: he's a tall man, and Doodie's just a short little dude and smells pretty bad. He isn't gonna be in my cabin, is he?"

My informant went off with his counselor to a different cabin, and I considered what I'd learned.

With a Swahili warrior and a movie star named Duke who didn't quite have his shit together, it was shaping up to be an interesting camping season, with larger-than-life personalities popping up all over the place. As I continued to register the boys, I considered asking them what their nicknames were, but I abandoned the idea. Sometimes it was better not to know.

As it turned out, Dukie became something of a camp mini-hero. For his age he had a lot of guts. This little guy was one of the few campers willing to go off the high dive at the lake. Though he wasn't the Duke, he was certainly the king of the dramatic moment. He'd haul himself up the diving tower and stand, meditating, as if he were concentrating on producing an Olympic dive worth ten points. What he was in fact doing was waiting for his friends to notice him and say, "Look! It's the

Infamous Diving Platform.

Duke up at the top of the platform." When a majority of the campers looked up and noticed him, then and only then did he commence his dive. He reminded me of a great matador preparing the coup de grace for a charging bull. Then he'd cut through the water like a scalpel and would surface with a huge smile on his face, swimming to shore with the confidence of an Olympic champion. With his sense of dramatic timing, he quickly became a camp personality. As for that other problem, we pointed out the usefulness of pine trees as emergency lavatories and saw to it that his pockets were always stuffed with paper napkins. After that he stopped being the butt of so many jokes.

Oha Bougah on the other hand possessed a ton of drive, which soon had him on the fast track to becoming a CIT. He was responsible and proved competent in any task we assigned him. He also developed into quite a leader. Don't ask me why—I hope it wasn't because of his unorthodox diet. Anyway, Oha Bougah was always on the lookout for ways to qualify for the CIT program.

One of the constant concerns of the Kamp Olympik staff was that some camper might wander off into the forest, especially at night. I understood the attraction. The pine forest, especially when lit by moonlight, looked mysterious and inviting to our nature-starved city kids. But inviting or not, wandering off, even for a moment, could have serious consequences. Though the Jersey Devil tale was effective in keeping the kids in camp, I was forever looking to add to my arsenal of terror to combat any after-dark excursions into the woods.

It was a red-letter day when I thought to include vampires in our nightly ghost story session. "Sometimes you see them when they arise from their coffins, huge bats flapping low over the rooftops, coming closer, looking for an open window, searching for fresh blood."

The eyes of my audience were saucers in scared little faces, but an insistent voice piped up, "The vampire in the movies got a black suit an' a long cape. If you stay away from dudes like that, you gonna be safe. Won't you?"

"You believe everything you see in the movies?" I asked.

A low moan of "Noooo" circled the campfire.

"Right. See, vampires are treacherous monsters, and they can dress any way they want," I said. "Hey, guys, anybody could be a vampire. You never know till it's too late." As the kids looked suspiciously at each other and at their counselors, I added, "So that's why you always keep your flashlight handy. Vampires hate light."

"I heard you gotta shoot 'em with a silver bullet," somebody piped up.

"That's the Lone Ranger, dummy," came the quick reply from a buddy, but one little kid wanted to get back to flashlights.

"It's gotta be flashlights to keep vampires from grabbin' you and suckin' your blood?"

"No, no," I reassured them. "Any kind of light works: vampires hate light—daylight, spotlights, lamplight. Even flashlights." As they were considering this, I stretched, yawned, and said, "It's getting late. Grab your flashlights and let's take a quick jog around camp before hitting the sack."

It wasn't really all that late, but I knew the counselors were preparing a special pre-bedtime surprise for our campers. Since Oha Bougah had qualified to be a CIT, he had to have an initiation ceremony, and the counselors scheduled it for that night.

As I mesmerized the campers with ghostly yarns, the initiation committee found a likely-looking pine tree at the end of the jogging trail and strapped Oha Bougah into a makeshift harness. He put his clothes back on over the ropes, and the counselors hoisted him up the tree and snuck back to the campfire.

Before we started running, I turned on the big spotlight in the center of the cabin area, about fifty yards from where the jog would end. "If we should run into anything spooky, make a dash for this light and shine your flashlights on your faces." I shined a light on my own face from below, making it look like something that'd escaped from the morgue. "Vampires always go for the neck, and you want to keep 'em away from there."

"Okay, kids. Let's move," called Barry, involved up to his eyeballs in the counselor's surprise. He started running, and the campers scurried after him like a herd of anxious sheep. Then as the kids came to the end of the course, Barry skidded to a stop and let loose with a blood-curdling scream. "Holy crap, what *is* that?" He directed his flashlight onto something swinging from the upper branches of the tree. Every camper followed suit, and soon a hundred beams of light were trained on the gently swinging figure. It was Oha Bougah.

Shrieking "Mommy!" at the top of their voices, the campers wheeled as one and sprinted for the safety of the big spotlight, just visible in the midst of the cabins. I have no doubt that the Olympic record for the fifty-yard dash was broken that night. By the time I caught up to them, over a hundred kids were crowding into an area about the size of a normal living room. Struggling, determined to get into the vampire-defying light, they were scrambling all over each other like puppies who thought they'd missed dinner, each grimly keeping a flashlight trained on his own face.

Before unfettered hysteria set in, I addressed the heap of struggling campers.

"It's okay, kids," I shouted, trying to be heard over the moaning and screeching that was going on. "Oha Bougah's just fine. It was all a joke."

I kind of regretted telling them that anyone could be a vampire, because the kids gave me this look that said, "Like we're gonna believe you?" Not until we produced Oha Bougah, laughing and smiling in his pj's, would the campers believe they'd been hoodwinked but good. Then each one claimed that *he* had known the spoof wasn't for real, though all of his buddies had fallen for the corpse-in-a-tree gag. There was plenty of good-natured razzing, so it took the kids a while to settle down, much to the chagrin of the counselor on cabin duty that night.

The rest of the counselors headed to the dining hall for leftover food, continuing to relate their versions of the night's events.

"Those kids will be too scared to even go to the can tonight," Barry predicted glumly. "Gonna be a lot of wet bedding in the morning."

"I'll tell you what we should do," suggested counselor Stevie Brown. "Why doesn't somebody put on a mask and go into one of the showers. He closes the curtain and waits. When a bunch of 'em come in to do their business, he jumps out, and then … "

"Are you nuts?" I cut in. "We'd be spending the rest of the night prowling around in the woods searching for lost campers. Enough is enough!"

Then in comes Oha Bougah. "That was great. I've never laughed so hard in my life." He looked at us, kind of biting his lip. "So am I a CIT now?"

"You bet," I said, and the counselors joined in congratulating him.

"I almost believed the vampires got you myself," said Barry, slapping Oha Bougah on the back.

"Yeah, you did great!"

The kid still stood there, biting his lip, looking embarrassed as hell. He finally blurted out, "Then can I have some anti-itch cream or something? Those bugs bit the hell out of me. I'm one huge hickey!" Everybody laughed, and we got him some salve from the first aid kit. I was ready for bed, but the counselors were still jawing about playing more scary tricks on our campers.

"That's it," I trumpeted, shooing them out of the dining hall. "Go play basketball under the lights down on the court. It's safe from the vampires and the Jersey Devil. Mess with those kids' minds once more, and you'll be awakened in the middle of the night by a real Jersey Devil …. ME!"

We really prided ourselves on providing our campers with three weeks cram-packed with activities that weren't part of their everyday experience. Their number-one job at Kamp Olympik was to improve their academic skills, but outside of class, it was strictly blast-off time. The only problem was that between swimming, Tarzanville, outings, making pot holders for Mom, and claiming their turns in canoes or on camp cycles, way too many of the campers scrimped on a few basics, like opening their suitcases, showering with soap, or changing clothes. That the kids occasionally wore yesterday's clothes didn't usually bother me. Camp was a place to get away from everyday routines, after all. Occasionally, though, things got a little ripe.

I remember sitting in the dining hall one day, my nostrils full of the aroma of Yolanda's homemade triple-cheese lasagna, when a whiff of something foul drifted under my nose. Since when was Limburger cheese an ingredient in my mother-in-law's epicurean lasagna? Turning my head to and fro, I sniffed suspiciously, eventually following the odor outside. At first the stench hinted of rotten meat in sulphur sauce, and I suspected something gross was festering in the swamp. Then I realized the oddly cheesy smell was reminiscent of discarded, decaying jockstraps. That's when I decided the odor wasn't mere carrion, but rather of human origin.

By this time a few counselors had assembled, and were observing my impersonation of a bloodhound with growing interest. I turned to the closest one and asked, "What the hell is that smell?"

"If you had to sleep in the cabins like we do, you'd know right away, Mr. Bragg," he said. "That's just the way campers normally smell after the second week. What do you expect? They forget to wash, and they wear the same clothes night and day."

"Wait a second," I objected. "They each bring a suitcase full of clothes from home."

"Uh-huh, but do they ever wear 'em?" demanded another counselor. "Their moms must think we're the greatest camp in the world, 'cause the kids come home with a suitcase of clean, nicely ironed clothes. You know why? The kids are too excited and too busy having fun to worry about grabbing a fresh shirt or pair of pants. Ever."

That did it. "Okay, everybody, listen up," I said. "When we go for the general swim today, have everybody bring a bar of soap to the beach." My first inclination was to have them strip down and leave their clothes on the beach, but that would have defeated the purpose. Clean little boys plus reeking clothing still equaled a nauseating smell. The weather was nice and hot, so why not march them into the water wearing the odoriferous clothing, and then have them wash the clothes? They could leave them on the beach to dry while they washed themselves and enjoyed their swim: problem solved.

When the kids were finally assembled, each one holding his bar of soap, I made the announcement.

"You kids are starting to smell like something that died. Now, maybe that's good for keeping the Jersey Devil away from you. And it might keep bugs away—not even Jersey mosquitoes are that desperate for blood. But your counselors just might smear you with tar and cover you with feathers to get rid of the horrible smell. So get in the water, wash your clothes, lay 'em on the beach or on the cedar-rail fence, then wash up yourselves. Let's go."

My counselors were congratulating me on my innovative solution to the assault on our olfactory centers when I detected another faint trace of the carrion smell, and it was very close at hand. The evil odor seemed to have filtered onto my trusty band of counselors. "You guys could do with a wash yourselves, if you take my meaning."

Without a word of protest, the guys dropped their clothes on the beach and galloped into the water with whoops of delight, a troop of Huck Finns liberated from the bonds of decadent civilization.

Our only real concern with skinny-dipping was the fact that we did have some females on the property, mainly our two young daughters and their little girlfriends from the RV campground. Two of the younger Priest girls were helping out in the kitchen at the time, but Yolanda was on top of the situation. Once unadorned hind ends started showing up down at the beach I heard Yolanda yelling, "Stop hanging out the window and give me a hand with these biscuits."

At the time, Renée was almost ten, and her rambunctious little sister Tracey was about eight. To keep them from acquiring a more complete grasp of male anatomy than we thought was a good idea, we corralled them and their two little friends in Uncle Joe's old cabin until after swim period.

A lot of good that did. Irrepressible Tracey climbed onto a stool, peeked out the window, and narrated all the naked goings-on down at the beach to her avid audience. But when the counselors stripped down, she fell off the stool helpless with laughter, and the room filled with nonstop giggling and little-girl shrieks. So much for our male mystique.

Theresa heard the commotion and marched over to the cabin to check it out, but her daughters saw her coming. They hurriedly pulled out Uncle Joe's checkerboard and started to play, nearly strangling on their badly suppressed giggles. Theresa walked into the cabin, took one look out the window and added two and two, hoping the answer wasn't four.

"Have you girls been looking out the window?" she asked.

Renée looked up with big, innocent eyes. "Out the window? Mom, we're playing checkers."

The other girls had bowed heads, and their shoulders were shaking. Theresa just stared at them for a minute. "I see," she said, glancing at the board. "Is there some reason you've got checkers on both black and red squares? That's not how I play checkers."

"I guess we were in a hurry and got mixed up," said Tracey, which stimulated fresh spasms of not laughing from the others. "Checkers is so fun, Mom."

"What about the stool? Why is it lying on its side?"

"We heard a big bang and checked to see if anybody had a gun out there."

"I didn't hear anything," said Theresa, narrowing her eyes and giving the group The Look that every experienced mother has mastered.

"It happened much earlier," said one of the other young partners in crime, tears of merriment brimming in her eyes. "Way before the checkers."

Theresa had no choice but to accept their explanation. "Okay, just see you stay away from the beach till after supper."

Stepping outside, my wife heard an explosion of laughter from the four children. She listened to the gales of laughter until she started laughing herself. Shaking her head over the mysterious ways of little girls (that she knew very well from experience) she headed back to the dining hall.

Once our newly sweet-smelling campers left the beach, a souvenir of bath day lingered on. The entire swim area was covered with soapsuds, as if a giant had treated himself to a bubble bath. Slowly, majestically, the frothy mass drifted downriver on the current, dissipating as it moved away. The very next day, the tall tales began to circulate through the Pinelands. Fishermen from the state campgrounds swore to having seen shoals of bubble-blowing catfish cavorting on the river. Others spoke of turtles coming onto the beach with iridescent bubbles glistening on their shells. Years later, I even heard stories about a snapping turtle who'd once eaten a bar of soap and turned the river white by blowing bubbles.

So bath day was a great success. It was wonderful to go into the dining hall and not have the glorious aroma of Yolanda's lasagna at war with a pervading presence of BO. We might not've ever reached the status of a spit-and-polish camp, but after bath day we sure smelled a lot better. From then on daily inspection was amended to include a stern reminder to change clothes at least every other day. The idea of the giant bubble bath was a big hit with the campers, so every so often we'd have a repeat. It was a kick to see a couple of hundred kids all lathered up, splashing in the river, their hair foaming like giant Brillo pads, their well-scrubbed little butts shining in the sun.

It's funny how they seem so young, constantly on the go, just having fun.

Too old to hold and cuddle, now engrossed in their life's struggle.

—*Don Bragg, "Kids"*

Our four kids also thrived in the atmosphere of Kamp Olympik. Of course, Theresa and I, as parents of active, imaginative kids, soon got pretty familiar with Hammonton Hospital's ER, especially after our sons became proficient on the mini-cycles. During the thirty-minute trip to the hospital, and then again on the way home, Theresa and I would lecture the boys about not taking chances, which I don't think affected Jeff's or Mark's ER statistics in the least. The problem was that both boys took to the little cycles like otters to mud slides, and that phenomenon took its toll in bumps and bruises. And though both boys loved to ride, Jeff was the cycle fiend. Constantly looking for new challenges, he'd test his ability against anything. One morning I complained to his mother, "Just look at your son! He's trying to ride his cycle up the sliding board into Fort Bragg. It's no wonder he's already crashed his cycle twice."

"Hold it right there," Theresa responded. "*Whose* son? I'd say yours, not mine. I didn't buy him the doggone cycle, did I?"

Chapter Ten

While Jeff would try anything at least once on his cycle, Mark was the first to develop perseverance and skill as a racer. It was really exciting when they started entering the motocross races that were held in the state forest. Once camping season was over, RV campers would flock to the park, hauling their cycles for practice runs on the actual racecourse. With their mutual interest in cycles, my sons quickly got friendly with these families, and Theresa and I also joined their circle. At their campfires the ambiance and conversation was always lively. The RV folks talked cycle racing but also discussed every other subject under the sun. The food ranged from the expected hot dogs and burgers to the exotic: elk steaks, marinated bear steaks, and every kind of seafood imaginable during fishing season, including perfectly grilled striped bass filets and numerous jars of homemade pickled herring. Damn, but they were tasty. But those elk steaks took the prize. "These are fantastic," I told the guy who'd brought them. "What did you put in the marinade?"

Beaming proudly, he shook his head. "No marinade. This is what these suckers taste like. Best eating there is!"

It was in this convivial atmosphere that Mark had his first cycle race. It was kind of bittersweet for me as a parent, since it signified a rite of passage: my eldest son was on his way to becoming a man.

Since I had to work, I wasn't able to attend the race, but Roy, an RV camper who was the starter for the race, filled me in that evening at the campfire. The idea was this: groups of four cyclists would take off at the sound of the starting whistle and tear down the ten-mile course through the forest. Forty yards into the course they faced their first hazard: a narrow passage between two trees with room for only one rider. The first one to reach that passage had the advantage. In Mark's race the three other drivers had full-size cycles with both impressive horsepower and an extra kick of acceleration. Since Mark was riding a bike with a fairly small engine, nobody thought for a minute that he could match the speed of the bigger bikes. "You should've seen 'em," Roy laughed. "The betting was really heating up over who'd reach the trees first, and not one of those jackasses had the sense to bet on your son and his kiddie cycle."

"And?" I prompted.

"The second I blew that whistle, Mark shot away from the pack and reached the narrow passage first. Those guys couldn't believe it when they saw their bets go up in smoke. Boy, were they pissed off."

We all laughed and enjoyed another beer, and I asked, "So what place did Mark take in the race?"

Roy just chuckled. "You know, when we design a course, we make it as tough as we can, making use of the most varied terrain and ensuring there are some obstacles, the wilder the better."

"Yeah, sure," I responded. "Otherwise what's the point?"

"Right, so about three-quarters through the course, we have a series of depressions, say three feet deep. Now you know what the weather's been like."

"It rained like hell last night."

"And what we got on the course is a bunch of serious water hazards. I was waiting at the finish line, and when a cyclist came in I asked him if he'd seen Mark. 'Sure did,' he replied. ''Bout five miles back, I got through the worst of the water hazards, but then I bottomed out, and my vehicle stalled. I was trying to get it restarted when I heard a splash right behind me. Sure enough, the kid was floundering around in the water like he was drowning. So I fished him out and threw him up on the bank. Then I got my bike started and took off.'"

"But he's okay?"

"Yeah, but he's not finishing this race. He's got guts, though." Laughing again, Roy finished his beer. "So I said to one of my buddies, 'Take your pickup and go find Mark, will you?'"

"So he never finished the race?" I was still proud as hell of Mark for getting as far as he did.

"Yes and no. We're standing around, and here comes Mark, carrying his cycle. Once he got it over the finish line, he just about collapsed on the ground. And then the kid says, 'I'll never do this again unless it's a dry day.'"

We laughed as Mark and Roy's kids came tearing by on their cycles, oblivious to everything but the joy of riding, then the two of us settled down to enjoy the fire. That always took some doing. First you had to be sure you'd collected sufficient firewood to last the entire evening. Otherwise, you'd just get comfortable when you'd have to go fetch another log.

And you had to be into two-faced temperature control as well. The front of you might be baking in the fire's heat, but at the same time your behind was starting up its own sno-cone concession. Sensible Theresa always brought a shawl, but I was too macho for that—for the first few chilly nights. Then Macho Man brought along a shawl, too, if only for the back of his chair.

Planning exactly where to sit also took some cunning. First you took note of the direction the wind was blowing, but that was never enough. You had to use an eso-teric combination of calculus and soothsaying to determine where it would probably shift to in an hour or so. Nobody wanted to sit with wood smoke and ashes pouring down their throats all evening.

So Roy and I sat on as the autumn night turned cold, talking about our kids, about hunting and fishing, enjoying the scent of wood smoke in the chilly air. Then, almost imperceptibly, the conversation slowed down, then stopped as we both watched the dying fire. We used different types of wood in our campfires, long-burning oak, fra-grant pine, and, sweetest of all, cedar logs. Surrounded by the silent forest, staring at the radiant embers, I kind of turned inward in an almost trancelike state and focused on the aroma of the burning wood. That's pine, I'd think, and then I'd get a whiff of the delicious scent of cedar. Watching the fire, I'd lose myself in the essence of the various woods circling around me as the night wind sighed through the forest. It was something that always made me feel that things were right with the world. And then I looked over and saw Roy staring at the fire as well, hypnotized by the gently flickering flames. Like me, he was lost to time and place as he drifted in a world of benevolent tranquility.

At night, that which moves is still till the still begins to move through the

darkened eyes of night. It begins to be, to live within its flight till

morning brings the dawn.

—*Don Bragg, "Night Moves"*

Camping is always great, but when the campfire dies out, and it gets too cold to sit there any longer, I was always grateful we could just mosey over to our cabin just on the other side of the camp and flick on the gas logs. At heart I'm an outdoorsman, but no matter how much I enjoy living outdoors, I'm happy that I don't have to lie on the cold ground with pine cones grinding into the most inconvenient parts of my anatomy. I also like the fact that I don't have to climb into a camping trailer and try to cram myself into a dinky little bed with my head poking into the wall and my feet hanging off one corner. The best part of the great outdoors is that I can go into my own cabin and get in my own commodious bed right next to Theresa. That's the part of camping I love the most.

In order not to lose the rest of my marbles while running Kamp Olympik, it was absolutely imperative for me to delegate whenever possible. And one thing I made sure I delegated was the onerous chore of cabin inspection. Since I divvied up the workload, each counselor got stuck with that detail several times per season. I didn't expect that Kamp Olympik's spirit of competition would muddy what should've been a straightforward chore. So despite my best efforts to unload some chores, I was forced to keep an eagle eye on what my counselors were cooking up.

If one counselor made another look bad on the basketball court, the offended party wasn't above inventing infractions come inspection time. More than once I had to break it to a vengeful staff member that infractions like not having the pillows all aligned with the equator didn't transform a cabin into a pigsty. Nor did a cabin's having a dusty ceiling make the cut as a major offense. I regularly had to factor in the possibility that spurious inspection violations grew out of plain bummed-out jealousy. Some counselors were superb leaders, and their campers tended to conform to all our rules. This resulted in more than a few bogus demerits come inspection time. However, if I received a bad report of a cabin, only to find it in good order when I checked it out, staff fur did fly.

The younger cabins could be the most demanding on a counselor because of the emotional needs of little ones away from home for the first time. The youngest were in Cabin 1, those a little older in Cabin 2, and so on. The counselors in the youngest cabins sometimes had bed-wetting to contend with, and the older cabins did not. Happily, we were able to designate some of the older, more experienced campers, especially those who exhibited leadership ability, as CITs. They'd stay in the younger cabins, helping to keep things running smoothly. They liked the fact that their expanded duties entitled them to stay up at night and participate in late-evening fun and games. It was a pretty good experience for the kids, and they liked the idea that we valued and rewarded their efforts.

One of the things we hoped to inculcate into our campers was the satisfaction received from doing a job—any job—well. Occasionally we'd run across kids who possessed a real affinity for carpentry. They became handymen, lending their skills to the constant repairs necessary to keep the camp going. Screens, for instance—they were constantly being torn, and if we didn't want to be eaten alive, they had to be kept in good repair. And I do mean eaten alive. Those Jersey mosquitoes make vampire bats look like amateurs. If a cabin constantly flunked inspection, penalties were assigned to the losers as a curative. Some cabins never did figure out what the hell inspections were about, and these unfortunates seemed to be permanently on morning cleanup assignments. Jobs such as bathhouse and kitchen cleanup as well as trash duty with Uncle Joe were at the top of the campers' shit list.

Then a mysterious tide of events rolled in. Cabins began volunteering for the trash duty gig with an enthusiasm that got my antennae agitated: they had to be up to something. It wasn't hard to figure out. The work detail would pile into Uncle Joe's pickup, some up front, the others in the back where they could easily load the trash cans from around the camp into the truck. Easy-going Uncle Joe didn't care what was on the radio, so the kids could tune in their favorite station. When everything was loaded, they'd take a ride over to the dump and drop everything off.

On the way back to camp, Uncle Joe would take a detour to Mick's Country Store and spring for Popsicles. He loved this system; hell, he never had to get out of the truck, let alone torment his bad back by picking up heavy cans. Problem was that his habit of treating his helpers was setting my carefully designed penalty on its ear. It had become a sought-after perk, so I had to step in and ruin the kids' little racket.

After canoe trips downriver, somebody had to pick up the canoes, since the younger kids couldn't have managed the return trip. Once again, Uncle Joe grabbed a crew of helpers and drove down and collected the canoes. Once again, volunteers began to pour out of the woodwork, and Uncle Joe had his pick of dozens of eager helpers. However, the more kids in the pickup, the fewer canoes we could fit in, so instead of one trip, Uncle Joe and his enthusiastic crew were making several. This time I was on the problem immediately.

"Uncle Joe, after you pick up the canoes, what happens next?"

"Are you nuts? I bring the canoes back to camp."

"You come straight home, right? No side trips?"

"Course not." He stopped, rubbing the back of his neck. "Well, we usually stop to check gas at Mick's and maybe get a few refreshments. But that only takes a few minutes."

So the attraction was a trip to the candy factory! Again, I had to trim my uncle's sails a bit, but it was gratifying to see the kids settling into camp life. After a few days they wanted to be a part of it, even if that meant shouldering a few chores. This is not to say the results were always even. Sometimes absolutely nothing got accomplished, especially if the duties were less than desirable. Despite all I had to do, I found it necessary to start creeping around in the woods, peering through the greenery to find out just who was doing what—and who wasn't.

No clear picture emerged. Sometimes only the counselors would be hard at it. Sometimes only the campers. Now and then I'd see a counselor put his campers to work and then sprawl in the shade to catch forty winks himself. If I returned in half an hour, the counselor would still be snoozing under a tree. What really brought the wrath of Bragg down on their unfortunate heads was any attempt to pretend he'd just started his nap. "Hi, Mr. Bragg. We've been working so hard we had to take a break from the heat." Once in awhile a camper would break into mocking laughter, prompting the counselor to amend his statement. "Well, maybe I've been resting a little longer than they've been."

With thunder in my voice, I'd tell the rest of the cabin to take a swim break and beckoned for Mr. Naptime to come with me. Then I would give him a special assignment or two that required every ounce of his well-refreshed energy. Later on, as his campers were returning from their swim, they'd observe their great leader peeling potatoes behind the dining hall, which told them there was justice at Kamp Olympik. Yolanda would come to the kitchen door and marvel, "Wasn't that sweet of that young man to volunteer for such a tedious job?"

"Yup," I'd reply. "He's a real sweetie pie."

The biggest enemy to any camp's discipline is boredom. Idle minds—and hands—are mischief magnets, so in addition to academics, sports, cycles, arts and crafts, and so on, we always tried to incorporate entertainment as part of the camp regimen. That way, there was always something waiting just around the corner for the kids to anticipate. Field trips were wildly popular, but we had a rich menu of fun and games right in camp. A mainstay of this program was Dave Miller, one of the campers' favorite counselors. He was the lead singer of a rock band called the Pinecones, which performed several times for enthusiastic camp audiences. The kids really enjoyed the live entertainment with microphones, speakers, and all the other neat professional gear. But what really turned them on to the music was the fact that they all liked Dave, who had a truly winning personality. There was, however, a huge dichotomy between easygoing Counselor Dave and Dave the Performer. Microphone clutched in one hand, he strutted the length and breadth of the stage, belting out lyrics with the gut-grabbing intensity of a true rock god. A few people were surprised when he went into the ministry, but I wasn't, because of something that happened during one of his performances. His band was playing outside on the basketball court, and an unexpected little squall blew in from the ocean. Rain inundated the band, the audience, and the equipment. Right in the middle of "Jumpin' Jack Flash," the speakers shorted out, and the microphone, spitting sparks, damn near exploded in Dave's hand. For a second his eyes bugged out, his hair stood on end, and he flung the mike away as if it were a viper. The kids thought it was part of the act and applauded like crazy.

"Mr. Bragg, I'm sorry we cut the show short," Dave apologized later, "but I got one helluva shock!"

"No, I'd say you just had your first taste of religious enlightenment," I shot back. No wonder he became a minister!

Should we float with the stream of thought, enveloped and absorbed in dreams it's brought?

—Don Bragg, "Fantasies"

Another guest entertainer was Peggy Sue, the daughter of one of Uncle Joe's friends. Only twelve years old, she was cute as a button, which made the hearts of her teen and preteen audience beat a bit faster. As she ran through her repertoire of magic tricks, everyone would holler, "Do it again—we know how you did it!" She would anticipate the audience response and set them up for a double hit both magical and humorous.

With her ventriloquist dummy perched on one knee, she invited a volunteer, of whom there were many, to assist her on stage. The deal was that the willing participant had to answer a series of questions, and the last one was impossible for anyone to answer. As the camper racked his brain for the answer, the dummy would roll his eyes and shake his head, putting the audience in stitches. Finally, when the poor volunteer admitted he was stumped, the dummy would eye him slyly and ask, "So who's the dummy now?" That always brought down the house. And though the entire camp laughed at the volunteer, embarrassing the hell out of him, for the next few days he was the camp hero.

What I enjoyed the most, though, were the Kamp Olympik talent nights that featured the various talents of our own campers. I couldn't believe the creativity the kids exhibited, and we were delighted to provide prizes of candy bars and Kamp Olympik

T-shirts for the three acts that earned the highest accolades. At the end of each session we'd have the kids reprise the best acts at the final camp celebration.

At that time Flip Wilson was one of the top comedians, and one of his greatest creations was a character named Geraldine, a sassy black gal with a talent for giving folks a hard time. So the kids went wild when Geraldine sashayed out onto our stage in a dress and wig, clutching a patent leather purse. The kid playing Geraldine had a real talent for zeroing in on some personality trait, then exposing the inherent contradictions in it. Wearing a costume provided courtesy of Aunt

Camper playing "Geraldine" in talent show.

Ruth, the camper circulated around the audience, making fun of everyone in camp, including me. One hand on "her" hip, Geraldine said to me, "So you think you're the boss man? Well, you're not!" and she started whacking me with her purse. Talk about hitting the bull's-eye. His comments were uncommonly perceptive and brilliant, and I wouldn't have been surprised if our Geraldine had gone on to stardom.

We did, however, capture several of these acts on film, and one was a real standout. It occurred near the end of the season, and it involved a group of older campers who presented a commercial for Ultra Piney Protective Sun Tan Lotion. It was so polished that I could hardly believe it'd been created right in the South Jersey Pinelands.

It started off on a serious note, with grim-looking "scientists" presenting the dangers of overexposure to the sun and its damaging affects. To illustrate this, they shoved a white camper under the spotlight.

"Look at this guy! If he keeps his sorry self in the sun's ultraviolet rays too long, his butt's gonna be toast."

This of course prompted a roar of laughter from the campers. Then they blacked out the stage, played a little lead-in music, and turned the spot on again. The lightest-skinned black camper was standing there.

"Just take a look at what only three days' use of our Ultra Piney Protective Sun Tan Lotion did for this pathetic white guy! No red splotchy patches of skin peeling off his nose. His feet are turning brown, not blistery purple. All the harmful UV rays have been blocked out!"

Then followed some inspired scientific double-talk. "The Lini Lagniappe Indians discovered the secret of this lotion in the disgusting, crappy iced-tea water of the Wading River." Peering over borrowed glasses, the lead scientist produced what looked suspiciously like a beer bottle and waved it mysteriously. "However, only after years of lavatory research have we been able to isolate these unique medicinal qualities and put them in our magnificent product."

To the accompaniment of the victory theme from *Chariots of Fire*, they doused the lights again, and then the spotlight came back on, only to reveal another subject, this time a counselor with exceedingly dark skin indeed. With a flourish of his bottle of the magic elixir, the head scientist presented this final stage of the magical transformation from a white-bellied catfish to a gloriously bronzed all-American boy. "After only one week, yes, that's right, just seven days, my friends, you too can have results like this."

Bringing out the white guy and his slightly darker buddy, the scientist lined them up beside the finished product and concluded his spiel. "And if you cannot believe the evidence of your own eyes, just perform this simple test. Put on a nice white bathing suit and drench it in Ultra Piney Protective Sun Tan Lotion." At this point all eyes turned delightedly toward Theresa, since everybody knew of her battle to keep her lovely white bathing suit out of the murky cedar water. Needless to say, my wife had practically laughed herself out of her seat. But the scientist had a bit more to say. "Immediately you will see this liquid start to darken the material. A miracle happening before your very eyes!" Their act ended with *Chariots of Fire* blasting on the speakers, which brought all the kids to their feet, convulsed with laughter, but applauding with all their might. Some started yelling demands for a product that would do the reverse.

"Yeah, then we could fool our parents when we get off the bus."

One kid, who was a bit of an operator, called out, "Nah, they'd never recognize me. So give me my deposit back!"

Say *what*? The other kids were quick to call him on his larcenous scheme, however. "What deposit you talkin' about, you turkey butt? We all got in free!" That was a good conclusion to a great night. This skit could've been created and presented by New York's finest writers, so come one and all to the Pines—you just might bump into your creativity.

It was after one of these talent nights that we celebrated my son Jeff's seventh birthday. The entire camp had cake and ice cream, and everybody boisterously sang "Happy Birthday" and cheered when he received that mini-cycle. We had to rein in our little Evel Knievel during camp season because our campers were constantly

Jeff, cousin Craig after receiving cycle for birthday.

urging him on to greater feats of daring. It was as if they regarded him as their little brother, vicariously proud of his roaring off the homemade jumping ramp and tearing through the woods. By the end of the session, we all felt like family, and it was damn hard to say goodbye to the campers.

In addition to entertainment nights at the camp, the campers also eagerly anticipated field trips. Although taking the kids on outings was an enrichment for them, I often ended up being enriched to just this side of gibbering madness. The campers would get so excited and involved that sometimes they'd do the damnest things. No matter how carefully we planned, something utterly off the wall would usually occur. For the safety of a busload of kids and to preserve my remaining sanity, it was essential that my staff and I kept control of our camp outings. Consider the land mines involved in the simple exercise of going to the beach.

In Kamp Olympik's third year, it occurred to me that taking the kids to the Jersey shore once a week would be a fantastic outing. Hell, almost none of the campers had ever seen the ocean or played in the surf. To ensure everybody's safety, I recruited our best lifeguards for the excursion. Once we'd loaded the bus with towels and picnic supplies, I figured we were on our way to a carefree day at the beach. This fantasy lasted until we got the bus parked and we headed toward the water, when I vaguely wondered what I'd gotten myself into. With the kids bouncing around like electrons on speed, I went ahead and alerted the beach's lifeguard staff to the fact that our campers had never set a toe in the ocean and had no idea of the potential dangers. When I requested them to keep an extra eye out for our campers, they looked at me as if I were a nervous schoolmarm. They said they'd do it though, so that was fine.

So we come over the dunes and the kids get their first sight of the mighty Atlantic.

"Look at that sucker," somebody whispered. "Hey, Mr. Bragg, I can't see the other side!"

"That's 'cause it's a zillion miles away," another boy informed him, looking as if he'd given up on ever seeing his mother again.

Staring at the breaking waves, somebody muttered, "And they expect us to go walkin' into *that*?" A dozen pairs of reproachful eyes turned in my direction, and I knew we were headed for an outstanding disaster.

I simply hadn't calculated the probable consequences of this wonderful experience. Here we had kids whose idea of a lot of water was a gushing fire hydrant or a jam-packed city pool. For the first time in their lives they were locking horns with billions of gallons of water coming at them like an implacable gray-green battering ram. The first ones to get up to their ankles in the surf yelled in alarm as the backwash tore the sand away from under their feet, causing them to sink into the sandy bottom. "Damn," one kid hollered. "This beach is tryin' to eat us. That what it's supposed to do, Mr. Bragg?"

In retrospect, it was kind of funny, as our bunch of kids tried out the delightful experience I had arranged for them. That morning in camp, I'd explained how powerful the waves would be, as well as outlining the dangers of the undertow, and the kids had sat listening obediently. However, I don't think they really grasped exactly what they were going to be swimming in. Our camp lifeguards had to scramble to keep up with the casualties. Kids were turning unintentional somersaults in the water and coming up with draggles of seaweed clinging to their hair. Upended by waves, the campers crashed into one another, then bounced up on shore on their butts. One little guy staggered stiff-legged out of the water complaining, "Something took a crap in my bathing suit!" Stifling their laughter, the counselors showed him how to rinse the sand out of his swim trunks. The kids were game, and even after mishap upon mishap, they trudged back into the water, cautious, but drawn to the power of the unending line of waves. But after a while they began to eye me strangely, as if they finally believed that all white people really were crazy.

Then ten campers formed a line and waded out to meet the breakers. The camp lifeguards were practically on top of them, so I assumed the kids would do just fine. They were in water about up to their knees when a larger-than-usual wave crashed into them. All ten kids disappeared into the foam, but when the water retreated, only three remained standing. The camp staff was on the emergency immediately and started towing kids to safety. The beach lifeguards came charging in as well, launching a surfboard to retrieve the kid who'd gotten the farthest out. Of course the kids who'd been in the temporary clutches of the undertow all competed for bragging rights as to who'd been the most heroic, who'd gotten the most seawater up his nose, or the most sand packed in his swim trunks. They were ready to go right back in the water, but I'd had enough.

"Okay, kids," I told them. "Nobody goes into the water again. Just play in the sand and build sand castles."

"Build what?"

"Big forts with towers and tunnels and big, thick walls. Make 'em out of sand. It's fun." As they continued to give me blank stares, I added, "We'll have ice cream for the best construction." So most of them got busy and started on their castles, once they knew what the hell I was talking about. Every so often, they'd stop their digging and just look at the ocean, communing with something new and wonderful. They also loved playing with the sand crabs, digging frantically to unearth the little beasts before they vanished in the beach sand. Busybody gulls had to fly down and check out what the kids were doing, and of course the kids had to chase the gulls. The gulls merely rose in an undulating wave, and then resettled on the beach, a grey-and-white quilt resting on the damp sand. One little boy nicked a toe on a shell, and after administering first aid, I showed a rapt audience of campers the reason this particular crustacean was named the razor clam. After fingering the sharp edge reverently, the children raced down the beach in an avid hunt for seashells.

Before we left the beach, we paid a visit to a nearby lighthouse. The many steps were immediately perceived as a challenge, and a race to the top became the order of the day. The counselors had to join in, and, displaying his signature stamina and endurance, Barry Ross emerged the victor. It was great watching the kids as they learned what the lighthouse was for, and how the lighthouse keeper kept it functioning. With faraway looks in their eyes, the youngsters scanned the horizons, as if imagining themselves on duty, standing between ships and catastrophe when a nor'easter came howling out of the sea.

When we finally started back to the bus, one of the pro lifeguards came over, grinning. "So you're leaving? Good. We've worked harder in the last hour than we've had to all season. Those kids are quite a workout."

My sentiments entirely. As we nudged the last few campers onto the bus, Barry Ross said to me, "Well, that was quite an experience!"

"You said it," I replied. "But that's really what Kamp Olympik's all about: giving kids different experiences, new windows on life." We followed the last of the campers up the bus steps, and with a shudder, the metal monster came to life and slowly headed for home with its waterlogged crew.

From my point of view, the best diversions for the kids were the ones that involved sports in some way. During my own sports travels I naturally became good friends with quite a few athletes, many of whom had become celebrities. One of the most gracious of these was Jersey Joe Walcott, the former heavyweight boxing champion. He really loved kids, and participated in many youth programs throughout the state. This heavyweight

Jersey Joe Walcott with camper.

champion visited the camp whenever I asked him to, which was often. He mingled easily with the kids as they went to class, went swimming, and played basketball. He even took time to admire their arts and crafts projects. He ended each appearance by making a motivational presentation to the group on the basketball court, and when he spoke you could've heard a pin drop.

From time to time, former Olympians would drop in and tell the kids about their experiences. One of them was Russ Hodge, the world record holder in the decathlon. This guy was incredible. He raced with the kids, high-jumped with them, put them through all the components of the decathlon. The kids took one look at his impressively muscular stature and knew he was a world-class athlete. When he threw the discus and shot, the campers stood in reverent silence for a minute or two before cheering their hearts out.

Now Russ had pulled a groin muscle severely, and didn't make the Olympic team in 1972, but he managed to convince Theresa and me that we had to go to Munich for the ill-fated Olympic Games by offering to put us up at the villa he'd already rented. In later years, Russ also became the chaplain for the U.S. Olympic Team.

Don and Russ Hodge, decathlon champion.

Now you may wonder how Theresa and I were able to just take off from our camp duties and go to Europe. Because we had incredible help, that's why. Not only did Yolanda pitch in with almost evangelical fervor, but my old buddy Frankie Dougherty stepped up and gave his all as well. The interaction between these two strong-willed individuals could fill another book and it wouldn't be pleasant reading. But suffice it to say, they both had tales to tell when we got back.

"He tried to take over my kitchen! Do you believe that?" an incredulous Yolanda demanded, as we walked in the door.

All Frankie said was, "Are you sure Yolanda's Theresa's mom? I thought she was gonna poison me!" Thank God Dominick was there to keep an eye on both of them.

Another frequent camp visitor was Dave Wottle, who gold-medaled the half mile in Munich. Dave pulled off an incredible upset, charging from dead last to victory. But one thing about Dave: he always wore a hat. His hair was a little thin—maybe it was to keep his head from sunburn—but that hat was simply a part of him, wherever he went. So there he was on the medal platform while they played "The Star-Spangled Banner." His hand was over his heart, he was kind of teary eyed, and his hat was on top of his head. I guess nobody reminded him it was there. Anyhow, the press trumpeted charges of disrespect to our national whatever in huge black headlines, completely ignoring the fact that he'd earned his country an unexpected gold medal. Damn, but I hate that kind of crap.

Larry James, who won both silver and gold medals in 1968, often came to the camp to play Hare and Hounds with the campers. And the kids ate it up. Patty McCormick, the 1952 Olympic diving champion, came by and brought her husband and gymnast daughter. The little girl went wild in Tarzanville and went off the high dive as well, swinging, spinning, soaring—while the campers watched in utter amazement. "And she's a *girl!*" I heard one of them exclaim. Little did any of us know that she'd become an Olympic diver years later.

Larry James, Don, and Theresa at Olympic fund raiser.

The athletes all hit the same themes: if you work hard and have the courage to follow your heart, true excellence was possible, no matter where you started from. The kids listened attentively, and I'm convinced these guys were instrumental in influencing the kids to the positive side of life. These athletes skillfully presented information in such an entertaining way that they kept the kids from turning off and tuning out before they heard the essential message.

Since the 1976 Olympics had just been completed, and since they'd met so many Olympians at camp, I was sure that the kids would love to see some Olympic champions in action. When I heard an international track meet was scheduled at University of Pennsylvania's Franklin Field, I knew I had to get some of the kids there. There was no way we could've afforded tickets for more than a few kids, so I contacted a friend and did a little finagling. When I was done, I had fifty tickets, and all I had to do was present some of the awards, including those for pole-vaulting. Since I couldn't take all the kids, we organized an Olympic Day at Kamp Olympik. We set up a variety of events: short- and long-distance running, swimming races, long and high jumping, along with basketball foul shooting. The top three contenders in each one got to go to the track meet. The kids weren't the only ones who wanted that trip to Philadelphia, though. Since the kids had to qualify for the trip, the counselors should have to as well. So I added five events for the counselors, but only the top contender qualified for one of the precious tickets.

Talk about motivated! I'd never seen the campers galvanized by such determination, and it was one ramped-up bunch of kids who piled into our bus for the trip.

On our way into the stadium, we ran into a friend of mine, Rocky Aoki, a Japanese wrestler I'd met during the 1960 Olympics. We greeted each other cordially, and then I said, "Rocky, I'd like you to meet some of our Kamp Olympik athletes." Rocky was great with the kids and joked with them for awhile before heading into the stadium. As we made our way inside, the kids commented, "He's a wrestler, huh? Cool guy. But he's kind of small to wrestle, isn't he?"

"Not at all," I told them. "In Olympic wrestling, you compete in your weight class, so there's no such thing as too small. And by the way," I continued, "have you kids ever heard of the Benihana restaurant?" Of course they had: everybody had. Since Clementine Paddleford's rave review a few years before, Benihana was one of the hottest dining spots on the East Coast.

"Yeah, we've heard of that place."

"Well, the guy you just met owns Benihana. He put up the money for this meet."

The kids were amazed. "And he was such a cool guy!"

Once inside the stadium, the kids found a million things to look at. They watched intently as the runners adjusted their feet to the blocks. "That's so they can push off good, Mr. Bragg?" These kids were sharp, knowing intuitively how things fit into athletic performance. They nearly jumped out of their skins at the starting pistol, but the speed of the sprinters had them on their feet, cheering their heads off. "How can they go that fast?" one kid asked.

"Easy," countered another camper. "You'd run too if you had some old dude firing a gun at your butt."

"He could shoot my butt clean off, and I still couldn't run that fast."

"You might if you really wanted to," I intoned, the ever-present oracle-jock.

Watching the milers circle the 400-meter track, the kids were all admiration. "Four times! I couldn't keep up with them once!" It was great to hear them analyzing their own ability and experience and measuring them against these superb performances. You could almost see their horizons broadening as they watched the competition.

They were delighted with the high jumpers' head-first and backwards assault on the bar, which was called the Fosbury flop. "That must take heaps of practicing."

"If I tried that I'd bust my rear, but I'd still like to try it."

You tell 'em, kid!

Since most of them had given pole-vaulting a try at camp with poles from the woods, and since they'd see me do some vaulting, the kids were fascinated by the pole-vaulting competition. They sat there like seasoned coaches scrutinizing the vaulters' every move. "His steps are screwed up," one of them whispered, smiling sagaciously. His neighbor nodded agreement.

"For sure. He's gonna hit the bar with his butt." Which the guy did. What a kick those kids were! Afterward, the campers scurried around getting the Olympic champions' autographs and usually a handshake, from which they came away beaming. The local paper took pictures of all our gang in their Kamp Olympik T-shirts, and they all looked pretty sharp. Not only were the campers ecstatic for the entire trip, quite a few folks complimented their behavior. In short, it was one terrific day for our kids and for me. So Kamp Olympik scored a victory at the meet as well as the athletes.

But of the many track stars who visited the camp, it was Larry James who left an indelible mark at Kamp Olympik.

It was business as usual to have Kamp Olympik inundated by visitors. I guess the word got out that it was the place to be for fun and games, though Theresa insisted that the fact that there was a lunatic-in-residence also had something to do with it. The only problem was that since we were involved so heavily in the ongoing activities, we usually had little time to enjoy our drop-in company. We were delighted when the state troopers who patrolled the area would stop by the camp and walk through it, mingling with the campers, who bugged them unmercifully to turn on the sirens on their police cars. This was great for the campers, since sometimes the relations between the police and their home neighborhoods were pretty tense.

But there was one black trooper who came around frequently. In fact, every time I turned around there the guy was. But unlike the other troopers, the kids weren't his main focus. Bragging about himself was. To hear him tell it, he burned up every track his feet touched. "That's right. Maybe I didn't win an Olympic medal, but hey! I never had the chance to try out." This was bullshit of the highest order. The kids were impressed, but not half as much as this trooper was … with himself. "And who do you think they put in charge of training new police recruits?" he'd ask nobody in particular. "Me!"

How did I know a self-involved braggart when I heard one? Because these self-glorifying traits fell pretty close to home. But please don't tell Theresa I said that.

Theresa: *Honey, I think the cat's already out of the bag!*

During camping season we always had an Olympic Day with races and field events. This trooper actually took it upon himself to become involved in these races, running against some of our fastest staff members. Of course the campers wanted me to challenge him. I'd gone through some spinal surgery not that long before, and I didn't want to throw my back out of whack, but the kids were adamant. "C'mon, Mr. B. This guy's beating all our counselors. You go kick his butt!"

So I went lumbering out on the track, and of course the trooper kicked butt—mine. Then he started bragging about how he took on an Olympian and ran him into the ground. I tried to explain that beating a retired pole-vaulter didn't signal the second coming of Jesse Owens, but he wouldn't surrender bragging rights.

But he gloated too soon. On one of our special activity days my good friend, former Olympic medalist Larry James, came by to watch the goings on. Now Larry hadn't competed for a while and was a little overweight, but the man was in the Marine Reserves, hardly a slouch outfit. So I just happened to mention to the trooper that one of our visitors was pretty fast, and that if he really wanted a match to show his speed, this was his chance.

Now Larry tried to put the guy off. He wasn't in strict training, and didn't feel he'd run his best. The trooper smelled blood, or so he thought, and continued to wolf on Larry, saying, "I don't care how good you are, I'm gonna win. But I'll take it easy on you."

You don't talk to a champion like that. Then the trooper really dug his grave. "Hey, let's add a few more yards to our little contest. That'll give you plenty of time to catch me. Okay?" Big mistake. Larry is a quarter-miler, and really can turn it on at the finish. The irony of this blowhard setting himself up wasn't lost on my friend. The little smile that kept curving Larry's lips wasn't there because he looked forward to eating the trooper's dust.

We gathered at the camp entrance, and then marked off about 200 yards on the road that led to town. Running out and back would be close to a quarter mile, a distance both men agreed was perfect. Only problem was, the road curved into the trees at one point, so the runners would be out of sight after about a hundred yards.

A minute or two before the race started, a delivery truck jounced into camp, and the driver wanted to know what the crowd of kids was doing right at the entrance. Uncle Joe told him, and the driver smacked down a bet on the trooper. A good betting man all his life, Uncle Joe took that bet and sat down beside the driver to watch the race.

As I expected, the trooper shot to the front from the starting line. The deliveryman immediately asked Uncle Joe if he wanted to up the ante, and Uncle Joe loyally took him up on the offer. The race was in full gear, and the guys seemed evenly matched. Then they disappeared into the trees, and when they emerged, the trooper was in the lead. I was beginning to think we were going to be humiliated by this cocky pretender to the throne. We'd never live it down, either: the fool would talk endlessly about it for the rest of his life. When the trooper was within a hundred yards of the finish, we notice Larry gliding up behind him with no discernible effort. Larry matched strides with the trooper and started to mess with the guy.

"You run like a turtle, man! Watch out," Larry called out, with an immense grin, "because here comes the hare! C'mon, get the lead out. There are little kids watching." With a final "See you around," the Olympian streaked off, leaving the trooper to eat his dust.

Larry reached the finish line about thirty yards ahead of the stumbling trooper. The guy had no word of congratulation for Larry but returned to his car in silence. He put on his shirt and buckled on his big gun, and without looking to the left or right, started his car and left camp. We seldom saw him after that, and when we did, there wasn't a peep out of him about his running prowess.

Of course, when the deliveryman heard that an Olympic champion had beaten his guy, he cried foul. "No fair. No wonder the guy beat the trooper. He's an Olympian! So give me my money back."

"Hell, no," said Uncle Joe, pocketing the bills. "This is Kamp Olympik. Who in hell would be racing here *except* an Olympic champion? Tell me that!"

And the deliveryman, with a bewildered look on his face, didn't say a word.

Chapter Eleven

As long as the weather was halfway reasonable, we had no trouble keeping the kids engaged, but when it rained, the entire staff was hard pressed to keep boredom at bay. We showed movies in the dining hall, and these were pure salvation for the staff. Summer storms could last for three days, and, despite our ingenuity, by day two of the squall we'd all be tearing our hair out as we racked our brains for more things to do. However, I didn't want the kids watching just retread cartoons or B movies. I had several Olympic films, including footage of my 1960 Olympics, which were a welcome treat. Other than that we depended on comic books, bingo, and checkers to keep the kids occupied. As long as the storm wasn't dangerous, we'd let the kids go swimming, and they loved the sensation of swimming in the rain. All too often, however, those unwelcome storms included the rumble of thunder and flickering lightning, so indoors we all had to stay.

Then another Olympic champion—the best of the best—came to the rescue. I'd met Muhammad Ali during the 1960 Olympics, and through the sixties and seventies we kept in touch pretty regularly. He called one day and, out of nowhere, asked, "What do those kids do on rainy days?"

"What you'd expect: cards, bingo, and games like musical chairs. Then more bingo, cards, and games."

"I get the picture. You've got a projector that will take sixteen-millimeter film, right?"

"Sure. Why?"

"Well, I've got a film of my fights they might like to see."

"That would be great. Which one?"

"You're not listening to the Champ, Tarzan. This is a film of *all* my fights, from the very first pro fight right up to the present day. You interested?"

Was I! The film had to include some of the greatest fights ever to grace a ring. The kids couldn't get enough of Ali, so I decided to make an occasion of it and originated Fight Night at Kamp Olympik: popcorn, sodas, and fight films of the greatest fighter ever.

Muhammad Ali really did love kids, and not only visited the camp often, but was more than generous in donating equipment that made their camp experience even better. Whenever he came around, they were always out of their minds with excitement. Here he was in the flesh: their idol and living hero, who thought that spending some time with them was worthwhile. That did so much more for them than any pep talk I could give.

I remember the first time he came to the camp, right after they'd stripped him of his title, and I had to pick him up in Philadelphia. He was living in the western section near City Line Boulevard. Before we left, Ali made sure that his wife, Belinda, had cab fare and our camp phone numbers. She was very pregnant, and he wanted to be sure she could get to the hospital just in case things got interesting before he got back home.

Theresa, God bless her, had welcoming banners flying and both campers and staff lined up at our entrance. With the Priests and many of our other local friends as well as members of the press on hand, the mood was festive and electric. When the Champ arrived, there was a flurry of people snapping pictures and maneuvering for position to snag a handshake.

We gave our guest a fast tour of the camp, and then he got down to business. With the entire camp assembled around the outdoor basketball court, Ali stripped to the waist and, wearing well-pressed slacks and impeccably shined shoes, he boxed everyone who wanted to challenge him. The first to enter the ring was Rich, our camp director. Rich's approach was unique. He sort of went creeping around the ring like an immense tortoise. I assumed his unconventional battle plan was dictated by some martial arts strategy. Whatever it was, it got nowhere against Ali, who seemed amused by Rich's strategy.

Years later, though, Ali fought the professional wrestling champion of Japan. Experts and bookies predicted Ali would knock him out, but all this wrestler would do was lie on the floor and kick The Greatest in the shins. When the Champ got home after the fight, the blood vessels in his lower legs were broken and bruised. So the wrestler was not without skill. So anyway, the fight with this Japanese champion dragged on, and Ali's wondering what in hell to do with a guy who looked like a baby trying to kick off his leggings. If the Champ got in too close, he risked being entangled in some wrestling grip, so common sense dictated he keep his distance. This high-kicking performance was roundly booed, but the press couldn't resist making a lot of nothing. "Ali Fails to Knock Out Japanese Champ," the headlines blared. What was Ali supposed to do, sit on the wrestler's chest and beat on his head? I assume the peculiar prone position at least kept the wrestler from getting his head handed to him on a platter.

Anyhow, after Ali eliminated Rich with a few well-placed jabs, the cocky counselors and even some of the campers tried the challenge. Ali toyed with everyone, keeping his punches feather soft with open fists, even the brilliant shots he occasionally threw to keep the opposition on their toes. The cheering was deafening, but the laughter at Kamp Olympik's hapless contenders was even louder. Shuffling his new shoes around the concrete court, Ali seemed to love every minute of the horseplay. Just when we thought the show was over, however, someone called out, "Fight Tarzan."

Ali heard that, of course, and alerted immediately. "Yeah, give me that big galoot next," he said, a slow grin spreading across his face. "The one who thinks he's the king of the jungle. I'm the only king around here, so bring him on!"

Standing at his side while I laced my gloves, I decided to razz the Champ a little. "I ought to tell you that I've been studying your style of fighting, and I think I've got your technique analyzed," I said, all macho. "I believe I've figured out how to hit you."

With amusement dancing in his eyes, Ali looked me over. "You're a pole-vaulter, right?"

"Yeah, but … "

"If you think you can hit me, Tarzan, you better wake up from your dream." As we walked to the center of the court, he added, "And you'd better lay off the bad coconut juice while you're at it." Starting slowly he began dancing around the ring, intersersing his demands that we "rumble in the jungle" with Tarzan yells. I lumbered around after him, a lead-pawed bear trying to catch a butterfly, or rather a bee with one helluva stinger. Moving like lightning, Ali smacked me with several shots. I never saw him throw the punches, but felt the light touch on my cheek.

Nonetheless, I felt a surge of hope when I realized he was falling into the pattern I'd taken note of while watching his fights. Ali would throw several shots, and then back up in a more relaxed position, dropping one hand then the other to below his waist. The minute his opponents would lead with one foot, trying to get close, Ali raised his hands again. What was to stop me from getting a good one in before he had a chance to raise those lethal fists? I reasoned that if I could get to him before he raised his hands, I'd be able to hit him. Wait a doggone minute, Bragg, I told myself. This isn't theorizing while you watch Ali's fight films with beer in your hand; it's happening right now. Mess up and he'll jab you someplace excruciatingly painful. But what the hell, I thought. I knew I'd regret it if I didn't try.

So the next time he danced backward, I raised myself on my toes and hopped at him. This rabbit-like gambit not only speeded up my approach, it caught him off

Bragg children and nephews with Ali.

Ali sparring with Director Rich Cheung.

Ali boxing with counselor.

Ali sparring with camper.   Tracey, Reneé, and Ali's daughter.

guard. I planted one foot and threw a shot that landed squarely on his nose. Then, instead of getting out of there, I grabbed his shoulders and asked, "Do you want me to do that again?"

Before I could draw a fresh breath, punches began to rain down on me. Hooks, jabs, uppercuts, you name it, I got it. Not that it hurt. Though his gloves came at me at the speed of light, Ali gentled each blow on impact.

Thank God!

As he proceeded to demolish me, the campers were going crazy. Finally, I threw my hands up in helpless surrender. Ali stopped the assault, jumped back, and screamed to the kids, "Did I hit Tarzan or what? Who's the king of the jungle now? Who can swing from the biggest tree? No one but Ali!" Some campers were crying from the unbelievable excitement of an event they'd remember for the rest of their lives. It took forever for the crowd to quiet down, and the staff and I finally gave up on trying to get the camp back on track for the rest of the day's activities.

Theresa: *Ali's visits were always exciting, but we never knew if they'd actually happen until we had him trapped in the Pine Barrens. Trapped? You bet! Twenty-five miles of twisting country roads separated us from the outside world, so for a few precious hours he was ours. My mom had to have a meal ready in a heartbeat because we didn't know when he'd feel like eating. So we prepped several of her specialties and waited on pins and needles.*

We took Ali over to the dining hall for a meal. Yolanda had a three-inch giant steak all ready for him, and that sucker overflowed the platter. Though he immediately thanked Yolanda, he looked concerned as he perused the array of other dishes she'd prepared. That surprised us, but I then remembered that as a Muslim he couldn't eat pork. He passed on the salad, but my mother-in-law realized why and speedily made another without bacon bits.

Hungry after his exhibition matches, Ali wolfed down the food and a few gallons of water. As we talked during the meal, he kind of cocked his head on one side and said, "You've really got a great setup here. I suppose you wouldn't consider selling it? I need to get myself a training camp."

Ali and Don boxing.

"No, Champ," I said, almost wishing I could, "we're doing great. And most of the properties around here would bring a pretty good price. Did they leave you with enough money to handle that?"

"Nope, attorneys do bleed you dry," Ali answered. Just then the phone rang, and I heard Theresa answer it. A minute later she ran up to the table, big-eyed and breathless.

"Belinda went into labor, and she's at the hospital," she blurted out. Buttoning his shirt as he tore across the dining room, Ali made a beeline for our Pontiac. Never have I seen anybody move faster. The campers, hearing that Ali's baby was on the way, went nuts, and Theresa grabbed me by the arm. "Honey, I can drive, but I'm not sure I'm up to handling this many berserk kids. Let me drive him to Philly." Since the kids were close to running laps around the ceiling, I stayed to bring order to the pandemonium.

Theresa: *Getting out of the Pines took forever. Ali was rocking back and forth in his seat, saying something over and over just under his breath. He finally gave me this eloquent look as if to say is this as fast as you can go? So for the first time in my life I put the pedal to the metal, and we flew down those backcountry roads. Meeting a trooper didn't worry me—I knew most of them—but if a deer darted out in front of us we'd really have a problem.*

What a relief it was to make it over the Philadelphia Bridge and head down City Line toward the hospital, but traffic was bumper to bumper, and the Champ was clenching and unclenching his fists. His murmuring grew louder, and I realized he was praying, calling on Allah to watch over his family and bring his child into a free world. I touched his hand gently. "I'm praying to my God, too, Champ, so everything's covered."

Ali laughed, then glanced at the speedometer and said, "Let me take over the driving, Theresa."

My stomach turned cartwheels. They'd taken away his license when he refused to go into the army and kill people who'd never done him any harm. "Champ, we could both get into real trouble."

He nodded, then leaned toward me with eloquent eyes. "Please. Belinda needs me." Now what could I say to that? I pulled to the curb, and he leaped out of the car. As I slid over, he jumped into the driver's side, gunned the motor, and we were off on what would put most roller-coaster rides to shame. Though we were driving fast, he began to weave in and out of traffic with surgical precision, cutting it close, but getting through. Traffic was becoming more congested, and I was sure we'd be stuck in gridlock. As if in answer to prayer, however, a wide shoulder materialized, and just past it, an empty sidewalk.

Of course, Ali saw all this too, and he glanced at me with a boyish grin. I told myself, he's not going to do what I think he has in mind. And that's just what he did. Veering out of traffic, he bounced the right wheels up over the curb and onto the sidewalk. It felt like we were riding at a ninety-degree angle. I clung desperately to the door to keep from sailing out Ali's open window. I shut my eyes, but that didn't give me much comfort. He kept slamming on the brakes every fifty feet or so. I could only imagine that the frantic braking was giving equally frantic pedestrians the chance to scramble out of the way. Stop and start, stop and start, until my insides were ready to abandon ship. I smelled something burning, and I prayed it wasn't anything expensive. As we progressed, I began to wonder what would happen if the floorboard gave way. Then we bounced back off the sidewalk. I breathed a grateful prayer and opened my eyes—just in time to see us tear through a red light.

Now Ali did look both ways, but that cut little mustard with the police car that roared after us. As soon as I heard the siren, I was sure the next stop would be jail. Mom would have kittens.

The officer leaped out of the squad car and charged toward us, stopping precipitously when he recognized the Champ. He stood there, his hands held out in supplication as he tried to take all this in. Finally he managed to stammer, "What in the heck are you doing?"

Ali didn't miss a beat. "My wife's having a baby. I have to get to her before the child's born. Can you help us?"

The officer pursed his lips, nodded, and said, "Follow me." With his mars lights flashing, he escorted us through the heavy traffic to the hospital. Our vehicle was now the focal point for everyone on the road, and when people realized it was Ali, waving hands, peace signs, and cheers came billowing toward him. In his uniquely loving way the Champ acknowledged them all with nods of his head as he kept on the squad car's tail.

When we arrived at the hospital, I thanked the officer profusely, but the Champ gave him a bear hug before bolting through the doors. Of course the staff was anticipating his arrival, and a delegation hurried him along to the maternity floor. I hastily parked the car and followed Ali inside. They'd escorted him right to Belinda; it was as if both she and the baby were waiting for him. The moment he entered her room, all hell broke loose, and they rushed her into the delivery room.

I waited alone in the waiting room pacing and praying and wondering if the distracted new father would even remember I was out there. He could very well slip out the back door when everything was over, and I'd be waiting till hell froze over. Just when I thought I should think about driving home, Ali burst through the doors with an immense smile on his face. He swept me up in his arms and thanked me for getting him there on time.

"But Champ," I said, "what about the baby?"

He blinked, and then grinned again. "Twins, Theresa, and they're just fine. In fact, they're all kinds of wonderful." We chatted for a minute or two, then I offered to drive him to his house, but he shook his head. "Somebody'll be picking me up shortly, but right now, I want to go back to Belinda and those babies."

Dizzy with relief, I called Don and told him the good news, and then I practically floated out of the hospital, got in my car, and started home. But I hadn't even driven two blocks when I realized that the brakes felt funny. Hemmed in by city traffic, I decided to keep going, but soon found I had to depend on the emergency brake. By the time I got back to the Pines, the car was smoking like a Texas barbecue.

Theresa's call came while we were all eating dinner, and when I shouted, "It's twins!" both campers and staff alike erupted with screams of excitement. The kids really felt they'd been a part of a very special day in the life of one of their heroes, something they'd treasure as long as they lived.

It was truly a day of miracles.

The first miracle was that Ali hadn't killed me when I bopped him in the nose. And there was the even greater miracle of two healthy babies.

Later that evening I was standing by the door of the dining hall, when I got a whiff of the Jersey Turnpike. A minute later Theresa drove up in a cloud of choking smoke. I pulled her out of the car, and she told me what happened. "Damn it all, Honey, why didn't you just pull over?" I asked.

"I had to get home and tell you all that happened. Besides, Mom and I wanted to get an early start on breakfast prep. Come on, we don't want to miss campfire."

So there were yet more miracles. The car made it back. Both the brakes and floorboards held up. The last, most important miracle? My wife. 'Nuff said.

Of course it fell to me to deal with the innards of our Pontiac. By the time Theresa got it back to the camp, the brakes had just about breathed their last. She was damn lucky to have made it home in one piece.

"But it's a brand-new car. The hospital's only fifty miles away—a hundred round trip. Could that little bit of driving hurt anything?"

Uh-huh.

The nice lady at the dealership was at a loss, too, but since the car was under warranty, she accommodated me immediately. She even secured a loaner car for me, a nice big Cadillac, so I could certainly return to the camp stylin'.

As she walked me to the caddie, the woman voiced her puzzlement again. "But you've only had the car a few weeks. How could the brakes have burned out so fast?"

I shrugged my shoulders. "Beats me. All we did was make one quick trip to the hospital."

Theresa: *That lady was so gracious, but I'll bet she'd have been impressed if she'd known whose foot had been pounding that poor brake pedal so energetically!*

The next time Ali came to the camp, he'd moved from Philadelphia to Cherry Hill, New Jersey. This was just across the Ben Franklin Bridge—much closer to the camp. Nick Werkman, Seton Hall's standout basketball star, kept me company when we traveled to Cherry Hill to pick up Ali. I pulled up in his driveway, but the moment we stepped out of the car, several large bodyguards swarmed out of the house and surrounded us. Nick was more than just a little scared; he certainly wasn't expecting an in-your-face-who-the-hell-are-you style of welcome.

The pain and suffering of that pursuit emanates from the basic root of all mankind and his consuming goal.

—*Don Bragg, "Identity"*

Then I heard Ali laughing as he strolled from the interior of the garage. "That's just Tarzan coming for a visit. He won't hurt you," he told his guys as he beckoned Nick and me into the garage. "Come on in and have a look at this." There were several vehicles in the garage, including a motorcycle, but the apple of Ali's eye that day was a brand-new reproduction of the old Model T Ford. "Look at the workmanship on this car," he said with awe in his voice. "I just got it, and I want to drive it to the camp. The kids'll get such a kick out of it."

"Are you sure you'll be okay driving up there alone?" I asked. "I could ride along with you."

Ali gave me an ironic look. "You've got your car, Tarzan. I've got mine." And that was that.

He led us into the house and through the kitchen where his wife Belinda was cooking something that smelled fantastic.

"Champ, is your wife coming with us today?" I asked.

His reply was succinct. "There be but one star in this family, and that is me." He ushered us down to his rec room, very contemporary, with a sumptuous leather couch. Turning on the television, he slipped a cassette into the VCR. "Why don't you watch this while I finish getting ready?" he suggested and disappeared up the stairs. When he hadn't returned in about fifteen minutes, Nick looked at his watch and glanced at me, his eyebrows raised in the unspoken question: he *is* coming back, right? I waved off his concern. I was, after all, extremely grateful that Ali was visiting the camp, and there was no way I'd put a negative twist on this trip.

Not that we weren't enjoying the film with its restored footage of some of the great fighters of the past. One of them was Jack Johnson, and we relived the highs and lows of his career as well as those of Jim Jeffries, the so-called Great White Hope, and Gentleman Jim Corbett. I knew the Champ loved the style of these great fighters, who were known for their social skills as well as for their speed and endurance. "I'm like them, you know," he'd joked one time. "Only prettier and smarter." However, I knew hundreds of people were waiting for his arrival at the camp, including Yolanda. She wouldn't be the happiest of campers if the feast she was preparing had wilted by the time the Champ sat down to eat. I don't believe that even Ali would want to take on Yolanda. But I kept reassuring Nick that everything would work out. "Just be patient," I advised, sounding more like my wife than I wanted to admit.

Then Ali appeared in the stairwell. "Are you two gonna sit there watching old movies all day? Let's go. I've got a camp to visit." Nick's jaw dropped—we'd been waiting over an hour—but he just flipped off the TV and, with a grin, followed Ali and me up the stairs.

Nick and I jumped in my car and pulled away, with Ali in his Model T right behind us. As we headed toward the camp, Ali had some fun with the Ford's truly obnoxious horn, saluting every car on the road with the sound of a goose being castrated. Then, out of nowhere, a large black sedan screamed past my car, then slammed in front of me, cutting me off. I braked, avoiding an accident, but boy, was I pissed off. Hitting the gas, I lit out after him, and when I caught up to him, I gave the jackass the flashing lights treatment. He jammed on his brakes and pulled over, with me right behind him. A very large black man swarmed out of the car. His impeccable suit covered a mountainous, well-muscled frame—a pro wrestler or football center, I surmised. But at 6′ 3″ and 245 pounds, I was hardly a shrimp, so I jumped out of my car, too, and headed for the guy. When he'd walked to within a few yards of me, his steps faltered, then he hauled tail back to his nice shiny car and took off, leaving the smell of burning rubber in his wake. Boy, this made my day! By this time Nick had joined me.

"Did you see that?" I crowed. "I guess that proves I still look pretty intimidating."

"The hell it does!" was Nick's immediate rejoinder. "Just look back there." I turned, just in time to see Ali climbing back into the Model T. Nick continued to dot the *i*'s and cross the *t*'s, just in case I'd missed the point. "Your size didn't have a damn thing to do with him skedaddling. It only proves that he wasn't crazy enough to try to beat up a guy who has Muhammad Ali watching his back." Much chastened, I got back in our car, and the three of us proceeded to Kamp Olympik. But Nick was right: the Champ'd had my back and had put the fear of God into my worthy would-be opponent.

We finally arrived at camp. With banners flying and kids cheering themselves hoarse, Ali waved and smiled as he drove his Model T all around the grounds. The kids then treated Ali to a demonstration of their prowess in swimming, sprinting, and foul-shot shooting. Ali was graciously attentive, praising the kids—and rightly so. They'd put everything they had into their exhibition for the Champ.

Once the kids had done their thing, we retired to the dining hall for all the hoopla of picture taking and reporter interviews. I gave Ali one of my Kamp Olympik T-shirts and laughingly mentioned that they cost me ten bucks each. Ali laughed too. "Take it out of my appearance fee and throw in a couple of kids' shirts for my family."

Was I embarrassed—and for one of the few times in my life. I remembered the Champ saying once that he'd been asked to visit another camp facility and that they'd offered him $10,000, but that he'd refused. "Your camp is more my style, 'cause those campers you've got come from the same background I do. Besides, I like putting up with a big old sissy, Tarzan, and that's you." And I was about to quibble with this guy over a few T-shirts? Hell, no!

After eating one of Yolanda's great meals—this one totally Muslim-friendly—we sat outside relaxing. He looked up, a little wistfully, like a kid sitting on a daydream and, in an offhand way, mentioned that he might have a shot at fighting again.

"I'm working on a deal with Atlanta and it looks pretty promising," he said, turning to survey the tree-studded terrain of Kamp Olympik. "You still not interested in selling me your camp? I'll need somewhere I can train in peace."

"Sorry, Champ, things are going great, and we're even looking to expand the program here. But you might touch base with a good friend of mine, Gene Kilroy. I introduced you to him in Philly, remember? Well, Gene keeps informed about what real estate's available around here, especially in the Pennsylvania mountains."

Ali looked thoughtful. "The altitude would help me build lung capacity, and it'd be pretty private, which is what I need." Shortly after that Gene found him

Don with Gene Kilroy.

a good piece of land in Deer Lake, Pennsylvania, where Ali built his camp. It was an ideal location for him to train, tucked well away from the distractions of city life.

Even after he took down Jerry Quarry in Atlanta and began his successful quest to reverse his draft-evasion conviction, Ali continued to make time for the Kamp Olympik kids. Once he drove into camp in his beautiful Rolls-Royce, and one of the kids asked him how much it cost. When Ali told them, the kids were stunned. They started to rub their hands over the Rolls, tracing its beautiful lines. I'd been pretty impressed with the price of this vehicle, too, so I told the kids to stop touching the car.

Immediately, Ali jumped in. "No, let them see it, touch it, and dream that this could also be a reality for them one day." So I shut up.

Later that season we took two busloads of campers to Ali's camp, and since Mike Douglas was shooting a TV show, the kids enjoyed a doubleheader that day. Because I'd appeared on *The Mike Douglas Show* in the past, Mike was extremely cordial to the kids and very complimentary to me. He told the kids about my appearance on his show, and that I'd pole-vaulted down the middle of Market Street into the Cloud 9 pit.

"That's what we've got at the camp," one young man whispered excitedly, nudging his neighbor. Mike's comments gave the kids a new perspective on my career, and some of them eyed me with awestruck eyes. That felt pretty good.

"One other thing I had to do because of this guy," Mike continued in the same vein. "To get an idea of what it was like to come off a jump the way Don does, the producers had me jump off a ladder into that Cloud 9 pit." He wiped mock sweat off his brow. "But the cameras were rolling, and as they say, the show must go on. Never again, though." Then here come a couple of gals bearing a set of enormous golden boxing gloves. I mean these were built for King Kong, about the size of the exercise balls the ladies use today. So Mike stepped into the ring and started sparring with Ali with these damn things strapped on his hands. Ali just looked at him for a minute, and then said, "Okay, now I'm going to whup this guy with the big old lopsided hands." All the spectators, including our campers, the press, and Ali's staff, roared with laughter. What an incredible experience for these inner-city children. I was so proud of them. Despite the hilarity and excitement, they were as well behaved as any Anglican boys' choir.

The show was taped for later airing, and some of the kids were already back home when it was finally shown on TV. They called us up and even wrote letters to let us know they'd seen themselves on the show. It was a once-in-a-lifetime experience for the kids, the counselors, Uncle Joe, and even a certain retired pole-vaulter.

For years thereafter, Ali never forgot to invite Theresa and me to his fights, be they in New York, Puerto Rico, or wherever. He always treated us royally, including us in his circle of good friends. So Theresa and I were there in Vegas when he lost to Holmes.

Steve Brown with campers at Ali's gym.

Ali and his daughter at his camp kitchen.

Mike Douglas exhausted after sparring with Ali.

Ali at press conference with Don and boys.

We sat with Angelo Dundee's family, and all of us were stunned. It was absolutely heartbreaking to see The Greatest fall. We were so honored to have participated in even a part of Ali's life. To my mind, he'll always be "The Greatest of All Time."

There was another man who not only was an incredible support to Kamp Olympik's kids, but whose life was also interwoven with Ali's. In fact, it's hard to think of Ali without having Gene Kilroy come to mind. We'd met about 1964 at the Philadelphia Boys Club and soon became good friends, despite our aggressive style and mutual tendency to arrogance. Maybe birds of a feather really are happier flocking together. When I opened the camp, Gene was still working with the NFL's Philadelphia Eagles, and he generously arranged for several players to visit the camp. They just showed up and surprised the heck out of the kids, who were thrilled out of their minds.

And it wasn't just football players. Gene had contacts with an unbelievable array of legendary artists. As a result he was the rock-solid entertainment expediter par excellence. Whenever I traveled to New York indoor track meets (though now only as a spectator) he always provided Broadway show tickets or reservations to the finest restaurants not only for me but for my close friends as well. Whether it was front-row tickets to Frank Sinatra or to anything that toured Philadelphia, like the Ice Capades or the Barnum & Bailey Circus, Gene could get 'em.

Later on I introduced him to Muhammad Ali, during one of the Champ's appearances in Philly before he returned to boxing. With his network that spread throughout the entertainment world, Gene quickly made himself invaluable to Ali, eventually becoming his business manager and overall confidant for many years. Though Ali was definitely of the hands-on breed of chief executive, Gene took care of the details that would've driven the Champ wild. Thus, Ali didn't have to waste his valuable time running around securing tickets for his friends for championship fights or just doing small errands for his family. Gene was one person the Champ could trust to take care of his own family's needs. I always knew Gene would make sure that I had tickets and accommodations to attend most of Ali's fights.

Gene's devotion to our campers came from the heart: he was another one who genuinely cared about the kids. Every now and then when camp was in session, he'd pull up by the dining hall in his luxurious Cadillac convertible, with a different sports celebrity in tow. Jim Ringo of the Eagles, the 76ers' Wally Jones, and Jersey Joe Walcott were among those who accompanied him. Sometimes Gene would pop his capacious Cadillac's trunk, and it would be crammed with autographed footballs and basketballs from the Philadelphia teams as well as pairs of Everlast boxing gloves and headgear. These not only helped the kids with their boxing, but prevented them from killing each other bare-handed. Gene never forgot the kids and was constantly coming up with little things that would add to their summer fun. I know he was the one who reminded Ali to block off time to come to Kamp Olympik. So unless his schedule made it impossible, Ali was there for my campers.

Having traveled from Vegas to Africa and around the world with Ali, Gene could certainly write a book about his experiences. Somebody asked him recently what he expects in heaven. His answer was typical of the man. "I don't care. I've spent over ten years with Ali, and that's heaven enough for me."

Gene did everything he could do to make not only my camp, but my life and my family's life infinitely more exciting and rewarding. He was a very special part of my life and I cherish our continued friendship.

Chapter Twelve

Although I had some of the best times of my life at Kamp Olympik, there were days when I felt almost overwhelmed by the stress of holding everything together. Sure, I had great help, but I was the one with the motto "The buck stops here" nailed to my rear. When the dog days of summer rolled around, and the heat and humidity soared, everything got to me. I actually looked forward to the days when I went to work for the governor in the morning and then managed my health club till late at night before heading back to camp. Juggling two jobs in addition to overseeing the camp was a terrific antidote to the feeling I was being consumed body and soul by the camp. Theresa had a fantastic capacity for monitoring the camp daily routine and keeping current with all its demands. But while I got off-site regularly, she worked the property 24/7. During weekend visits she did the schmoozing with the parents while I stayed in the background, keeping all the activities functioning smoothly. I think she also wanted to make certain that my underdeveloped sense of tact was someplace where it couldn't get me into trouble. We worked well as a team, though. We'd both get frazzled occasionally when some problem threatened to go supernova, but something funny or touching always occurred just in time to prevent an utter implosion. At least most of the time. Now I was used to the tension of competition and had developed the ability to pour on that superhuman burst of power when it was needed. The constant slow grind of running the camp was very different, and utterly inimical to both my nature and experience. At times, had Theresa not been right there to soothe the savage beast, I know I would've gone ballistic.

There was one particular incident of mental meltdown, however, that even my wife couldn't comfort away. We'd had five straight days of temperatures soaring over a hundred degrees, with the humidity in the eighties. One day of this delightful weather we could tolerate, but after five days of it, the staff was beginning to crack. The counselors—who were on their feet all day—were exhausted. The kitchen staff, sharing their work space with blistering-hot grills and cauldrons of steaming vegetables, to say nothing of my intrepid mother-in-law, were just about at their breaking point. After the second day of this hellish heat I just plain stayed out of Yolanda's way. The heat didn't deter her in the least: it made her more energetic than ever. How she still produced delicious meals on time, regardless of the hot weather, I'll never know.

In a way, the campers were the best off. We shifted the tutorial program to the dining hall, with the giant fans running full blast. The second their class work was completed, we took them down to the beach for a marathon swim period. Getting into the cool river water was the only relief we had, but it felt great and was free. Despite the swimming, though, we had to be on the alert for any sign of heat exhaustion, which plastered another layer of concern on the thinly stretched staff. When the kids began to comment that they were turning into prunes, we wondered how long we could continue our cool water therapy. We didn't want to return them to their parents looking like the keepers of the crypt.

And of course there were flare-ups as the heat got to somebody or other. My counselors were individuals with strong personalities and strong opinions. Good guys with mile-wide competitive streaks. In this punishing heat any insignificant comment was liable to be blown up out of all proportion, and tempers rose with the temperatures.

One incident went like this: a CIT came running up to me, perspiring and gasping for breath, to alert me to an altercation in progress.

"Okay," I responded wearily. "Where are they?"

"The bathhouse," the kid answered.

"I'll take care of it," I said. "You get a cold drink from the kitchen and sit in the shade until supper." Inside the bathhouse I found two counselors—who should've known better than to act like ill-tempered roosters—circling each other warily, glaring for all they were worth. My entry interrupted one of 'em in mid–cock-a-doodle-doo.

"Enough," I snapped. "Now what the hell is this about?"

"He made a crack about the Cubs," one of the combatants mumbled.

"What the hell do you care?" I demanded. "You're a Red Sox fan."

"Yeah, well, my dad's from Illinois," he growled.

"How 'bout you?" I asked the other one.

"What he said, I guess."

These two dingbats didn't know what they were arguing about! Grabbing each of my banty roosters, I hauled them outside, still squawking and flapping, and got to the bottom line. "Go to the beach and sit in the water up to your neck."

"How long?"

"Till I say you can come out. Now go!"

The last straw for me this particular day was when my wife said, "We'd better make a run into town today. We're just about out of staples."

It was like being goosed by the Grim Reaper. Staples? "God almighty, Theresa, how could we be out of food with the grocery bill I just paid?"

"Calm down, Honey," she said, giving me The Look. "The stapler's almost empty, that's all. Don't be so paranoid!"

Paranoid? Me? I was the one who risked getting hit upside the head by a well-aimed skillet if I ventured into the kitchen. My own sweet daughters were raiding Mick's blueberry fields at the behest of Aunt Ruth, a latter-day Ma Barker in grandmotherly disguise. And my own undershorts were being snatched right out from under me, victims of my lovely wife's laundry fetish. As I struggled for breath in the humid, overheated air, I realized how fragile my little empire was. What if Yolanda quit? Or Dominick stopped bringing truckloads of fresh vegetables? We'd be eating canned spinach and pumpkin, and all the campers would run away.

I tottered into our air-conditioned cabin, collapsing onto the bed. And then I heard it: the telltale patter of raindrops on the metal roof. Leaping for the door, I flung it open and stepped into the gently falling rain. "Damn," I exulted," It's cooling off! Just feel that breeze!" My earlier gloom dissipated like a desert mirage. "C'mon everybody," I bellowed, striding through the camp. "Everybody into the dining hall for bingo. Cash prizes, or would you rather have candy bars?"

I called to campers who were running to grab clothes off the line. "Never mind that. Leave 'em right there. They could do with a good rainwater rinse."

I lifted my face and let the chilly rain soak in. What a great camp; what a great life! Waving at Uncle Joe, I yelled, "How 'bout you run into town and buy another 500 Popsicles? Take as many kids as you want with you." I shoved open the dining hall door, and roared, "B-25, I-83. It's bingo night. Let's go, go, go, as in G5, O7!"

When the weather was temperate, however, the kids were always up for an excursion to Batsto Village, a kind of mid-Atlantic Williamsburg. When we observed how they soaked up information about colonial life on the old plantation, we expanded our visits there to include even more of the exhibits. While the kids always enjoyed the glassblowing, they also became intrigued with colonial life in general. The main house on the plantation was crammed with antique furniture, but the items that caught the kids' eyes were the spinning wheels. I saw one kid thoughtfully fingering his shirt as if he were imagining the work it would've taken to make it a couple of hundred years before.

One presentation the campers especially enjoyed was the story of the runaway slaves who were given sanctuary in the old mansion, which was part of the Underground Railroad during the Civil War. This of course was the antislavery network that helped slaves escape from their masters. The tour guide made the kids feel as if they were actually hiding with the fugitive slaves in the secret chamber above the dining room while proslavery dignitaries dined below on extravagant meals. Eventually, Theresa knew the stories so well that she conducted tours herself. The kids were even more attentive when my wife was telling them the history of the place.

Those kids were so sharp: they took in every detail of the quaint village. At the old-time sawmill, they were fascinated to see how the colonists controlled the flow from the water gates to start and stop the spinning saw blades. They seemed amazed that even with his primitive equipment, the millwright was still able to saw cedar logs into ruler-straight planks.

Since Batsto Village had originally been a stagecoach stop, it had a barn for the horses that pulled both the stagecoaches and wagons. Cows were also quartered in that barn; they provided milk and butter for stopover guests. But when our urban cowboys got a look at the horses out in the pasture, they went wild and started campaigning for rides. They climbed up on the fence rails and waved handfuls of hay at the horses, trying to entice the animals to within hopping-on range. Of course, the horses noticed the hay and came galloping over to sample the free eats. The thing was that they were all draft horses, absolutely huge animals with hooves the size of dinner plates. The thunder from those hooves made the ground vibrate, and the racket would've scared the devil out of John Wayne. The kids leaped off the fence with wide eyes, still offering the gigantic beasts the hay, but at a respectful arm's length through the fence.

Don and campers at Batsto Village trip.

Everybody wanted to send postcards home from the original colonial Batsto Village post office. The kids watched attentively while their cards were postmarked by hand, and walked out with ear-to-ear grins on their faces. It really doesn't take much to make a kid happy.

We'd always served refreshments before the trip home, but all the new experiences and sights got the campers almost too keyed up to eat. They stayed that way, too, well into the evening, practically ricocheting off their cabin walls at bedtime. So I thought, why not let them work off some of that energy by hiking home?

The trip to Batsto was fifteen miles on the road that skirted the state park most of the way. But the colonial village at the center of the park was just shy of three miles south of Kamp Olympik as the crow flies. There happened to be a deeply rutted dirt road that led from Batsto almost to the camp's front door, and it was perfect—as long as you were on foot. The bus would never have survived a trip over the road's bumps and ruts. It wasn't too hot, so off the kids went, in the care of the counselors. Barry and Rich followed in the pickup truck, but not too closely, so the campers would feel like they were trekking through the wilderness on their own.

I drove back to the camp with Theresa, but it wasn't that long before the campers came streaming into the camp. In fact, it was only about half an hour since they'd left Batsto Village, and I didn't know what to make of it. They were running around squealing and high-fiving each other, yelling exultantly like Olympians finishing the marathon. They told me they loved their expedition through the woods, but the high point seemed to be that they'd made it back to the camp at all. When Barry walked up, I asked him what'd happened.

"Search me," he said. "At first, it looked like the kids were running races, but only sporadically, like they usually do. Then they took off, running like hell. It was hard for Rich and me to keep 'em in sight."

Upon hearing that, I collared a passing counselor. "You were with the kids just now. How'd you get back to camp so fast?"

"A couple of the counselors and some of the older campers began sneaking ahead and ambushing the others," he laughed. "You know, screeching and howling and jumping out at the kids, who were sure the Jersey Devil was after them. A few of the little ones grabbed their counselors' legs and hung on like grim death, hollering 'Don't let him get me.' But we got home in great time, huh?"

So that was the secret of the kids' record-breaking three-mile dash. I guess it really does give wings to your heels if you think you're about to be eaten. That night at campfire, we talked about our excursion, but when we got to the part about the trip home, all one little kid had to say was, "He didn't get me."

I asked, "Who?"

The answering chorus was deafening. "The Jersey Devil."

And we adults smile when the little ones shriek at the thought of monsters and such, but I heard a tale that sent shivers up my grown-up spine. In our part of the Pinelands, and I guess in forested areas all over the country, hunters have constructed and furnished deer clubs. Walt Priest and his brother Lou built theirs piecemeal during the last years of World War II. About a quarter mile off the main road, it faced into a remote area of the forest where deer were plentiful, along with smaller game. The Priest elders had furnished it like a mini-hunting lodge, with bunk beds, a cozy fireplace, comfortable chairs, and the all-important kitchen for cooking their venison, fish, and homemade pasta. Walt's nephew Cutt also moved into the Pine Barrens and built a home near Walt, which made for some lively gatherings in the Indian summer afternoons. There'd be an abundance of food and homemade wine as well as good beer kept chilly in tubs of ice. Theresa and I joined the Priest clan on more than one occasion before we moved to the camp year-round and started hosting get-togethers there.

As the party got rolling, the men competed at horseshoes, pinochle, and the Italian game of *morra*, where two guys would thrust their right fists out fast, displaying a certain number of fingers. Both players instantly had to shout out their estimate of the total number of fingers showing, and the guy who nailed the right number won. *Morra* could get incredibly intense for a game that only used the fingers, and sometimes the guys got a little argumentative. The wives usually put an end to that real fast.

And there was always engrossing storytelling. After Walt's son-in-law Tom Marshall whupped my butt playing horseshoes, I just sat back and enjoyed the tall tales of hunting prowess with bow and arrow. I had no pretensions of being the great white hunter, certainly not with a bow, and it was just as well. If I'd tried playing Robin Hood, I'd have been the first guy to shoot an arrow into his own butt. Walt's forty-two-pound bass won fishing honors, though not without heated debate. Cutt had the biggest buck, but since he shot it off-season, it couldn't be officially registered. So Walt claimed bragging rights with his buck whose size was noted in the state hunting register.

Against my better judgment, I got drawn into a nutty argument between Walt and Cutt about the height of Cutt's deer stand. Now the deer stand from which you actually do your shooting is located at some distance from any deer club, perched well up in a tree. The thing was that the deer stand couldn't be affixed permanently to the tree—that was illegal. Since no nails could be used to secure the stands to the tree, they were pretty precarious places to hang out. Thus, it was okay to shoot a deer from a tree, but only if the hunter risked falling on his head. What environmentalist dreamed that one up? After all, these Pineys weren't after deer heads to mount in their paneled libraries, they were shooting deer to put venison on their families' tables, even though they did love to brag on the size of the animal's rack of antlers. Anyhow, Cutt claimed his deer stand was more than thirty-five feet up in the tree. Now I didn't think you could hit a deer from that high up because of the angle in which you'd have to shoot the arrow. "Come on, Cutt," I said, "Thirty-two feet max."

"Wanna put some money on that, Bragg?" he came back at me. So Cutt, Walt, and I headed out into the woods, trailed by Tom and some of the others. It was painful going, mainly because we kept bouncing off the damn trees.

Did I mention the beer?

We paraded solemnly through the forest, Cutt leading the way. Walt brought up the rear, carrying his special measuring tape with the solemnity of a surgeon preparing for a heart transplant. I marched along in between the two of them, reflecting that this was how men were marched to execution. And why would I think that? Because the idiot that Theresa Fiore married had agreed to be the one to climb the tree. Perhaps the beer had something to do with that, but I was stuck. You don't go back on your word if you've given it to a Priest.

Our bet was that the measurement had to favor Cutt's or my estimate by at least three feet. Walt supervised as I climbed the tree, voicing all manner of concern that I take care of his tape measure. Nobody seemed to care if I fell on my ass, but since I didn't care either, I couldn't hold it against anybody else.

I struggled up to Cutt's deer stand, uncomfortably aware that the wind was picking up. Measuring with inebriated care, I let out a hoot of triumph.

"Thirty-two feet even. Cutt, you owe me money."

When I reached the ground, Cutt argued that I hadn't measured all the way up to the top of the deer stand. "Hell, Bragg, that tape measure barely touched the bottom of it." He was sure I'd screwed up, and I knew I hadn't. We were fixing to stand out there arguing all night until we got a whiff of wind-borne smoke enhanced by the hickory and cherrywood Walt used to fire his grill. Hell, that aroma would seduce any living being to come closer, be it man or beast. So Walt, the self-proclaimed patriarch, called our wager a draw and proclaimed that nobody owed anything. Case closed.

As we approached the deer cabin, the tantalizing perfume of Walt's barbecue sauce and the chicken he'd anointed with it hit our noses and reminded us that we were ravenous. Man shall not live by beer alone. Fried striped bass and incredibly delicious barbequed chicken are also necessary.

We sat around a shaded table outside and had a superb meal, the norm at the Priests' parties. The surrounding forest was always beautiful, but especially so when, like today, the pines glistened in the sun and the oaks started taking on that rich olive-gold hue that spoke of the coming autumn. That day seemed particularly wonderful and peaceful as the season ripened to its perfection. Then somebody commented that their area had more deer than any other in the vicinity.

Walt slapped the table. "Hell, boy. That's because while you guys are sittin' on your butts in the city, I'm workin' mine off carrying baskets of apples and potatoes to bring the deer in close where you can get 'em. I'm a slave to your hunting pleasure."

With a wicked glint in his eye, Cutt said, "Thanks a lot, Walt. But you do realize that's the only reason we let you move in down here."

Walt started roaring, and a family feud seemed well in the making, but Virginia intervened, saying, "Now who wants ice cream with their apple pie?" Since her homemade pies were renowned throughout the Pinelands, everybody shut up and held out plates for their share.

There is a tree in yonder wood where angels fear to tread. Its timber tall,

it stands alone with crooked branches spread. 'Tis cursed by druid hands.

—*Don Bragg, "Demon Tree"*

After we'd all eaten our fill, the general conversation diminished, then trailed off. After a long, easy silence, people began to joke about the Jersey Devil. Of course no adult believed that childish nonsense. Of course not. That's when Cutt commented that there'd been lot of weird noises emanating from the dark and dismal marshlands of late. "I'm used to foxes yapping during mating season and the way owls can scream, but these noises were different."

"Been nipping at the homemade dago red again, have you?" a cousin laughed.

But Cutt just looked thoughtful. "Maybe I have. But two months back, a farm down the road lost a bunch of pigs. Had their throats torn out, and blood was all over. There's something just plain spooky living in that swamp."

We all looked at each other. Those marshlands weren't that far away from where we were sitting eating apple pie.

"I'm not saying it's the Jersey Devil or anything, but some damn peculiar things have been happening around here." He caught my eye and grinned. "Take the tree where my thirty-five-foot-high deer stand's at."

I stirred at his renewed boast but said nothing.

"I've climbed up and down a hundred times, but this one time I was going down, and it was like I got distracted for a second. Next thing I knew I was falling. Lucky for me I wasn't too far off the ground. Twisted the hell outta my damn ankle though, and I had to hobble all the way back to the cabin."

"Awwww," a voice broke in, but Cutt kept going.

"And all the way back to the cabin, I could've sworn something was stalking me. Few years later, Dottie Priest's son headed out for that same tree, and never came home. We found him lying beside it dead with his chest all bloody. We figured that he hadn't put on the safety when he lowered the gun out of the tree, and the damn thing went off. But that boy knew the right way to handle a gun, and that's a fact. Something must've spooked him."

Nobody had anything to say. Cutt stared at the sunlight dappling the treetops. "And a few years after that, Lou's son, Louie, was hunting in the same tree. He'd reached the top and was just starting to buckle up, when he heard this noise and turned toward it."

"What kind of noise?" I asked, realizing I was gripping the arms of my chair pretty tightly.

"All Louie said was that he knew it didn't belong to the forest, but he didn't have time to think about it because he lost his grip on the safety belt and fell like a rock to the forest floor. Luckily, he hit a few branches on the way down, which probably saved his life."

"So he wasn't hurt?" I asked, as the ignorant newcomer.

"I didn't say that," said Cutt. "Louie said he landed with a resounding thud and couldn't move his legs. He knew he was fading in and out of consciousness, but he had a sense that something was near him circling around the ground where he lay."

"So what happened?" Theresa demanded, on the edge of her seat.

Cutt nodded at Tom Marshall. "Tom's son Vincent realized Louie was long overdue from hunting, and he went looking for him. He found the poor guy lying all crumpled up at the foot of the tree and called the paramedics. A chopper airlifted him to the hospital."

Staring at the smoke haze gently rising from the stone barbeque, Cutt lapsed into silence, so Tom took up the story. "The funny thing was, afterwards when doctors had him all plastered up in his cast, Louie kept jabbering, makin' no sense. He kept asking my son Vincent if he'd had to walk all around the area searching for him before he called for help. Vincent said, 'What? Why in hell would I do a dumb thing like that? I followed the path right to the tree, and there you were.' And Louie, lying in that hospital bed, got a little bit paler and said, 'Then something else was. And whatever was prowling around was creeping closer. Hell, I could hear the damn thing snuffling: sounded like something between a boar and a buck deer during rutting season. Didn't think I wanted to meet it lying flat on my back in the middle of the woods.'" Tom grinned over at Walt's wife. "Of course, Virginia here thought he was hallucinating, and she had to go call a nurse. Then the nurse started shushing Louis and telling him he was just imagining things and to go to sleep. Then she chased the rest of us out of the room. 'Out of here, all of you,' she said. 'The poor man needs his rest.' Leave it to a woman to ruin a good story."

The spellbound audience let out a little sigh, then laughed, as if relieved that the spell of the tale was broken. Cutt kept laughing a little longer than the others. "But you want to know the damnest twist on this yarn? The forest rangers came in with the EMTs, and their contribution to Louie's rescue was to give the guy a ticket for using an illegal stand. The rungs leading up to the deer stand were nailed to the tree, and that made them permanent, therefore illegal. Louie always bragged that he was the only guy in the history of the world to get a ticket for breaking his back. But he never went anywhere near that tree again."

That something so weird had been going on in Kamp Olympik's backyard felt a little unnerving, and I decided it was time to change the subject. "Enough storytelling. Let's head over to Kamp Olympik for a swim and ice-cold watermelon." I wasn't the only one who wanted to leave the swamp demons be and go have some fun. Everybody got up and headed for the cars. "Let's see if Cutt's up to climbing my diving tower and jumping off," I said. "It's the same height as his thirty-two-foot roost in that tree."

Tom laughed as he climbed in his car and said, "That I'd like to see."

So the afternoon ended on a cheerful note. But after that day, whenever I was driving in the neighborhood of Cutt's deer-stand tree, I was always aware of something eerie. I'd remember the peculiarly gray-green light that always played around the tree and the uncanny silence that seemed to watch over the spot. Even in my car I never felt quite at ease, as if something were watching me with unfriendly eyes. So I'd goose the gas pedal and get the hell outta there. But of course, like Virginia thought, it was probably all just a hallucination.

Then heart of camp operations was the dining hall. It was where we were entertained, where we hung out, where we laughed and played pranks. It was the wellspring of information that flowed through the camp. It's where we kept the phone for emergencies and the first aid kits. But more than anything, it was where we kept the food. For though it was our command center, Yolanda, as chef extraordinaire, was the one who ruled the kitchen and maintained the entire dining hall as her private fiefdom. It was kind of like the Vatican, a state within a state that commanded the respect of everybody.

And I did respect the lady. The matriarch of the Fiore clan, she knew what she wanted and went for it: basically my favorite kind of person. The only problem was that she almost never wanted what I wanted, and that led to an interesting relationship. I will always maintain that, since the both of us were born under the sign of the bull, it's a major miracle that we two Tauruses both survived her first week of Kamp Olympik.

Once, when we'd scheduled a trip for the kids, I decided it made sense for them to eat a little earlier. When I informed Yolanda we'd be eating at 11:30, she gave me her biggest smile and said, "No."

Let's cut to the chase. You know that bit about the irresistible force meeting the immovable object? Well, after locking horns with his mother-in-law for about ten minutes, this irresistible force stormed out of the dining hall and wreaked his wrath and frustration on the first sizeable tree limb he found. Then he felt like an idiot, especially since he had to pick pine bark splinters out of his knuckles for days afterward.

This incident turned out well, since it put Yolanda in at least temporary awe of me. Not only was she a mite more amenable to my suggestions, she also began to use me as her enforcer when necessity demanded it. The first time she called on my unique interpersonal skills was when a state health inspector swung by the camp to check us out. Yolanda had just taken four mammoth sheet cakes out of the oven. They were cooling on big wire racks, and their fresh-baked aroma floated through the camp. The tantalizing smell alerted anyone who had a nose that there'd be cake for dessert.

The inspector looked down his nose at the cakes. "Cover up those cakes, ma'am. They could become contaminated."

In an icily quiet voice that would have caused any sane man to run like hell, she demanded, "So you think my kitchen is dirty?"

"I didn't say that, ma'am. But all food handlers are required to cover displayed edible items at all times."

"Who taught you to cook, *stunade*?" she demanded. "If I fed these children hot cake fresh out of the oven, they'd all get sick in the stomach. You know nothing."

"Ma'am, they've got to go in a cooler." He flourished his clipboard. "Regulations."

"So your regulations say I have to ruin the taste and texture of these children's dessert? Ah, *finabola*, you and your rules. Go find somebody else to annoy."

"Ma'am … "

"Those cakes are staying right where they are. If you want to argue about it, go see the owner. He's right outside."

By this time the guy was hugging his clipboard like he was trying to hide behind it. "You mean that huge guy I saw when I came in? The one who was leaping around and yelling at those counselors like he was nuts?"

"Exactly," she said, turning away to tend to the pot of sauce Bolognese on the stove. "And he's nowhere near as pleasant as I am."

Now I was just standing outside, minding my own business, surveying the camp. But I saw the guy scurry out of the dining hall, hop in his car, and light out of there liked a scared rabbit. When I found out what'd transpired, I expected notification of a heavy fine or the impending closure of the camp. But we never heard from the guy again. Game, set, match to Yolanda!

Maybe if the state inspector hadn't implied that Yolanda's regime was less hygienic than an operating room, he wouldn't have gotten in hot water, for absolute cleanliness was an article of faith for my mother-in-law. No bug, microbe, or pestiferous fingerprint had a chance of surviving in her domain. I really felt sorry for the cookie boys who did cleanup along with kitchen prep and serving. They tended to go around nervously scrutinizing everything, from the floor to the salt in the shakers, and I understood why. Yolanda's idea of cleaning was closer to hand-to-hand combat than simply removing visible dirt from any given surface. Dirt offended Yolanda; the fact that it ever had existed in any particular location was license to insist on repeated cleansing even when the surface in question already sparkled. And she expected the cookie boys to share her enthusiasm.

They didn't exactly share it, however.

Just when they thought their duties were completed, she'd pounce on them over a dusty windowsill. "Why didn't you tend to the windows? Today's not a holiday, you know."

They'd mop under the dining hall tables, and then head out to the lake for a swim. "Come back here, you two. Didn't I tell you to mop under the tables?"

"We did that first thing, Mrs. Fiore."

"Then you didn't do it right. March right back here and finish the job."

I peeked in the dining hall as the two young men stood peering in befuddlement at what looked like a perfectly clean floor. They mopped the area again, though, and were just about ready to make a dash for the door when Yolanda halted them in their tracks. "Where do you think you're going? The grease traps in the kitchen are disgusting."

"But we already ... "

"Not good enough, you didn't," she cut in. "Get busy!" If the kids were lucky, they'd have time for a quick dip before starting dinner prep, and even then Yolanda's approval was grudging. "Well, it's far from perfect, but it's okay. This time!"

Thank God I didn't have to work under the steely-eyed supervision of our chef. And yet, there was never a shortage of volunteers for dining hall duty. The reason was Yolanda. She had a knack for knowing when a cookie boy needed a kind word or a piece of chocolate cake and a glass of ice-cold milk on a blistering afternoon. And the kids learned how to work under a tough manager, not a bad life lesson. But hell, I didn't need any such lessons. Besides, keeping an eye on the growing roster of camp pranksters was already a full-time job.

If I had to name the counselor or staff member who was innocent of pulling any pranks, I couldn't come up with a name if I pondered the question for years. But the biggest prankster? No contest: that would be Steve Brown. His mischievous nature wasn't even neutralized when he took a day off. Hell, that's when he armed himself for future skullduggery at the expense of the other counselors, campers, and staff.

Now Steve was a great guy and a good counselor, but he wasn't into the spit-and-polish aspect of things. Unfortunately that was the aspect that made for a great showing at cabin inspection time. Ricky, the counselor in Cabin 12, was just the opposite. You could bounce a coin off the neatly made bunks in Cabin 12; the shoes were always in ruler-straight rows, the floor immaculate. Steve rarely passed inspection, however, and he felt that something was skewed in the universe because Ricky passed so consistently. Goody Two-Shoes, that's what Steve called Ricky, and one day Steve decided to bring his rival down a peg or two.

On his next day off, Steve spent the day in Atlantic City, kicking back on the beach, chasing girls, strolling down the boardwalk. And while strolling, he ducked into a novelty store, the sort that sold rubber false teeth, hand buzzers, whoopee cushions, and all the fake dog excrement any fool could wish to buy. Guess which item Steve snapped up?

Back at camp, a few days after making his purchase, Steve slipped away from his table during breakfast and meticulously arranged the pile of counterfeit doggie droppings right alongside Mr. Clean's front step. No doubt cackling in fiendish glee, Steve returned to the dining hall, all casual, and waited for the results of cabin inspection to be announced. Barry Ross finally came in with the bad news: " … and failing inspection are Cabins 5, 9, and 12."

For a full minute Ricky just sat staring, jaw gaping in disbelief. He came to, leaped to his feet, and sprinted to his cabin, sure a mistake had been made. But there'd been no mistake. There beside his cabin step, gleaming in the morning sun, was an unmistakable heap of shit. They say he shouted the name of what he found all the way to his reading tutorial class, which was next on his schedule. He was on pins and needles until the class was dismissed, and then, still hyperventilating, he led his kids back to their cabin.

"Just look at that," he bawled, pointing to the area beside the steps.

The ten kids crowded around staring at the bare ground. "Look at what?"

"At this," Ricky snarled, pointing at nothing at all. "Okay, who took it?"

"Took what?" the kids wanted to know.

Breathing hard, shifting his weight from foot to foot, Ricky said softly, "Did anybody take a crap out here last night?"

"Why in hell would we do that? We know where the toilets are."

"Maybe somebody cleaned it up," Ricky said. "Or maybe some animal ate it. They do that sometimes."

"Uh-huh." They continued to stare at their counselor as he searched for his missing pile of shit, then they asked, "Can we go now? We're supposed to be in Tarzanville."

Ricky continued to pace around, mystified, then headed for Tarzanville himself, thinking what's done is done. Case closed.

Oh no, it wasn't. So the poor guy goes back to the cabin to change into trunks for swim period. He opens the door and stops dead in his tracks. Right in the middle of the cabin is a huge pile of brown things, and flies are circling it appreciatively. I guess Steve's top dressing of a little honey made things look pretty realistic—or appetizing— depending on your point of view. Ricky charges out the door, and a few minutes later he comes back, followed by Rich, the camp director.

"Just look at that," he squawks, pointing at the nicely swept floor.

"Very nice," says Rich, "but I've got a meeting with our lifeguards, and … "

"Noooo," moans Ricky. "I'm telling you there's a pile of dog shit somewhere, and I want you to see it. First it was outside, then it went away, then it comes in here, and sat right there."

"Let me get this straight. Your pile of shit came up the steps and waited in here … to ambush you? We're talking a conspiracy? Give me something, here, Ricky." Ricky just stared, muttering incoherently. "Okay," continued Rich. "It's been hot as hell for nearly a week. Heat affects some people more than others. Now maybe you've been hallucinating. Just a little?"

"No way! I know shit when I see it, and I saw it, and then I didn't, and it came back, and yes, it came up the steps and sat right where you're standing."

Rich took a giant step backward. "Okay, fine. Better get down to the beach with your kids. But stay out of the sun, will you?"

Well, Ricky twitched for the rest of the day but began to settle down just before lights-out, when the counselors gathered for their late-night snack. Anyhow, Yolanda was serving pizza, his favorite. He ran down to the bathhouse with the other counselors to wash up, and then hurried into the dining hall. Everybody'd been served; even the absent counselors had plates at their places, their contents kept warm by overturned paper plates.

Already salivating, Ricky whipped off the cover, and there on top of his pepperoni and sausage pie reposed one of the tapered turdlets that had been haunting him all day. Freshly sprinkled with a little water, the brown object sported a fresh, newly minted appearance. The artistic properties of the damn thing didn't soften the blow. "No! Not another dog turd," he wailed. Shoving himself away from the table precipitously, Ricky flipped his chair over backward with a crash, and the rest of the counselors exploded in laughter.

As Ricky picked himself up, Barry, who'd assisted in the turd placement, picked up the object of Ricky's dismay, and sort of nibbled one end judiciously. "No," Barry declared with certainty. "Not dog. I'd say possum." More laughter ensued as everybody realized the entire turd caper had been built around phony poop, not the real deal. Ricky and the horrified cookie boys, Richie and Bobby Morello, eventually joined in. Everybody thought it had been a great trick.

Except Yolanda.

For my mother-in-law, food was a sacred thing, and God help anybody that took its name or essence in vain. So the next morning when she'd heard about the desecrated pizza, she came down on the cookie boys like the chef from hell.

"So you think it's funny to put poop on my pizza. I'll teach you just how funny it is." Richie and Bobby spent the rest of the day doing—and redoing—the most disgusting chores. While they were scrubbing their fingers down to the knuckles, Yolanda stalked around the kitchen, smacking kettles with ladles, rattling cutlery, and growling evil-sounding Italian phrases at the unfortunate cookie boys. After supper, she made them scrub the pots and pans. Twice. Then there were trash cans, baskets, and salt-and-pepper shakers to sanitize. She kept them at it until 11:00, when the salt shakers were finally dry enough to refill.

Were they ever pissed! Since they were ignorant of Steve's orchestration of the entire Great Turd Caper, they blamed Barry. They figured he'd enjoyed the entire episode too much to be innocent of their fate at Yolanda's hands. So from then on Barry's name was mud so far as the Morello boys were concerned. At least until they concocted a suitable revenge. Barry, however, held his fire, but turned prophetic. "Some day Steve Brown's gonna get his payback. Just wait and see!"

We didn't have long to wait, either, and the source of the payback was the grand-daddy of all dirty tricks. But if Steve Brown could've seen the unintended repercussions of his prank, he might've had second thoughts.

It was usually fun and games whenever any counselor returned to camp from his day off, because he always brought something back. It might be anything from a new baseball glove or basketball to a scary mask, a fright wig, or some crazy outfit. But whatever anybody would spring on the camp to startle or terrify everybody, it wouldn't be long before Steve Brown would try to top it.

The week after the Great Turd Caper, Steve had another day off and followed his well-worn path to the novelty store on Atlantic City's boardwalk. Steve was Mr. Showbiz around camp: it was in his blood. All his brothers were entertainers; in fact, one of them wrote the song "Tie a Yellow Ribbon Round the Ole Oak Tree" that Tony Orlando made famous. But Steve's special gift was magic, and he loved to perform his act around the campfire and often stole the show on talent night. So he was always on the lookout for something to liven up either his act or set the hair of the entire camp on end. And when he was buying his fake dog doo, he'd seen something he just had to have.

It was a bearskin coat with the full head and well-clawed paws attached. Our camp dimwit spent an entire week's salary on the moth-eaten thing and carted it back to camp in triumph. He didn't clue in any of the other counselors, though, and they were dying of curiosity. Rich was the only one he took into his confidence, and the two of them plotted a deliciously wacky stunt. I knew Rich was sensible and decided his good sense would keep anything truly outlandish from happening.

Yeah, right!

The ceremonial campfire was planned for that night, and I expected Steve to make some unique contribution, but the end of the campfire ritual was coming up, and not a peep had been heard from Steve. Then, without warning, Rich jumped into the campfire circle and called for silence. Directing his flashlight into the woods, he began shouting, "What the hell *is* that?"

As he spoke the bushes began heaving and shaking, and the sound of growling and grunting rolled towards the wide-eyed campers. Then we saw it: an abominably hairy creature shuffled into view, its massive head swinging from side to side as it took the human scent. Growling even more ferociously, it advanced toward the fire. The light from the flames glinted on its exposed fangs as it came closer.

Then somebody screamed, "It's the Jersey Devil!"

The rest of the campers roared in unison, "Kill it!" Grabbing anything that might serve as a weapon—rocks, heavy branches, shoes, flashlights—the kids charged the monster, determined to protect their turf from this terrifying predator. In a remarkably short time, the kids toppled the beast and proceeded to stomp on him en masse.

Caught flat-footed by this unprecedented show of bravery and solidarity, Rich and I led the other counselors to the rescue of the poor creature. The kids were beating their monster pretty fiercely. In fact, we had to throw the kids off the thing before we could reach it. The other counselors had their hands full trying to calm down the campers, but Rich and I were finally able to lift the exhausted monster from the ground. From deep inside we heard noises that might have been words. Rich and I looked at each other, and I put my ear down by the brute's mouth, which drew an admiring sigh from the kids.

As I listened, the noises morphed into words: "Shoulder...ribs...arrgh!" We hauled away the hairy skin, and there was Steve, crouching in a fetal position, groaning about his ribs. When the campers saw it was just the camp court jester, they quieted immediately.

Barry drove Steve to the hospital, but the guy was lucky. He only had bruises, a wrenched shoulder, and a few cracked ribs. They taped his ribs, put his arm in a sling, and sent him home, where his real torment began. He had to bear the brunt of taunts and ridicule from the entire camp. He always defended himself, though. "Don't give me that crap. I had everyone in a panic and scared to death. Top *that* if you can!"

I tapped him on his good shoulder. "Yeah, Steve, you're right. But you almost got killed."

Big laugh. "Yeah, I just about did," he said proudly.

Since he'd blown his salary on the damn bearskin, Steve was a little hard-pressed for cash when his next day off came around. "I don't have the bucks to get home this week, so would anybody want to buy a mangy, hole-ridden bear outfit?" No buyers came forward, so Steve just kept the moth-eaten monstrosity as a blanket on his bunk. However, he began having nightmares of campers attacking him in his cabin, and he laid the blame on the bearskin. He finally gave it a burial on the Wading River; half the camp watched respectfully as it floated downstream. I wish I could've heard the comments of weekend canoers who encountered it. As it was, I heard third-hand stories about the floating carcass of a mythic wild beast that had dwelled deep in the forest years ago. Folks opined that it had probably been the last of its kind. What a pity it had drowned in the river.

"Yes," I responded with a solemn face. "What a shame we couldn't have saved the pelt and sold it to the Franklin Institute Science Museum in Philly. We have a very deserving young man back at camp, and he could sure use some help paying some doctor bills and buying a bus ticket back home!"

Chapter Thirteen

Now Richie and Bobby Morello were the only cookie boys who survived for five entire seasons, and their names became legendary at Kamp Olympik. Despite their alleged part in the Great Turd Caper, Yolanda swore that those two guys were the best assistants she'd ever had. It was great for the Morello boys, too. They not only got the idea of what food prep and service was all about, they hung out in the kitchen whenever they could, picking up culinary lore from Yolanda. During this period, Barry Ross often took his breaks in the dining hall with his buddy, Dave Miller. Barry, now assistant camp director, took his job very seriously and frowned on any infraction of camp discipline.

Actually, the friction between Barry and the Morello boys worsened because of Yolanda. Grateful for the great job Richie and Bobby did, she'd let them take off and go swimming outside of regular swim periods. That just irritated the hell out of Barry and of course his ever-present sidekick Dave as well. Sometimes during swim period, the two counselors would vent their frustrated sense of propriety on the unfortunate cookie boys by way of horseplay that verged on drowning. The Morello boys were no slouches, but Dave was 6' 4" and Barry more physical than either Richie or Bobby at that time. The younger guys had their moments as well. Whenever Barry and Dave would pass the dining hall, the Morello boys, under Yolanda's protection, would razz the older guys. "Boy, it must be a hundred degrees out there," Richie would holler through one of the dining hall windows, as the two sweating counselors would walk by outside. "Boy, it's a lot cooler in here!" Stuff like that.

Now occasionally Yolanda would snag somebody passing through the chow hall and get them to taste-test one of her creations. Knowing this, Barry constantly found reasons to cut through the dining hall en route to just about anywhere in hopes of getting one of her tasty handouts.

The day the Morello boys decided to even the score with Barry and Dave, Yolanda was making her killer vegetable soup. She beckoned the dynamic duo as they cruised by. "Come have a bowl of my soup," she invited, turning the heat off under the boiling cauldron. Snapping her fingers, she directed Richie and Bobby to fill two bowls. "But be careful," she admonished. "It's terribly hot."

At the word *hot*, Richie grinned at Bobby and got to work. Now Pete Italiano, Dominick's good friend, had just delivered a basket of his blazing hot peppers, which we all loved—in minute portions. One bite of the unseeded pepper would've knocked the Wizard of Oz back to Kansas without need of his balloon. Every summer Pete would save the seeds of the hottest peppers for planting, thus insuring his peppers would retain their signature heat. So while Bobby ladled out the soup, his brother ground up a handful of these dried fire sticks, adding

Rich laughing at "Hot Pepper" escapade.

them, seeds and all, to the soup bowls as a fiery garnish. Placing the bowls carefully before their victims, the Morellos kept poker faces in place while casually waiting for the fireworks. Both counselors attacked the soup like ravening vultures, but Barry dropped his spoon after a few mouthfuls and went flying outside to the bathhouse. I was told he stuck his head under the faucet and just let the water gurgle down his burning throat, almost drowning in the process. While all hell was breaking loose in the bathhouse, Dave calmly ate his bowl of soup and finished Barry's as well. Spooning up the last drop, he said, "That was terrific, Yolanda, but you were right. It was a little hot." Richie and Bobby exchanged unbelieving looks when they heard this, not knowing if he was serious.

When they told Pete the story, they asked his opinion. "So did Dave really like what we fed him or was he putting us on?"

"Only one way to find out," Pete chuckled. "Watch him when he sits on the john. If he starts screaming, he was bullshitting you. If he doesn't piss and moan, he was giving it to you straight, and he's the all-time pepper-eating champion. But in that case, make sure he keeps his rear end away from the campfire and from any open flames in the kitchen. You don't want him to blow up the camp."

Barry didn't catch up with the culprits that night, but the entire camp heard his tormented yells promising to visit a horrible revenge on his tormentors. Since all cookie boys were supposed to immediately clean up any messes that occurred in the dining hall, Barry was able to twist camp regulations to assist him in his vengeance. As soon as the food was on Barry and Dave's table, Barry would decorate the floor with ketchup or soup and then would summon the Morellos to wipe it up. "And clean it up right, or you'll be back to do it again," he said, imitating Yolanda. But the minute the servers turned their backs, another mess would mysteriously appear at Dave's end of the table, and back Richie and Bobby would come to clean that up.

This went on until Yolanda collared her cookie boys and snapped, "Enough with the soap and water. Come help serve: we're falling behind, and the food's getting cold."

Before long, though, these four nuts abandoned their vendetta and celebrated by treating the campers to a homemade chocolate nut cake, prepared by Bobby and Richie. It was, however, devoid of the hot peppers. Like I said, Richie and Bobby were the two best kitchen workers that Yolanda ever had, but of course, they were Italian.

Although many tricks were played on unsuspecting targets at our camp, I was not usually one of them, thank God. When I was, it was usually my wife who spearheaded the attack. One time, in fact the night Jeff received his first motorcycle, Theresa brought out a special gift for me as the camp celebration was winding down. The large box was exquisitely wrapped in lovely paper and just dripping ribbons. What a great present, I thought; then it struck me that the cheering was a little wild and that the air suddenly snapped with extra excite-

Cookie boy Morello escorting Ali to the dining hall.

ment. Thus, it was with more than normal caution that I began to slip off the ribbons. Almost immediately I felt a movement in the box as I tilted it, and something in it slid to one side, then shifted again. What the hell is this, I wondered as I pulled away the paper. Whatever it is, it's alive. Is Tracey giving me the puppy she's been pestering her mom about? Then my still-anonymous gift started shifting around in the box on its own, and in a most unpuppylike manner. No way in hell was I opening the box, let alone reach in to grab its contents. By now everyone in the hall was screaming with laughter. They kept assuring me that the present in the box was just beautiful and that I should reach in and pull it out. How dumb did they think I was? No way! I thought, as I rose and backed away from the table. Finally one of the counselors stepped forward and gently removed my gift from the box and presented it to me. It was a six-foot pine snake as wide as my wrist, and it was coiling itself around the counselor's arm in that possessive way snakes have with a prospective dinner. He kept saying, "Mr. Bragg, just touch it; he can't hurt you. These snakes are harmless!"

Of course, some wiseass had to shout, "Dump the snake on Mr. Bragg's head!" The snake charmer heard it too, and advanced toward me with a wicked gleam in his eye. But I nailed him before he could sign his own death warrant.

"You want to tag me with that snake, that's okay. But if it bites me, so help me, I'll break your jaw. So before you do anything rash, consider not being able to chew for three months!" Those few words made him reconsider the folly he was plotting.

Now I know there are people who get on television and assure us that spitting cobras and black mambas are beautiful creatures. Hell, they all but cuddle them. Me, I think these snake people are demented. Generally speaking, where snakes are concerned, I'm with Indiana Jones: he couldn't stand 'em, either.

So despite the pleading of a hundred voices to touch the damn thing, I kept backing up. And there was my beloved wife, laughing so hard that tears were pouring out of her pretty blue eyes.

Meanwhile, the counselor was busy comforting the snake. "Don't you worry, you can come stay with me."

Fine. They deserved each other. The thing was, not all the counselors knew that a snake had taken up residence in Cabin 7. The guy on cabin duty that night started making his midnight rounds and worked his way around to number 7. He told me later, "Here I am, making sure everybody's safe and sound, and then my flashlight beam hits the bunk in the corner, and I nearly drop dead. Here's this humongous snake coiled on the counselor's chest." He flew out of there, almost right through the screen door. "No more cabin duty for me," he told Barry. "I'll clean the bathhouse instead."

For several days after I backed off from the damn snake, I was the camp joke. The campers kept laughing and hollering, "Tarzan is afraid of snakes." But then an interesting incident occurred that restored my reputation to its former sheen. On Parents' Day, one mother had a frisky little dog on a leash, the sort of pooch that bounces and yaps ceaselessly. She entered the dining hall with her dog, and a counselor went to find her son. When he returned with the camper, the counselor had his pet snake coiled around his neck. The serpent glared at the fluffy thing that was bouncing around like a demon-possessed volleyball, barking urgently, alerting the world to the fact that there was a S-N-A-K-E in our midst. In one fluid motion, the snake slid off the counselor's neck and dropped to the floor. It immediately retreated to the corner where it coiled into a defensive posture. As the mother tugged her pooch to a neutral corner, the counselor reached out to retrieve his pet.

I have never seen a happy snake, not even in a photograph, but I could tell this one was mightily pissed. I yelled, "Look out!" but bang—in just the blink of an eye—the snake bit the counselor on his hand.

The kid looked stunned, and glanced over to me for help. I knew the bite was indeed harmless. Hell, the counselor had told me so himself. "Don't worry," I said. "Pine snakes aren't poisonous, remember?" I had one of the other counselors take him to the hospital, but I couldn't resist razzing the snake charmer a tad more. "The worst that can happen is that the bite might get infected, and your hand might swell, but the doctor will take care of that. Let's hope he doesn't have to amputate."

One of the other counselors who was into snakes removed our bad-tempered guest from his corner. He released him in the woods a couple of miles from camp, much to the relief of the other counselors. When the snake's former landlord returned from the hospital, he was a much-chastened kid. Maybe it was the shot the doctor gave him, but I never heard him mention snakes again. The entire camp had to bust on him, though. "How's the hand, Nature Boy? Has it fallen off yet?" Anyhow, Tarzan didn't look quite so foolish, so all turned out well. This incident showed the kids that where nature was concerned, you had to be aware of the law of the jungle, even if you were in the middle of New Jersey.

In addition to the satisfaction Theresa and I felt at the intellectual and social growth our campers made, we had the added plus of watching our own kids mature tremendously. All our nephews as well as our kids spent time at the camp learning responsibility and integrating themselves into the camp system. I was proud of the way my two sons, Mark and Jeff, shouldered their various responsibilities. Not that they weren't above goofing off on occasion. But Theresa and I both knew the overwhelming feeling of being on call at the camp for the entire camping season, so we were more than ready to cut them some slack. Both Mark and his cousin Mike eventually became counselors, but of course that engendered a whole new set of problems. Most of the campers enjoyed buddying up to the owner's kin. But there were a few who did not.

Whether it was coursing testosterone or just plain jealousy, I don't know, but there were kids who needled Mark and Mike incessantly. Others picked fights. Of course, physical confrontations were not that unusual among the campers, and when they occurred, our solution was simple and invariably cleared the air. We'd have 'em put on the boxing gloves and go at it, hell for leather, for a few minutes. If we merely broke it up, the combatants would be at each other all day, and we'd develop a champion-sized headache. Boxing was a good safety valve, and since we encouraged the antagonists to keep at it until both their hostility and energy were spent, it dissipated the situation. With the gloves on, nobody could do that much damage, and harmony would be restored to our domain. If it wasn't, we'd have a three-round bout at the campfire. Each period was two minutes long, and when it was over, the other campers would crown the winner by their applause. God help the pugilist who didn't accept the verdict of the camp, for instead of one opponent, he'd face a hundred.

Understand, Mike was a peaceable kid, perhaps too much so. Then one day he and an older camper really got into it. The camper was a helluva lot bigger and really poured on the punches, but I had a gut feeling that the fight would be epochal for Mike. He looked over to me, as if for support, but I said, "This is your battle. Fight back!" Suddenly my nephew yells, "That son of a gun just bit my arm!" and he looked over to his big Uncle Don for salvation.

"Then bite him back," I said.

Well, that day Mike became a young man. Charging his opponent like an infuriated bull, he kind of went wild, raining blows on the camper's head and midsection. After Mike tagged him with a right hook to the jaw, the other kid backed away. He'd had enough. After that, nobody fooled with Mike.

He went on in high school to become a member of the Delaware Valley all-star football team in two positions, linebacker as well as center. He had scholarships first to Vanderbilt and later on to Temple University. Mike's dad—my brother Bill—and I often reflected on that summer. Bill would say, "He came home from camp with so much confidence and maturity. From then on he dug into his life, his studies, and his sport as he'd never done before." We agreed that the Kamp Olympik experience was a real turning point for the young man. Well, that was the whole point of the camp: it was an environment that was conducive to truly growing up while having fun.

Mark had his share of boxing encounters and held his own pretty well, although he was more tenacious than talented in the art of fisticuffs. He just wouldn't give up. He especially enjoyed the bouts at the campfires where his audience appreciated his maniac style of boxing.

Like his brother, Jeff also was limited in his boxing techniques. But the kids named him The Closer, for though he might lose the first round or two, he always dominated the last one. Once, when he was taking a good beating, his mother told me, "Honey, stop the fight. It's over."

So I asked Jeff, "You ready to quit?"

He shook his head. "Nah, I'm okay."

Soothing his anxious mom, I said, "No, there's one more round; let's let Jeff finish this one."

The next round Jeff got in a roundhouse punch to the head, and, headgear not-withstanding, the other guy plummeted to the ground. My second son's confidence bounded to new heights, something we really didn't need. After winning this fight he was unstoppable—at least on his motorcycle—and started attempting even more daring jumps and stunts. I remember Theresa looking daggers at me one time as she put an ice bag on a huge bump on his shin. "If you'd only stopped that darn fight when I asked you to ..." she said. I knew what she meant, but Jeff's skill as a rider proved to be its own corrective. He figured out if he didn't change his approach to his cycle style, he'd be spending most of his time being patched up, not riding. So in a way it was a turning point for him and got him on the path to real excellence in his chosen sport, though he still ended up in the hospital every so often.

When I purchased the land that was to be the site of Theresa's and my dream home, I realized that the property, just down the road from the camp, would be ideal for another purpose: overnight campouts for the older campers. These kids were approaching adulthood and needed extra activities in addition to their normal camp schedule. An overnight apart from the younger campers would give them a heightened sense of being grown up. My new property had its own lake, and from there they could explore the back lakes and surrounding woods that were filled with wildlife. I thought it would be a win-win situation. But I'd miscalculated the power of negativity: some local folks didn't have a clue about what we were trying to do.

I simply couldn't comprehend their attitude. The part of Penns Grove where I'd grown up was full of black kids. They were my playmates, my buddies. When I started competing at track and field events, again, I was surrounded by African American athletes. We bonded as competitors, as equals, and as friends. So when people got all antsy about skin color, I knew they were nuts.

Unfortunately, the property was located in a township that didn't like the idea of black people running around in their woods. As soon as these folks got wind of the overnight campouts on my property, they began to interfere with the innocent fun of well-supervised young people. One night, the campers got a none-too-friendly visit by the town fire department. Without ceremony, the firemen doused the fire and claimed it was a violation during the dry season, a rule that hadn't been strictly enforced prior to this. Luckily, I arrived just after the fire brigade did, and I was able to help keep things civil. Theresa didn't believe this when I told her, but I saw to it that nobody said or did anything that could be misinterpreted. Being able to talk louder and faster than anybody else comes in handy from time to time. Anyhow, everything turned out all right, but the kids couldn't have their campfire. This certainly put a damper on the excursion. Hell, they could sit around in the dark on their own front steps back home. So from then on, whenever we scheduled an overnight, I applied for a campfire permit. Boy, what a runaround. They'd deny the permit, but when I cited the fact that the private campgrounds across the road from our property could get campfire permits, they'd reluctantly approve ours. The area grudgingly permitted our type of city program—why wouldn't they? I paid a handsome tax on the property. But they weren't about to cooperate in making the camp experience better for kids who weren't just like them.

Trouble was also surfacing in another area. Bureaucrats behaving autocratically toward kids who'd never done a thing to anybody in the community was annoying. But if you weren't born in the Pinelands, you stayed an outsider. So every time our counselors had a day off, they had to run a menacing gauntlet that would've tested the most seasoned warrior. And these counselors were just teenagers.

Whenever our counselors had a day off, they had to catch a bus to go back to Newark or Jersey City. The bus stop was on Route 9, which ran right through the middle of town, so one of the senior staff would drop them off. But the minute we drove away, the local punks descended on the waiting counselors. It started with name-calling and racial slurs, and the counselors just took it, determined not to be baited. They knew if they caused any trouble, they'd answer to me. So they never said a word about what was going on, not even when the confrontations got physical. Eventually Barry Ross informed me of the situation. So one day I dropped off the counselors and drove away like I was going back to camp. But then I doubled back and parked just around the corner from the bus stop. Nobody saw the six counselors who were hiding in the back of the truck. All seven of us crouched down out of sight and waited.

We didn't have to wait long. Several trucks tore up and slammed to the curb beside the bus stop. The township tough guys jumped out of the vehicles and started throwing punches at our young men. The seven of us lying in wait came charging in with an angry roar. We must've looked pretty fierce because the local gang took one look at us and dispersed faster than a flock of geese at first blast of a shotgun. Our guys cheered and high-fived each other. This incident created a fraternity among our counselors, and the sense of unity became evident in the way they handled their duties at camp from then on. Less petty razzing, and more teamwork.

Now this was good, but I didn't leave it at that. We'd made friends with a few of the state troopers, especially the only black trooper in the area. I let them know what was going on, and not only did they patrol the area more frequently, they'd cruise by and stop and talk to the counselors as they waited for the bus. This gave the counselors a heightened sense of security. I was certain that the town busybodies would spread the word throughout the Pines not to mess with the boys again. For they weren't just messing with a few vulnerable teenagers, they'd be taking on team Kamp Olympik, and that was formidable indeed.

As the camp grew in size, we tried to ramp up the variety of activities we offered. In addition to the first-rate academic program, we offered basketball, softball, and volleyball. There was motorcycling, Tarzan-ville, arts and crafts, and nature study. The swimming and boating classes were always popular, and there was a waiting list for the evening lifeguarding class for advanced swimmers, including counselors. Games of action like Capture the Flag and Hare and Hounds were a must, the first thing returning campers asked about.

All these things were an integral part of the daily schedule, which Theresa and I pains-takingly worked out as if it were the most complex algebraic equation. Now my father-in-law had acquired a large brass bell that had been used on a company locomotive at DuPont where he'd worked. He gave it to us, and we mounted it near the dining hall. It was ideal, not only for alerting the staff to emergencies, but for keeping the camp run-ning on schedule. When that thing rang, the entire camp reverberated with the sound. The excuse "I didn't hear the bell," just didn't wash at Kamp Olympik.

If the schedule's complexity made the life of the counselors difficult, the necessity of keeping it flexible drove them nuts. Why flexibility? First of all, because we were dealing with kids. Second, because searing-hot or stormy weather could throw us a curve. Now I've had potential counselors act like camp owners were doing them some humongous favor by paying 'em to play for the summer. But our camp was real life, not some Hollywood screwball comedy.

By the end of the third day of camp, a few counselors always quit, a few got fired, but the ones who stayed pretty much earned their doctorate in child care. The experi-ence of being responsible for ten little kids every minute of every day was a bit of a shock, but by the end of day three these teenagers began to morph into grown-ups.

Here's what goes on in a typical day in the life of a counselor:

He wakes up just as the sun is rising, about 6:00 am. The humidity's already about 80 percent, and the temperature is rising fast. It should hit the low nineties before noon. His nose tells him that one of his kids got hit with a bout of diarrhea and didn't make it to the can. He notices the screen by his bed has a rip in it about the same time mosquito bites all over his body demand to be scratched. Oh, yeah, two kids were roughhousing by the window the previous night. He makes a mental note to get the screen repaired before nightfall as he wakes the kid with the odiferous bunk and starts him cleaning it up. Now our counselor hotfoots it to the bathhouse, tears through a quick cleanup routine, and finds a place at the urinal while twenty voices are urging him to hurry the hell up.

He does hurry because cabin inspection will take place during breakfast, and everything had better be tidy. First thing, he scoots the sleepy kid who has waiter duty toward the dining room so he can set the cabin's table. The smelly bunk is outside being scrubbed down with detergent, and kids are making up their bunks, sweeping the floor, and lining up their shoes in even lines. The counselor glances at the time and herds his charges to breakfast as the bell starts pealing. Though he isn't quite awake enough to eat yet, our guy shovels in the food: it's gonna seem like a thousand years 'til lunch at noon. His stomach is in knots while he waits for the inspection report after breakfast. He knows that if the cabin fails, it'll draw the crappy duty of bathhouse cleanup or garbage pickup, and the kids won't be happy. With an admonition to the waiter to remember to stay and clean up the table, he checks to see if any of his kids are crowding around Mrs. Bragg for sick call. Since none of our counselor's kids are at sick call, he sets out for the first activity period as the next bell rings.

If his first activity is a tutorial period, he's got to be on his toes, since he's assisting the teacher. Besides, some of his kids are really beginning to get it. A catnap would go down great, but the teacher asks him to give some extra help to the little kid with glasses who's way behind in his reading level. Now the second bell rings and our counselor is hoping he draws softball. It's a nice easy game, and it can be pleasant to doze in the shade of a compassionate tree when nothing is going on. But today it's basketball, and the counselors are fully engaged in it. Not only is there no nap, but our guy has to deal with jabs in the ribs from the macho types who want to show off their athletic ability. He's hoping the camp owner cruises by and deals with the wild men, telling them to tone it down, but that ain't happenin' this morning. So he's bouncing around trying to keep track of the kids and his fellow counselors' elbows. But he has yet more problems to deal with.

If it's a sunny day, the sweat starts to drip down the counselor's arms and legs by midmorning. If it should be cloudy, there's an even greater treat in store: deerflies and strawberry flies! The damn things swoop down for their daily Dracula cocktail hour, leaving little bloody zits on any exposed skin.

Memo to self: use the doggone insect repellent Mom gave me!

By now he's starving and praying for the lunch bell, when it'll be his turn to grab a bite out of something instead of being the bait for swarms of flies. When it does ring, he collects his kids and goes in to eat. And I do mean eat—anything he can get his hands on that isn't on fire. Veggies, salad, pasta, meat, dessert, he wolfs it all down without being told. And people used to call him a fussy eater!

Now the hectic activity yields to quiet in the rest period after lunch. But for the counselor, it's business as usual. Some of his campers are still jumping around, agitating for a game of tag, and he has to go sit on them: they're his kids. So much for downtime.

During afternoon tutorial, he helps a kid understand his fractions, and that feels great, but as soon as class is over, things get really frenetic, with everybody wanting to do as many fun things as possible, since school is out for the day. Yesterday, he was stationed in Tarzanville to give the less adept swingers a hand if they needed it. Today our guy signs out the canoes and rowboats, always with a gaggle of kids at his elbow, wanting to chat. He obliges them. Relationships are the backbone of the camp, and he knows it. He looks hopefully at his watch. The afternoon ends with general swim time. Since he's not assigned lifeguard duty, maybe he'll be able to chill out and just relax on the beach. But he also knows some other counselor will probably challenge him to a swim race or to flips off the high dive. Since the honor of the cabin rides on his performance, he'll have to rise to the occasion.

Swim period comes and goes, and he rounds up his campers, and then gets them back to the cabin to hop into some dry clothes and get ready for dinner. Once our guy gobbles whatever's on his plate and maybe a few bites of the table itself, the pressure is off—kind of. If he's assigned to an activity station, he'll be keeping an eye on the campers, or he might be doling out the sweet treats at the canteen. If not, he'll probably challenge somebody to a basketball game. The counselor has gotten his second or third wind by now and may have to throw himself into campfire duty if it's his turn. That gets the adrenaline flowing again. There's always a "best campfire" competition between cabins, and the counselor may want his kids to show up a rival cabin. That cabin's pathetic campfire the night before is begging for a put-down. But tonight our counselor is free 'til lights-out. He's with the kids during campfire; then there's something else to do: a bunch of counselors challenge each other to a game of basketball. Like all the counselors, he's competitive as all get-out, so he shrugs off any fatigue he might feel and joins in the game. The game stops at lights-out at 11:00 p.m., when the owner comes galloping over, bellowing for them to turn the damn lights off and go to bed.

Since his empty stomach has started rumbling again, our counselor skedaddles over to the dining hall, where Yolanda is setting out dinner leftovers. Or a bunch of counselors may risk Mama Fiore's wrath by sending out for a pizza. Thus, the stage is set for a repeat performance of his wild day as soon as the sun comes up again.

At first, seeing all that those kids accomplished had me in utter awe of their energy and dedication. I couldn't imagine ever keeping up with them. Then I'd remember the time when I was a kid myself, when both golden dawn and silver moonlight were too precious to be squandered on sleep. At night at Kamp Olympik, though, as I started walking the grounds, I could still hear some of the counselors in animated conversation as if the day had been a serene walk in the forest. When I finally headed back to my cabin, I'd invariably find a few of them hunkered down around the remains of the campfire, mesmerized

Staff looking their best with Ali.

by the last glowing embers. I could hear fragments of the deep-down stories that flow most easily when men sense their shared humanity, with all the frailty, power, and potential that implies.

It was a treat to watch the counselors grow up right under my nose. The most interesting thing, from my point of view, though, was the transformation of these young people from self-involved teenagers into responsible protectors of the children put in their care. And the campers bloomed as they realized they were being cared for in this strange woodsy environment. The beauty of the whole scenario was that, instead of a couple of hundred individuals, the inhabitants of Kamp Olympik gradually evolved into family. Counselors were the big brothers who watched over the campers, who in turn adulated their young mentors. After several days, the routine became an agenda for fun, the clanging bell its herald. So any young man who took on these overwhelming job requirements and survived was unique. It only took a few seasons for me to realize that I wasn't doing these young men a favor by giving them summer jobs. They were doing me a tremendous favor by working at Kamp Olympik. They became ordained members of the Knights of the Forest, the most elite fraternity in the world.

Yet being a member of this fraternity could have painful repercussions sometimes. Take our one foray into organized football. One of the by-products of dredging out the beach was a terrific new playing area for Kamp Olympik, once we pushed all the fill from the dredging into the adjoining marshland, filling it in and reclaiming it for camp use. I reasoned that the newly turned sand—plus the gravel and few stones it also contained—would make a great field for softball, soccer, dodgeball, and anything that required a soft landing. For good measure, I installed two cedar posts at each end of the field. By topping them with two-by-four crosspieces, I'd created goal posts, a nice professional touch. These would be handy for any camper who hankered to practice kicking field goals. Then Andy pointed out the array of cedar stumps protruding from the sandy fill: most inconvenient to plough into head first. So we hauled the stumps out and were in business.

With such a fine facility available, we decided to inaugurate the Olympik Bowl at the end of the season. Kamp Olympik's First Annual Touch Football Classic would be played on this nice fluffy surface.

The campers thought this was a great idea and enthusiastically lined the sidelines as the two teams ran onto the field. Rich, our camp director, captained one team, seconded by his brothers, Magoo and Andy. Leading the opposition, I depended on Assistant Director Barry and his redoubtable friend Dave as the mainstays of my team. Rich and I then each chose six of our oldest and biggest counselors, which brought the tally for each team up to nine players. Somebody had to give us grief about that, of course. "Football, my ass. You've only got nine players each, and it looks like you're playing tag. Why don't you play girls-rules baseball?" I think Barry shoved the naysayer into the lake. Anyhow, we quickly organized our supposed touch football game, to the delight of the campers. The kids chose sides and cheered and hollered their lungs out, urging their team on to victory just like at a regular professional game.

Only problem was with the "touch" part of our game. Everybody who was playing rationalized that touching surely included tackling, pounding, chewing on, and sitting upon the opposition. Otherwise it *was* a sissy-type girls' game. But everybody was proud of getting battered and wore their wounds like badges of honor, as soon as the contusions stopped throbbing. Looking back on this gridiron classic, I'd say we scored more injuries than the entire NFL that year.

I quarterbacked my team, with Barry and Dave as my receivers. This sounds more impressive than perhaps it was. Barry was too short to be any good for receptions. When he got in position and looked around for me, all he saw were the armpits of the opposing guards as they intercepted the damn ball. Dave was tall enough, but he couldn't catch the ball to save his life. He said the shape was funny. Tell that to Peyton Manning!

Rich approached the game with his usual complex military strategy, which I'd say went right over the heads of half of his players. But I got a kick out of his super-serious attitude, and he usually did mine some fine precision playing out of his guys. His biggest stroke of genius was assigning his brother Magoo to chase me no matter where I went on the field. Magoo did just that, though with the difference in our weight, it was like a Chihuahua trying to bring down the mailman. But despite the fact that he couldn't stop me, he'd wrap himself around one of my legs and stay there. No matter how hard I tried to shake him, Magoo hung on like a limpet. So there I'd be, trying to pass to my short star receiver, the one who couldn't see where I was. Or I might try a pass to my tall receiver who was allergic to the shape of the ball. If I tried to scramble, I had this leech named Magoo growling like a Bears lineman down around my knees. I looked like Long John Silver, hobbling around, desperately looking for the treasure, which was any damn pass receiver downfield who might possibly catch the football. The rest of my team kind of milled around tackling the opposing guards. Or each other—just so they smashed into somebody.

When we were on defense, it wasn't much better. Rich organized his center as if it were a martial arts contest, and even Bruce Lee would've had a tough time getting at the passer. Unlike me, Rich's quarterback didn't have an Italian cement boot to lug around: *he* could run.

We did have a couple of referees, but they both were betting on the game, and football purists might frown on that. But hell, each one was betting on a different team, so we assumed their preferences would sort of cancel each other out.

Anyhow, we weren't quite following an NFL playbook. If a play to the sidelines went out of bounds, nobody stopped the game. We were out there to win, not play nice. The players would continue tackling and fighting for the ball 'til nobody could move. Once they galumphed out of bounds and right into the racks of canoes and rowboats—the first time my canoes were ever damaged on land. It was great fun sorting that one out, since players were entangled with life vests and each other, and bits of paddles protruded jauntily from various parts of their anatomies. Occasionally when unscrambling these sideline pileups, we'd come upon an entirely unexpected face. "Who the hell are you? You on my team?"

"No sir," a voice squeaked. "I'm just a camper from Cabin 11."

"What the hell are you doing here? You should be with the rest of the campers."

"But I wanted to get a piece of the action. It's a great game!"

A true fan! "Get your butt back to the sidelines and stay out of the game," I roared with some regret. Hell, I wanted to recruit him on the spot.

If we ran out of bounds on the other side of the field, the play would end up in the cedar swamp, on top of stumps, rotten trees, smashed frogs, and a few snakes. That's the only time I ever saw the camp staff unafraid of snakes, when they were in hot pursuit of a righteous tackle.

A few times, even with the ref's whistle proclaiming a dead ball, the play continued past the sidelines, spilling all the way to the bulkhead, then off into the lake. This never stopped the game. I think the refs called an unofficial time-out for a water break.

Now about that nice, fluffy, sandy field we were playing on. As big vehement feet pounded the surface, the sand precipitated to the bottom, revealing the malignant nature of our playing surface. Not only were we playing on impacted gravel, the gravel was dotted with stones. Big ones. So we were basically playing on a concrete surface pocked every few inches with jagged stones. What more could you ask of a playing field?

With concrete to contend with underfoot, nobody thought too much about the fouls that were being committed every second. If every personal foul that was perpetrated during that game had been called by a ref, we'd have had no time to play. There were foul-ups on every play, with players punching, biting, gouging, and twisting things that weren't meant to be twisted. When I was tackled, it was like being buried in a mound of ferocious dogs, each one determined to get his teeth into the meat I was holding. Sorry, I meant the football. But I developed a new respect for dog biscuits that day.

Part of the ferocity was due to the fact that they were using the field as a venue for payback. Anybody who'd ever dumped some odious chore on another guy or was more dangerous on the basketball court or always got to the fried chicken first at chow was fair game. It was even worse than suicide ball, with each guy determined to prove his toughness by beating the hell out of everybody else. My guys took their share of hard knocks. But though we laughed at Rich's Napoleonic approach with his team, we soon realized he was consistently outmaneuvering us.

Then somebody rang the big camp bell to signal the last play of the game, and my team controlled the ball. Barry ran up and pulled me aside. "Listen, Dave and I've worked out a secret play. This is one time the old Statue of Liberty play will be unstoppable."

"Yeah, I know that one," I said, heading for my place behind the center. "I raise my arm like I'm about to pass, you come around from behind me, take the ball, then run around the other end. Like a fake pass."

"Nope, this is Dave's and my own creation, a guaranteed winner. Just throw the ball to me."

"If I could ever see you, that might work, but I can't, so …" My protest was cut short.

"You'll see me this time, I promise."

Since it was the last play of the game, I thought, what the hell, why not?

The center hiked the ball, I grabbed it, and as usual, Magoo was right on me like a flea on a dog's butt. I floundered around struggling with Magoo, and I almost went down, but at the last minute, I spotted Barry. He was at least five feet above the other players, standing on Dave's shoulders right at the goal line. I spiraled the ball right into his hands, and I was sure they were going to score. The other team, however, saw this going on and attacked the dynamic duo like locusts. Slowly, like a giant tree being felled in the forest, the double-decker statue tumbled to the ground. Barry went headfirst into our abrasive playing field, dropping the ball for a fumble at about the three-yard line. The whistle blew, and the timer announced that the game was over. But the only sound we heard was a continuous chant from Rich's team. "Timberrrrr. We decapitated the giant!"

After what seemed like days of heroic struggling in the heat of late summer, we finished the game with a tie, the worst scenario possible.

And what's so bad about that?

Because every player was bragging about the special play when they really nailed somebody, but nobody had a victory to claim for true superiority. In addition, the campers couldn't wait to play Monday quarterback, changing the play calls, especially for those plays that ended upside down in the cedar swamp.

Even worse, all of us who'd played were limping and moaning our way through the camp activities for days. Lifting anything heavier than toilet paper was an impossible task. The camp was filled with the sound of suffering, as the owners of over-exerted muscles beaten black and blue cried for mercy. The bottom line was that the counselors and senior staff weren't worth a hill of beans. Theresa, who had to take up the slack for everybody, had a few well-chosen words about macho boys, and the blue fire in her eyes made it clear that she included me among them. And my dear wife wasn't done yet. "As a matter of fact, this is going to be the last time you play that game at this camp." She glared at us. "I mean it."

I beg your pardon? Standing tall as I could with my ricked back, twisted ankle, and throbbing knees scarred with Magoo's tooth and claw marks, I said, "We'll see about that. What I say goes." Theresa didn't say anything; she just gave me a scary hint of a Mona Lisa smile, and walked away.

Even now, as I write this, those nostalgic memories come back in force, and the memories are even better than the original. This time there isn't any pain, just a great adrenaline high!

Theresa: *And there are no great big pains in the neck for me to nurse back to sanity.*

Chapter Fourteen

During the first week of any of the three-week camp sessions, we let the campers get acclimated to both camp routine and its physical layout. Once they got the rules of the camp and the lay of the land down pat, we introduced two all-out games, Capture the Flag and Hares and Hounds, both of which involved all the campers. The first was a game of strategy for two immense teams. The second, Hares and Hounds, was a competition: campers versus counselors and staff. The kids had to chase down the counselors 'til they caught them or the counselors made it to home base, their sanctuary. They couldn't go charging right into home base, however. In order to prolong the game and make it more fun, the Hares had to let the Hounds pursue them for at least a half hour before attempting their run to safety.

It was a helluva lot of fun for everyone, but of course, Kamp Olympik had to develop its own set of rules to keep chaos at bay. The Hares had two defensive weapons, their speed and the Wading River, which all campers, that is, Hounds, were forbidden to enter. Each Hare wore a flag football belt to which their flags were attached by Velcro. They popped off the second somebody grabbed them, something the smallest camper could do—and did—during the game. Of course, it didn't take long for the campers to realize that if they all plastered themselves around the perimeter of the basketball court, no Hares could ever get home free. The minute they came in sight, the Hounds could tackle them and strip off their flags. What we'd end up with was the entire complement of campers guarding home base, with the staff and counselors skulking around in the bushes, waiting for their chance to charge home. And that wasn't going to happen, not before everybody in camp died of old age while waiting around. Since Hares and Hounds isn't a game that tolerates a stalemate, I drew a hundred-foot circle around the basketball court and announced that no one could enter it unless in hot pursuit of a counselor. I ruined the Hounds' defensive strategy, but the game became more fun and with a helluva lot more action as the Hounds got into the spirit of the chase.

But this game wasn't only played for glory. Any Hound who caught a Hare collected a carefully calculated bounty of Popsicles or candy bars. To establish the rate of payout upon capture, we'd rate the Hares according to their speed and their ranking in the camp hierarchy, and then translate that into candy bars. I am still proud that when I played the game, I was valued at ten candy bars per flag. With his tendency to pack on the pounds, our camp director Rich could make the earth tremble when he ran, but any camper, even one with two twisted ankles, could catch him with ease. He was our no-candy man. Since he couldn't run worth shit, he was detailed to officiate, something he did with great style as the field marshal on his trusty Honda cycle.

We assembled everybody in the cabin area, and our Hounds would be foaming at the mouth in expectation. They weren't lusting after the blood of the soon-to-be vanquished, however, just savoring the luscious taste of those candy bars they'd be winning presently. After Rich and I each gave a final warning to the Hounds not to go near the river, Rich solemnly rang the camp bell, and the game was on. The Hares got a fifty-yard start, with the Hounds shrieking with mounting excitement. The ear-piercing scream that went up from the Hounds as they started the chase was truly bloodcurdling to us Hares, enough to put the fear of God in our hearts and the wings of Mercury on our feet. But there was one particular session of Hares and Hounds that was especially memorable.

As the counselors scattered to their planned escape routes through blueberry fields, cranberry bogs, swamps, and plain old woods, I pounded down a deer path, cut across a cedar swamp, and slowly worked my way back to the dense sticker patch behind the cabin area. From there I intended to get to the river and slip across it. My roundabout route was about a mile long, but I could've done it blindfolded after doing the same thing every session with success. What made it nerve wracking was the continuous howling of the kids—menacing as air raid sirens. That sound was an undulating scream in our ears, fading and growing louder as they picked up the Hares' trail. And the sound was getting closer by the minute. Every so often I'd hear a spike in the clamor of the pursuers, and I knew another Hare had bought it. Not that I was surprised: some of the older campers could run like the wind. Their speed and youthful stamina overtook the slower Hares, and these speedy Hounds popped their victims' flags only five minutes into the game. But they hadn't gotten me. Not yet.

The playing field for this game was huge—all of Kamp Olympik's grounds, plus the contiguous areas of the state forest. The state forest only gave us extra maneuvering room, however, since the heart of the game was the basketball court, and nobody wanted to hike miles away from it—and then back. But if you've got two, three hundred Hounds fanning out in such a space, you practically trip over one every time you turn around. Since I quickly veered off the normal deer paths, however, the Hounds would be less likely to spot me when I reached the river. After I'd gone three-quarters of a mile, I crouched beside a ragged blueberry bush and listened. The sound of excited voices floated down the wind, so I dropped to the ground, burrowed deep into the leaf mold, and waited. Somebody laughed a stone's throw away from me, and then the voices faded into the ambient silence. Like a shadow, I rose and crept toward the soft sounds of gently moving water. It only took me a few minutes to wade across, and I began to move upstream until I was facing the other side of home base. If the vigilance of the home guard Hounds was aimed at the section of woods into which the Hares had disappeared at that first bell, they wouldn't notice my stealthy approach from the other side.

Then I was in my sweet spot, opposite the small island that would screen my reentrance into the water from the opposite shore. There wasn't a sound anywhere near me, but I still slipped into the water as slowly as I could. All I needed was one loud *kerplop* and I'd be up to my armpits in Hounds. Once safely in the brown water, I submerged up to my eyes, bobbing higher only when I had to breathe. Or chuckle. Hell, using my unorthodox water route, I was as good as home free!

I was just coming abreast of the island when a movement in the water caught my eye. Turning quickly, I recognized the telltale ripples of a swimming snake. Terrific—my least favorite of God's creatures was coming straight at me. It was just a water snake, taking a jaunt to find a quick midafternoon snack. But I couldn't assume I was not on its bill of fare. What if the damn thing wanted a sociable nibble of my nose as it went by? Want to or not, I knew I'd raise a ruckus that'd advertise my position to everyone in the county. Comforting myself that it didn't seem to be paying any attention to me, I relaxed a little. Too much. Voices down at our beach area alerted me to the presence of Hounds. Their voices pinged over the surface of the water.

"No, you didn't! You're dreaming," somebody said.

"No way. I heard something out there in the water." I watched, holding my breath as several pairs of eyes began to scope along the dark water, heading toward my location. I sank down into the murky depths, hoping whatever showed above the waterline would pass for a bird's nest or a really fat leaf. Then I felt other, colder eyes on me. Yup, my slithery swimming buddy had seen me. He seemed to hesitate—do snakes tread water?—considering what to do about me, his sliver of a tongue darting in and out. I was truly on the horns of a forked-tongue dilemma. If I got the hell out of there, the way every cell in my body was telling me to, the Hounds would pounce on me immediately. If I stayed put, that snake could have its way with my nose, not a pleasant fate for something that had served me well for so many years. Collecting as much saliva as I had at my disposal, I sent a shower of spit in the snake's direction. It kind of jogged to one side, but kept coming. Just then one of the Hares made his move to reach home base from the other side near Tarzanville. With shrieks of delight, the Hounds tore after him. I let fly at the snake once more, and this time I think my spitball tagged him. He gave me one dirty look, as if to say, "There goes the neighborhood," and glided majestically past me. Spitting is a great defense technique and must be learned by all; it's very effective, even if it is a little sloppy.

With the attention of all the Hounds I could see riveted in the opposite direction, I decided to make my move before I had any more uninvited guests. I swam quietly to Kamp Olympik's bank, heaved myself out of the water, and sprinted toward home base. Though I outran the nearest defenders, they hounded me all the way into the sanctuary of home base, ripping my flags off with undisguised glee. I let them keep those purloined flags just to be a nice guy. And because I was grateful that a certain wandering snake hadn't tried to make a meal out of my nose.

Along with three other captured Hares, I waited on the court as the others tried to reach base. Ears of corn would've had a better chance against a swarm of locusts. The minute any Hare showed up, he was mobbed immediately. We commiserated as we waited for the end of the game. Some of the counselors had hidden a hundred feet away in the swamp, waiting for over an hour for the right opportunity to race home. Dave commented sourly, "These bloody mosquitoes in the swamps don't wait for nighttime to start feeding. I'm bitten all over, including my eyeballs and under my toenails. I hope we've got plenty of calamine lotion: I plan to drink a few bottles, then take a bath in it."

We laughed as we compared our battle scars. Bug bites, a few ticks, a couple million scratches, a few cuts, and an accumulation of smelly bodies was all the damage the Hares had incurred. But a handful of counselors hadn't been caught, or seen in quite a while, and time was running out. At the last minute, we saw the guy who delivered our bread pulling his truck up by the dining hall, a couple of hundred feet away. As he swung open the back of the truck, the missing counselors spurted out, sending loaves of bread flying. With impossible speed they raced for the court, legs pumping, teeth clenched with exertion. Speedy Barry Ross made it home free, but the others were deluged by a wave of campers.

The captured counselors were mightily pissed. "Hell, if that guy had just driven by the court like we told him to, we'd have made it." What they were really mad about was the fact that they'd lost their bet with Barry that they'd make it home, and he wouldn't. And they'd have to pay up.

"Why didn't he drive you right to home base? Didn't you bribe him?" asked one of the Hares who'd been nabbed a few minutes after the starting bell sounded.

"We did," came the indignant reply, "but he said it wasn't enough to take on that mob!" He pointed to the dancing, jubilant crowd of campers. "He said he was afraid they'd grab him and destroy his bread truck. Hell, it's still loaded with more deliveries."

Who could argue with that?

At the insistence of the reproachful campers, however, I immediately amended the rules to include "No bread trucks." It wasn't exactly the Code of Hammurabi, but that's how the Hares and Hounds rules evolved—on the spot. We were still waiting for the last two counselors when the bell announced the end of the game and the beginning of dinner. I was concerned but knew some Hares invariably got lost. They always wandered into camp eventually.

When dinner was almost over, the phone rang, and I hear Walt Priest's matter-of-fact voice on the line. "Don, I got a couple of youngsters here, and they're all beat up and wore out. I found 'em creepin' around a cranberry bog. They say they belong to you. Shall I have 'em walk home or drop 'em off in my truck? Like I said, they're dead on their feet."

Good Lord, the kids must've gone over ten miles—and through some rugged terrain. I knew this for a fact because I hunt this section of the forest. "Would you drive the kids back? I'd appreciate it, and I know they would."

Half an hour later, the missing counselors were climbing out of Walt's truck. "How'd you get way out by Walt's place?" I asked. "That's one helluva run."

"Sorry, Mr. Bragg. But there was one camper hot on our trail. Whenever we rested for even an instant, he was on top of us. After about an hour he lost us and disappeared. By then, though, we were good and lost. We could hear the noise of cars and trucks from the road. It was pretty faint, but we walked toward that. Then Mr. Priest found us. And we've still got our flags."

"Who was tailing you?" I demanded. But they had no idea. So I addressed the dining hall. "I hear that one of you went on quite a trek and gave these two counselors a real workout. Who was it?"

Looking as if he didn't know what I planned to do to him, a young boy raised his hand and said, "Me, I guess."

Suddenly everything became quite clear to me. "Aren't you one of the Mays boys? Isn't your uncle Charlie Mays?" The little one nodded cautiously. I turned to the chagrined counselors, clearly embarrassed at being hounded by such a young camper. "Listen, his uncle qualified for three separate Olympic teams as a sprinter and long jumper. So you managed to dodge a pretty fast kid with the genes of a champion." This pleased the counselors, and when I presented their flags to Charlie's nephew, he beamed with pleasure and pride. All in all it was a great ending to an exhilarating day, except for Theresa. As Kamp Olympik's chief medical officer, she was up to her eyebrows in cuts, splinters, and bug bites, especially on the counselors. I don't know what the big deal was. "Count yourself lucky, Honey," I said. "At least there weren't any broken bones, and only a pint or two of blood spilled. That's nothing."

> **Cautioned not to do certain things, we continue to defy the warnings.**
>
> **Who suffers if we not listen?**
>
> —*Don Bragg, "Warnings"*

So you can understand why the first thing returning campers would ask when they arrived at camp was "When do we play Hares and Hounds?" Like Capture the Flag, we scheduled a game of Hares and Hounds once in every three-week session—until a horrendous incident nearly ended Hares and Hounds for good at Kamp Olympik. It was late one Friday afternoon in our fifth year at the camp, and I was hanging around the basketball court with a few of the captured counselors waiting for the last of the Hares to make a break for the safety of home base. The remaining Hounds were pacing back and forth, hungry for fresh meat, when one of them muttered as he walked by our group, "Well, I guess Willie is gone."

The counselors and I wheeled as one, demanding, "Willie who?"

"Dunno his last name, but he went into the river," the kid said in a shaky voice as he pointed downriver. "He went under and never came up." Nearly choking on the unsaid question "Why didn't you tell us right away?" I raced away, an icy feeling in the pit of my stomach. The youngster's trembling finger had been pointing toward one of the most hazardous sections of the river. I heard the alarm being sounded behind me in camp, and a glance over my shoulder confirmed that the counselors were tearing after me, with the campers following them.

A moment later we reached a spot about fifty yards downstream where a rambunctious tributary joined the three-foot-deep Wading River. At the point of confluence the flood of water created a funnel nearly eight feet deep, almost a whirlpool. Rich and Magoo immediately formed the counselors into two river-spanning lines, and they began working their way both upstream and down, with the best swimmers taking on the section of deep water, diving, surfacing, and diving again. The others kept low in the water, feeling their way, desperate to find our camper.

"Where did Willie go under?" I asked my young informant as gently as I could.

"There," he said, pointing to the whirlpool, the most turbulent section of river. "And then he just disappeared."

Jesus! "Why? We've told you kids a million times to stay away from the open river!"

"Yeah, but he saw a counselor on the other side, and he wanted to get 'im. The river was the only way over."

"And when did it happen?" Damn, it was hard to keep my emotion from putting an ugly edge on my voice.

"I dunno. I came right back to home base and told the guys. Then you asked me about Willie."

So at least ten minutes had elapsed, and perhaps it was too late for Willie. Suddenly one of the cookie boys surfaced, yelling for assistance. He'd found Willie upstream, but it was a struggle to keep the missing boy afloat.

We all raced into the water and hauled the missing camper to shore. Magoo immediately started mouth-to-mouth resuscitation. While he worked on the boy, I did some quick calculations. We'd found him about ten minutes after we'd heard he was missing. But he had to have been under for five minutes prior to our hearing the news of his accident. At least fifteen to twenty minutes. Too long? I couldn't be sure.

We eased Willie over to ascertain we'd drained all the water we could from his lungs. While Magoo took over the mouth-to-mouth work from Rich, other counselors started to massage Willie's legs and arms. A line of counselors certified in CPR formed, ready to take over from Magoo, and the counselors followed each other closely, making sure the rescue breathing continued without a break.

All of us were engrossed in Willie's condition and were jarred by the sound of a strange voice barking out the question "What's the problem over there?"

"One of our kids got caught in the current," I shouted back to the keen-faced guy in the passing canoe with his family. "He was under for quite a while."

In a few strokes he beached his craft and jumped out, bending over Willie. "I'm a doctor," he said. Positioning his fingers on Willie's wrist, he watched us continue with CPR for a long time. At last he raised a face that warned us what was coming. "I'm so very sorry. This young man is dead."

That frozen sensation in the pit of my stomach emanated waves of horror. I felt sick. Then I shook off the mantle of fear that was suffocating me. No, dammit! Nobody was going to die on my watch. "Keep working on him, boys. We're not giving up."

The doctor shook his head and went back to his canoe. He'd just gotten it headed downstream again when Magoo and Dave shouted, "Look at that. His eye just twitched!"

I shouted this information to the doctor, who shrugged, "It's just an involuntary muscle reaction. I'm sorry." The guys didn't stop working. It was dead still except for their labored breathing, as one counselor after another took over the CPR efforts.

Then several of the guys gasped. "Hey, his other eyelid just fluttered!"

Somebody grunted, "Involuntary reaction, like hell!" After an eternity the welcome wail of the ambulance materialized in the distance, growing louder by the second. It was an unspeakable relief when the uniformed EMTs took over. Taking his vital signs with incredible speed, they carefully transferred Willie to the ambulance.

This cannot be happening, I thought as I watched them put the oxygen mask over his nose and mouth. With all the force in my body and spirit, I willed the youngster to live. But the sight of Willie's motionless form didn't give me much hope. Theresa followed the ambulance in our car while I returned to camp to calm and comfort the other children. My wife and I agreed the other kids needed some symbol of solidity and safety, and that I needed to be there for them, especially for Willie's brother. So I had to watch the ambulance drive away, return to camp, and try to minister to some very upset kids.

But before I could so much as hug one child, I had to call Willie's mother. It was one of the hardest things I'd ever had to do. It was as if I were trapped in a bad dream, but it was one from which awakening would bring scant comfort. The mother took my news in shocked silence, finally breaking it to tell me she'd leave for the hospital that instant. She and her boyfriend didn't arrive at the hospital until Saturday morning, but in the meantime my wife and brother Georgie kept vigil by Willie's side. They kept us posted on Willie's condition through the night, but I hated the fact that I couldn't be at the hospital. When she arrived, of course, Willie's mom was distraught. Theresa told me that the woman kept sobbing that Willie was her brightest child, as her boyfriend tried to comfort her.

Though their own hearts were heavy with sorrow, my incredible team of counselors helped me hug and comfort the other campers. All of us were afraid. Though the hospital was getting some vital signs from the boy, they told Theresa that they doubted Willie would make it through the night. It was unearthly quiet in camp as the daylight died. The mood was somber, and it was clear to all the staff that each camper was praying for Willie in his own way.

Willie's desperate condition tore me up on a couple of counts. Here was this nice kid in terrible jeopardy because of a momentary lapse in good sense, a horrendous event to deal with. But the situation also forced me to revisit the death of our own newborn baby son years before, a terribly painful time for both Theresa and me.

I had a son who did not run, he did not play a game. I had a son who had no fun, we cast to none the blame. I had a son who never cried, he never had a pain.

I had a son who shortly died. He never had a name.

—*Don Bragg, "Unknown"*

My brother Georgie had escorted Willie's mother back to our camp, where she'd rested until Saturday evening. Then she and her boyfriend drove back to Jersey City to look after her other three children. Willie's brother, however, stayed on at the camp. My wife remained at the hospital and kept us posted throughout the night of his prognosis. But on Sunday morning, an elderly couple arrived at the hospital very early, and joined Theresa at Willie's bedside. The kindly silver-haired man said, "We're Willie's grandparents, ma'am, and I'm a Baptist preacher." Exuding a rare confidence, the grandfather held his grandson's hand and prayed silently. Then he made a simple request. "Let's all join hands. I have an important request to make." Theresa, my brother Georgie, and a few nurses all joined hands, forming a circle of prayer. Then he began to pray. "Lord, we're all here asking a favor for our little Willie," he said. "Give him one more chance with life. He's good child, and I don't believe he's really done with what he's got to do here on earth."

Everyone in the room searched Willie's little face, hoping to see some sign of a miracle, but the grandfather merely smiled and said to his wife, "We can go now, our work here is done. Everything will be just fine." With this he said his goodbyes and left the hospital.

Georgie was shocked by this incident. He'd never seen that kind of unperturbed faith before, and it kind of jump-started his spiritual life. After the preacher departed, Theresa left as well for a few hours but returned just before dinner time. She was exhausted with unrelenting worry and lack of sleep. Curling up in a chair in Willie's room, she eventually dozed off.

Theresa: *When I awoke, light was streaming into the room. I stretched, blinking at the brilliance of the morning. Then I sat bolt upright. When I heard a voice right next to me, I thought it was a dream. But I was awake—and alone—in Willie's room. I shook the remnants of sleep from my eyes and looked over at the bed. There was Willie, his eyes wide open, talking a blue streak. Jumping up, I found a nurse and dragged her to Willie's bedside.*

Regarding me pityingly, the nurse shrugged her shoulders. "That's just comatose rambling, dear. It doesn't mean a thing."

Well, I didn't contradict the nurse; after all, I'm not an RN. But it seemed to me that having a child looking around and jabbering was preferable to having him lying still and silent as death. Wild horses couldn't have dragged me from Willie's bedside after that.

In the early afternoon, the nurse had taken his vitals again and was exiting the room, when Willie sat up in his bed and began chattering urgently about horses.

"Nurse," I called. "Did you hear that?"

"He's only hallucinating," the nurse snapped.

"But listen to the way he's talking," I said. "He's certainly more coherent than this morning."

"Hallucinations can be deceiving," said the nurse, turning away.

That tore it; my patience snapped. "Enough of the doomsday prophecies. Let's think positive, for heaven's sake."

By now Willie was pointing out the window and describing the horses. "Look, a gold horse with a white mane," he cried. "And there's a black and white horse. Look at him pulling on his rope!"

I had to see for myself, so I ran to the window and looked out. Sure enough, a palomino and a fractious pinto pony were being led by the window down to the lake for water. For an instant I thought I might be hallucinating as well. I hurriedly rang for the nurse and triumphantly pointed at the animals. "Hallucinate that," I crowed in triumph.

Then Willie put the icing on the cake. He sat straight up in bed and said, "I'm hungry." All of us started laughing … it was an incredible moment.

The doctor wasn't having anything to do with hopefulness, however. He marched in and examined Willie with the glummest face I'd ever seen.

"This is all a mystery," he announced. "I just don't understand what happened." He sighed disconsolately. "Of course, even though he survived, this boy's brain was without oxygen for too long. The child may be alive, but he'll probably be handicapped."

I stuck out my tongue at his departing back and raced to the phone to tell my husband the miraculous news. Don's reaction was jubilant, but then he asked, "Now wait a minute. Where in hell did those horses come from?"

"There was a circus in town," I explained, "and they were taking the animals down to the lake to water them. Willie could see them from the bed, but the nurse couldn't."

What a glorious Monday!

We called Willie's family and told them the good news. Of course we also advised them that his motor skills probably wouldn't be up to their expectations right away. Best of all, I was able to inform Willie's brother that things had taken a turn for the better.

By Tuesday, Willie was off oxygen and doing well. On Wednesday, his mom took him home.

Theresa never did buy the doctor's grim diagnosis. "True, Willie seems a little confused now and then," she said a few days later, "and he's talking more slowly and with more effort than he used to. But he knows exactly what he's saying!" In fact, my dear wife was getting pretty hot about the way the doctor didn't seem to want to even admit that Willie had made a remarkable recovery. "The only thing that doctor seemed to want to do was to insist that Willie was handicapped!" And then she muttered something that was only halfway intelligible.

Now my wife's always been a perfect lady, even under extreme duress, so I guess I couldn't really have heard her say, "Handicapped? What a pile of poop!"

Once Willie went home from the hospital, those frantic days and nights took on a surreal quality. No one could believe what'd happened over those last few days. We went from having a nine-year-old camper pronounced dead to having him talk enthusiastically about playing games back at camp. We knew he wasn't quite up to that, so we made arrangements for him to return home to Jersey City, where he'd definitely receive a hero's welcome.

At the end of the season, I always had a lot of hurry-up work to get done before serious cold weather set in, draining the pipes before the water froze and burst them, and generally weatherproofing the camp. After I'd started working at a nearby college, Barry and Dave were primed to start classes there. However, they stayed on at the camp, soaking up the last fun of summer before the start of school. It was an unwise decision on their parts, for though it kept them around for the festivities at the Green Bank Clambake, it got their college year off to a shaky start.

Now Green Bank was an historic little community not far from Batsto, and, like that charming colonial showplace, was also on the Mullica River. The town was quaint, a fun place to visit. Its markedly woodsy atmosphere also made it ideal if you wanted some solitude. Green Bank was also a center for boat building as well as the predictable fishing and local hunting but was above all a neighborly place. When the town threw its annual clambake to raise money for the volunteer fire department, the entire community turned out for it.

The clambake had everything. For the kids there were carney rides and games of skill where every child could win some kind of prize. Music was supplied by local bands, every thing from rock to jug-blowing bluegrass groups. A local gal named

Eleanor would belt out a series of country hits, ending with the town's favorite, "I'm a Piney from Green Bank."

And of course there was food for every palate, though the barbequed deer ribs and fresh clam chowder were my personal favorites. As the Bragg's good luck would have it, my good friend Tom Marshall, his wife Joyce Priest Marshall, and the entire Priest clan ran food booths, ensuring that my family and I ended up with a little extra on our plates. So from 10:00 in the morning till late in the afternoon, this enormous block party drew people from miles around.

Problem was, the early fall weather was still hot, and the well-iced beer went down very easy. Too easy in some cases. Also, there was a certain amount of sipping on the sly from jugs of home brew that would turn a mule cross-eyed. After several hours, a few folks were crocked as owls, so arguments began breaking out here and there. Understand, I had my share and so did Tom and the Priests, but no more than was good for us. The general noise level began to rise alarmingly, and Tom and I exchanged knowing looks. Something was about to pop. There was a group of punks from the next town over who started swaggering around, disruptive as hell, bad-mouthing the world as they moved through the crowd. Tom and I both stood up, hoping our stalwart presence would quell any untoward physical outburst. I don't know who threw the first punch, but about twenty guys threw the second one, and a fine donnybrook erupted. An old-time bare-knuckle boxer like John L. Sullivan would've been proud of it. Parents drew their kids in close, but no one panicked. Hell, nobody wanted to walk out on something as interesting as an honest-to-gosh free-for-all.

Things took a serious turn when the fight spilled out on the road, which might have been fine if there hadn't been cars speeding by. Taking a right cross to the jaw is one thing; getting smeared all over the asphalt is another. Since people were tumbling right into harm's way, I assumed some right-thinking locals would put a stop to the whole thing.

Next thing I know, Dave and Barry go charging into the melee. Now when tempers flare into a pitched battle between well-oiled Pineys, the last thing that should happen is for two outsiders to try and break it up. Some guy I'd never seen before ran up behind Dave, picked him up, and body-slammed him onto the hood of a parked car. I thought, oh hell, here we go. But before I could go three steps, Barry intervened with incredible intensity. He may not be too tall, but you don't mess with his friends unless you desire a small tornado to rearrange your body parts. Which was the price the jackass paid for ambushing our tall Good Samaritan.

Since the occasion was a fund-raiser for the fire department, the firemen were attending in force. One of Green Bank's volunteer firemen edged into the fracas with a fire hose, and the torrent of water began to break up the fight. A minute later, however, a hefty guy from out of town wrenched the hose out of the fireman's hands and began hosing down the crowd indiscriminately. I was concerned when they jumped Dave, but seeing the fireman struggling to regain control of the gushing hose made me mad. Telling Tom to watch my back, I charged into the fracas to protect the fireman and get back the damn hose. The opposition immediately bunched into position and advanced threateningly, so I backed up and let a beat-up truck protect my back. The toughs surged forward, then backed up quickly as big Tom strode forward. I think the two of us could've handled 'em, but it still felt great when somebody hollered that the state troopers were on the way.

Within a minute, the troublemakers had scattered to their trucks and sped off. The trooper who showed up so speedily was a brother of one of the locals; when he heard there was a fracas, he was there in a heartbeat. The trooper took off after the departed troublemakers as the rest of us continued what had become a victory celebration with plenty of beer. Everybody had to recount his version of the fight. Dave and Barry, looking pretty banged up, hobbled over and began complaining.

"Take a look at my eye, will you? Somebody must've hit me with an anvil."

Dave had an injury to report as well. "I think I broke my elbow. God almighty, what're we gonna do? Classes start tomorrow!"

Tom and I looked at each other, then back to the wounded duo. "How the hell did that happen?" Tom demanded. "Don and I are just fine."

Barry exploded, "Sure you are. You just stood by a truck and made noise. We were in the thick of it. Why the hell didn't you help us?"

"But you rush into things," I said. "Figure out what the repercussions will be before you make your move."

Dave nodded, the student at the feet of the master. "Yeah, that's true. They were tougher than we thought." Barry gave me a Bronx cheer and told me to go soak my head. I didn't mind. I was just grateful that right had triumphed. Translation: I didn't get hit in the head. But it pissed me off that the troublemakers had evidently gotten off scot-free. I considered this while joining everybody in another cold one.

Others shared my mood, evidently, because someone suggested rallying at the local tavern known to be the punks' favorite hangout. "Right! Then we can teach 'em a lesson!"

Whoever said that never finished his battle plan because Joyce, Tom's wife, began shouting, "Are you out of your mind?" She looked mad as hell. Worse than that, Theresa and Virginia Priest were watching her back; they looked pretty irritated, too. And determined. "It's over," Joyce continued. "The clambake's closing, and the tavern's closed." She scowled severely at us. "And Kamp Olympik's closed for the season, so just forget about going over there to jump out of trees or pole-vault blindfolded or try to catch boulders with your teeth."

Virginia and Theresa joined their voices in a sweet chorus. "So if you guys are done with those beers, we're going home. Because they're certainly your last."

Of course, we guys had our male pride ruffled, so we strode off manfully toward our cars. Our macho gesture would've been more effective if we hadn't waddled away in the wrong direction. Luckily our pathfinder wives corralled us and hauled us back to our respective vehicles. But you can see why none of us would even think of missing the Green Bank Clambake.

It was in the off-season following Willie's tragic accident that I learned what the value of his life was: a mere price tag. His mother's attorney notified us of her intention to sue Kamp Olympik for damages. They claimed that since his near-drowning, Willie's thought processes were slower than they'd been, and that he now had a twitch in one eye. I recalled sadly that when his mother had arrived at the hospital, she'd told us—continuously and tearfully—that Willie was the smartest of her five children.

Long into the night, Theresa and I discussed what would happen to our camp if Willie's mom won her lawsuit; she was suing us for millions of dollars. I kept coming back to what my own reaction would be if something like this had happened to one of my own children. Knowing that we had done everything in our power to save his life and that this nice kid had ignored my admonition to stay away from the river was cold comfort. Damn, I thought. If he'd just followed the rules, this whole sorry mess would never have happened. I went over to the cabin window, and Theresa walked over as well, kind of leaning against me. With a sigh, she said, "It breaks my heart the way she said he was her brightest child." Then I felt her kind of tense. She looked up at me with narrowed eyes. "I wonder if he really was?"

How I blessed the care we'd taken in giving each camper thorough in-and-out testing with the Ohio and Metropolitan tests. They were designed to determine the campers' academic level before they started our remedial tutorial program. It not only showed the children's progress, it let us ascertain the efficacy of our program. And it nailed the brightness—or lack of it—of each camper.

When I retrieved Willie's test score, it was far below the acceptable level for a fifth grader. In fact, his test performance registered at a point between second and third grade. We subpoenaed his public school test scores, and they also indicated he was definitely below par for his age. Happily, we were able to arrange interviews with some of his school friends, and even with one of his brothers. Everyone we talked to assured us that neither Willie's activity level nor speech pattern had changed since his near-drowning. We also learned from all these sources that the little guy'd had a twitch in his eye since he was a toddler. Having this hard evidence made the ordeal that we were facing seem bearable.

On a brisk November day, Theresa and I were scheduled to give our depositions. I'd consulted our family lawyer, and he hadn't planned to attend this preliminary session. "The Kamp Olympik insurers will have their attorneys there," he'd told me. "And insurance attorneys are always well prepared." With the sheaf of hard evidence we'd gathered, plus the presence of these hard-nosed lawyers, I hoped things would go well.

Nonetheless, our trip to Jersey City was an anxious one. We arrived at the attorney's suite well ahead of time, and as we entered the elevator, a young black boy stepped on with us. Since Theresa and I were having a whispered conference, we paid little attention to the other passenger until he turned to us and said, "Hey, Missy Bragg, Mr. Don!" With a rush of emotion, we realized that this was Willie. Up to that minute, we'd only seen him in shorts and a Kamp Olympik T-shirt, running from activity to activity. We stared at this youngster standing before us in dress pants and shirt, looking exceedingly dapper indeed. After an instant of awkward silence, he threw his arms around Theresa and me, laughing excitedly.

Theresa was immediately concerned. "Willie, what on earth are you doing here all alone?"

With an innocent smile, he said, "My mama's going to be late, and she told me to take the bus on in to this hearing myself. And here I am."

"You came on the *bus*?" I was frankly astonished.

"No sir," Willie said emphatically. "I came on a whole bunch of buses." He then proceeded to rattle off the numbers of his buses, their routes, and the locations of the bus stops in great detail.

I stood there listening in shocked silence. How could this allegedly brain-damaged youngster manage all those transfers? Theresa and I had both been expecting to see a young boy out of sync with reality. We'd been dreading to find that the bouncy camper we'd known had been reduced to a child struggling to comprehend the simplest tasks of daily living. But here he was, sharp as a tack. Talk about a feel-good moment! The ordeal he'd been through at camp notwithstanding, this young person was okay in every sense of the word! We couldn't thank God enough for this miracle of life. Theresa had to brush tears of gratitude from her eyes. I don't get emotional, but I had to pretend there was a chunk of gravel in my eye that I had to deal with.

The principals to the lawsuit were duly deposed, and the insurance company's attorney made all kinds of points in our favor. He pointed that the incidence of injury ran far below those of other camps. "No doubt this is accomplished by limiting their campers' activities."

Huh? I sat there, keeping my face expressionless, but boy, did that comment gall me. Hell, one of the most important gifts we gave our campers was the chance to prove themselves. If they wanted to take a risk by diving off a tree or from the diving tower, we'd tell 'em exactly how to do it, and then a concerned camp staff watched their backs. That our kids were able to perform some action that had an inherent calculated risk with the safeguards that instruction and security provided was vital for their development. I remember all the times kids came to us wanting to try something they were a little scared to do, and we'd tell 'em, "Try it. We'll cover you." Success gave the campers a boost in the kind of confidence they'd need as men responsible for others. If you wrap a kid in cotton batting, you're not doing him a favor—just the opposite, really. And I had to sit there and listen to this attorney's bullshit and not say a word.

But who was I to quibble? The lawsuit was settled out of court, at an infinitely lower cost than the original claim. Even the insurance company was happy with it.

Not that the episode left things unchanged at camp. After seeing the unintended consequences to what was meant to be a playful game, I removed Hares and Hounds from our activity schedule.

And Kamp Olympik experienced its first full-scale mutiny. Campers dogged my footsteps whenever I showed my face on the grounds, demanding that their favorite game be reinstated. Pleading kids and entreating counselors gave me no rest until I decided to permit a modified version of Hares and Hounds in the schedule, which, among other things, insisted that nobody, including the counselors, stick so much as a toe in the river. We also severely restricted the roaming room allowed the players, which permitted me to station counselor lifeguards along the river as an extra precaution. Every session we told Willie's story and the horrendous events that flowed from not following the rules. The fear factor had its effect on the kids, and they stayed safe. But the game itself had lost its innocence, and was never quite the same again. That's when we put a stronger emphasis on Capture the Flag.

Hares and Hounds wasn't the only activity affected by the harrowing experience of Willie's close call. My staff and I burned the midnight oil brainstorming with the counselors on ways to make our fun and games safer. As a result, we were able to continue to make things fun and exciting for the campers, but all our precautions were tripled.

We did get some important feedback from Willie's experience, and it popped up several months after the accident. The doctor who'd beached his canoe to help Willie sent us a copy of the paper he'd completed on the cold water theory in drowning. The gist of it was that extremely cold water temperatures slowed the body's functions. This enabled the human body to stand oxygen deprivation for much longer than the medical profession had thought. His thesis was printed in one of the national medical journals, and there was one line that stood out as if it were highlighted in fire. It said that Willie's life was not saved by the hands of a hospital medical team but by the aggressive attack the Kamp Olympik team made on his behalf out there on the Wading River.

Wow!

That certainly brought a smile to a lot of faces and warmth to our hearts, knowing that we did indeed save a life when the chips were down.

Chapter Fifteen

W
hile we often entertained at the camp, nothing we did was bigger than one end-of-season bash for the entire staff. Though I'd only envisioned it for the counselors and senior staff, once our CITs got wind of the party, they begged to stay and enjoy the fun. Theresa contacted their parents to get permission, and of course our counseling staff did the same. I sometimes forgot that these very responsible individuals were still just teenagers. When they knew that their parents had given their blessing to what they considered some sort of rite of passage, our junior staff went wild with expectations of a truly memorable blast.

They were right—up to a point. Dominick and his Italian Connection supplied us with farm-fresh vegetables from my hometown, Penns Grove. We picked up a bushel or so of those delicious blue pincer crabs plus 300 cherrystone clams. We also provided fruit punch for the teenagers, to their intense disappointment. To the others I offered this admonition, "Drink if you want, but nobody drives anywhere afterwards. You can crash in the cabin or pass out in a tree if that's your thing. But no driving. Period."

In addition to the counselors and staff, we invited the entire Priest clan, including Tom Marshall and Joyce, of course. So we had quite a lively group gathered to celebrate the end of summer.

We chilled bottles of beer and wine in galvanized tubs. Though local merchants offered a nice selection of wines, we chose to go with the cold duck. That stuff might've only been Champagne's distant cousin, but it was nice and bubbly and a pretty color, which appealed to the ladies. Only one problem—the stuff went down like a lamb, but could turn on you like a lion. This was especially true if you were so unwise as to consider it akin to grape juice with bubbles and quenched your thirst with it. Talk about treacherous. It could give you a worse headache and a furrier mouth than straight rum.

Games of basketball, water polo, and softball continued throughout the day. Most of the guests brought bathing suits and took a dip or two. Not Theresa, however. Though we'd been at the camp for several seasons, she had yet to put so much as a toe in the water, and I really couldn't blame her. It wasn't only the murky color that put her off. Whenever a camper found an especially repulsive centipede or worm or slug, he'd hunt Theresa down and display his prize to her. "Hey, Missy Bragg! Lookit what I found!" they'd say.

Fighting an urge to gag, Theresa would manage to say, "Well that's certainly a good catch. Where'd you find it?"

The answer was always the same. "In the river." And I'd watch Theresa grimace as she made another resolution never to set foot in that awful water.

Our older guests took it easy with horseshoes and boccie, but some of their kids went off on motorcycles and didn't return for hours. Of course, every cyclist swore he was competent on the cycles, but evidently they'd missed the class that showed them how to steer. When they finally showed up back in camp, a few would-be cyclists were limping, wheeling cycles with bent handlebars aimed at all points of the compass, fenders that resembled kayak keels, and wheels in every shape but

Reneé with cousin Marc on cycle.

round. I made a mental note: no cycles next year. I couldn't afford such repairs even on an annual basis. When I inquired if perhaps inebriation might have skewed their alleged skills, I got hurt looks from the disheveled cyclists.

"Are you implying I can't handle a beer or two?"

"Hell, no," I said. "But a beer or eight? That's exactly what I'm implying."

My sister Dietzie was among our guests that day and had been playing tag with her nieces and nephews. She ran up, out of breath, and flopped in a chair, saying, "You know, I think I'd like to try a little wine."

I considered this. Dietzie seldom drank alcoholic beverages; her favorite beverage was blueberry juice. "Why don't you have some of this," I said, handing her a bottle. "It's got a nice, fruit taste."

I saw her pour herself a generous glass, then I sort of lost track of her for a half hour or so. Suddenly I was aware of a high-pitched, persistent laugh. It was Dietzie, laughing hysterically and fanning her face, which was pretty flushed. She then performed a couple of somersaults, and was fine until her finish, when she kind of collided with one of the tubs of iced beer. I saw Theresa helping her up, and then somebody else ran up, wanting me to get them something or other. The next thing I knew my sister had somehow gotten Theresa on her shoulders and was making a beeline for the beach. Theresa was screaming blue murder, but nothing was going to stop Dietzie, who had my wife's feet tucked behind her elbows. Dietzie plowed into the water until it was up to Theresa's waist. When it got higher, Theresa did this remarkable somersaulting dismount that she'd clearly swiped from the Russian gymnastic team. Galloping out of the water, she flew straight to our cabin to change and deal with whatever creatures she'd acquired during her dip. Dietzie wandered out of the water and began weaving toward the dining hall.

"That cold duck is nice. Gonna go have some more," she called over to me. I was about to bird-dog her, when Barry ran up, looking concerned.

"You know the canoers that left two hours ago? Dave said they were drunk as skunks. They'll probably end up in Jamaica." Collecting a few volunteers, I took the truck to the pickup point, but no canoes were in sight. Mentally crossing canoeing off the list of attractions offered at the next end-of-season party, I began to scout along the river, backtracking toward camp with the rest of the search party.

Unfortunately, we found the missing warriors. Most were sleeping soundly on the riverbank. One was singing lustily. A few had gotten their canoes stuck between rotting tree stumps, but the guys were still paddling for all they were worth. One of them roared a warning to me. "Stay back, Mr. B. The current here's pretty fierce." This idiot kept paddling even after we dragged him out of his canoe and threw him in the back of the pickup for safekeeping.

It was pretty funny, but at day's end, Larry Priest still hadn't been accounted for. Now I knew he was as familiar with the local woods as I was with the inside of my pockets. For him to be lost was unusual and unnerving. I was worried, too, because the stuck canoer hadn't been completely full of it. The river was moving pretty rapidly. Larry could swim, but accidents can happen to the best of swimmers.

Then somebody pointed to the sky over Piney Road, which led from the camp to the river. "Look at all the turkey buzzards circling. D'you think something died?" Barry Ross and Dave Miller took off to check it out. I followed at a slower pace, determined not to think the worst. As soon as I noticed that both guys were not only pointing to the ground, but also laughing uproariously, I began to breathe again.

"There's our missing adventurer," Barry said, in between guffaws. It was Larry, all right, his jaw and chin shining from his own slobber and beery drool.

Larry opened his little red eyes and glared at us. "See what you went and did! You scared them off."

"Them?" I didn't know what the hell he was raving about.

"My vultures. I was lying here pretending to be sick to see if any vultures would attack. Maybe I could grab one. It'd make a cute pet, huh?"

"They only land if something's good and dead, and though you may smell deceased, you're not fermented enough to bring in the vultures," I said, fairly disgusted, after my panic attack on Larry's behalf. "Come on, let's leave him here to play with his birdie friends. We're going back to camp."

We returned to the truck and slammed the doors, but before I could turn the ignition key, we all heard a thud in the back of the truck. We immediately checked, then had to laugh. It was only Larry. He'd climbed in the back and had promptly passed out. We took him back to the camp, but left him in peace to dream of turkey vultures, after we'd set a bottle of cold duck next to him.

But I'd had enough. The next party we threw at the end of the season would be absolutely booze-free! We'd feed our guests, but they'd have to make do with iced tea and blueberry juice—the real thing, not innocent-tasting cold duck that kicked like a brace of Missouri mules.

One of the things that immediately engaged my mind when I acquired the property for Kamp Olympik was that the varied terrain would be perfect for a rousing game of Capture the Flag. Most of us know it as a game that was played through the backyards of our neighborhoods when we were growing up. In principle, however, it's no different from what went on at Thermopylae, Gettysburg, or on Flanders' bloody fields. Us against them. War. Of course, Kamp Olympik's version of Capture the Flag wasn't a battle to the death, but rather for the victor's share of sun-sweetened watermelon. The principle was exactly the same, however. Of all the competitions we arranged at the camp, only Hares and Hounds equaled Capture the Flag in popularity.

Call the preparations creative, ingenious, or maniacal, they absorbed the camp for days before we actually played the game. I suppose the strategies the combatants worked out had to be complex, since the basic game was so simple. This is how it worked: we divided the camp into two equal areas, with the dining hall as the neutral zone that separated them. Capture the Flag was never Buffed Behemoths vs. Skinny Nearsighted Kids—both teams were pretty evenly matched physically. For fairness' sake we set odd-numbered cabins against the evens, with younger and older campers on each team. This way neither team had an unfair advantage. Each team placed a flag in some defendable locale. The other team tried to capture that flag, while simultaneously defending their own. Any player could be captured and be put in prison; he could, however, be freed by a daring member of his own team. Like I said, a simple game. It was a great vehicle both for fun and for boosting a sense of belonging for all the campers. The kids usually went all out, inventing team logos that they sometimes emblazoned on flags or banners. However, the fine print in the ever-evolving rules was as much fun to interpret as hieroglyphics, and I, the referee, had no Rosetta Stone to consult.

If we'd been able to definitively state who belonged to which team, my job would've been a lot simpler. We tried differentiating by shirt color, but the game turned into Shred the Enemy's Shirt. That left the guy who'd paid for those shirts—namely me—jumping up and down, tearing his hair, and turning purple with frustration. Armbands were an even worse solution: they were too easy to counterfeit. In the end we dabbed a mark on each participant's arm with washable paint, and that kept the teams distinguishable. And since I immediately put the paint buckets under lock and key, this system worked.

In the earliest years of our war game, I assumed leadership of one of the teams, Rich the other, and each of us was determined to win. When I realized Rich had placed his flag in the camp backfield, I was sure I had him skunked despite the fifty campers guarding the flag. After a long rainy spell, that field was mud up to our shins—and thus the defenders would be impossibly hampered in the case of a surprise attack. At the time, I owned a brand-new Citröen sedan, and though its engine labored at sixty, you could pump up its shocks to over a foot high. It would keep going through *anything*: my kind of car.

With Barry Ross as my aide de camp, I commandeered this primitive all-terrain vehicle from where my wife Theresa had carefully parked it. Silent as serpents, we made a wide detour through Mick's blueberry field, feeling smug as hell when we saw the muddy mire deserted, the flag unprotected. The moment we emerged from Mick's berry patch, however, the well-camouflaged militia materialized—hunting lions springing from the high grass to attack their prey. But what the hell, we had mile-high shocks and feared nothing.

Leaning out of the Citröen's window, Barry snagged the flag and waved it triumphantly as we took off. Problem was, the muddy field was swarming with highly indignant kids, all headed for our vehicle. I had to circle around and backtrack, until even our mile-high shocks were entombed in mud. I was still spinning the tires when crazed warriors attacked us, dragging Barry and me out into the mud. They marched us off to prison, and we stayed in stir for the remainder of the game. I don't remember which side won, just the cyclone that busted out of the dining hall when Barry and I drove up in the mud-encrusted heap. "What happened to our new car?" demanded Theresa in a voice pitched way too high for my peace of mind.

"Not to worry," I responded cheerfully. "It was involved in one of the major battles of the war and nearly captured the flag." Grabbing a broom, she started chasing me all over the place, with the campers cheering her on. "Honey," I laughed over my shoulder as I ran, "Where were you when our side needed you? You could've defended our flag against the Jersey Devil himself with that broom."

The various camp strategists decided our Citroën had been too cumbersome for a wild gallop across a muddy field. However, they evidently liked the idea of using cavalry, for the next round of Capture the Flag featured daredevil counselors on mini-bikes. At first, it looked like an ideal setup. The enemy positioned their flag near the basketball court, and the surrounding terrain would more than support the lighter-weight bikes. Keeping out of sight, the counselors watched the guardians of the enemy flag move onto the basketball court, seeming to be merely keeping a casual eye on their flag. If an attacker tried to play hero and grab the flag, however, the regiment of basketball players engulfed him in seconds. So this wouldn't be a slam-dunk maneuver, but the bikers figured that they had the advantage of speed. When the basketball game got going again, they made their move. Gunning their bikes, they shot out toward the flag, catching the defenders flat-footed. But when the bikers came within a few yards of their quarry, they were greeted by a massive barrage of unexpected missiles, as the defenders fired basketballs at the invaders' heads and upper bodies. One after the other, the cyclists went airborne, while their motorcycles spun out of control, spitting dirt and sand on friend and foe alike. The gleeful defenders rounded up the Wild Bunch and herded the crestfallen bikers off to prison.

One of the prisoners just couldn't figure out what went wrong. "This doesn't make sense. We had the cycles. There was no way they could stop us!"

The unsympathetic captors prodded them toward the prison area. "Yeah, you had the cycles, but you didn't anticipate the throwing arms of the home guards. So shut up and go to jail."

Now Uncle Joe wrote the last chapter in the motorized version of Capture the Flag. One day, in the midst of our war game, he ambled out of the dining hall and climbed into the bus, which was parked right outside. I vaguely wondered where he was going, but I didn't think much about it till I heard agitated voices screaming "Get him!"

What he'd done was this. He'd driven the bus just past one team's flag when three rival counselors burst out the bus's rear emergency door. They hotfooted it to the flag and snatched it up, but were tackled immediately. Their outraged captors also escorted Uncle Joe from his bus and marched him to the prison area as well. They were upset at what they considered to be the treachery of a trusted friend. I mean, they'd helped him pick up trash, and he'd treated them to ice cream. And here he was giving bus rides to the enemy! Absolutely shameful!

This bunch of teenagers gathered around him looking grimmer than the prosecuting attorneys at Nuremberg. "What in hell made you do such a low-down thing? We thought you were our friend!"

Uncle Joe was immediately apologetic. "They claimed they'd wash my bus and throw in a pack of cigarettes if I helped 'em out."

"Well, you're gonna stay here in prison for the rest of the day. That's what you got yourself into."

Looking mournful and desperate, Uncle Joe said, "I guess I got it coming, but I've learned my lesson." He patted his pockets dismally. "And I seem to be outta smokes."

The youngsters decided to take the high ground. "Okay, Uncle Joe, you're released on good behavior. But no driving for the rest of the game."

After Uncle Joe's fall from grace, it was unanimously decided that no motorized vehicles could be used in our war games. It was an easy call, unlike most of the acrimonious disagreements that would erupt over the taking of prisoners. After two or three seasons of Capture the Flag, I was forced to retire from active participation and devote my time to mediating prisoner-of-war disputes. This, of course, practically meant consulting the Geneva Convention to figure what in hell one did in these circumstances. It should've been so easy. Once a soldier stepped out of the neutral zone into enemy territory, he was fair game for capture. If you wanted to capture somebody, all you had to do was grab him and say, "One, two, three, you're my man," and you got to escort him to the incarceration area. Clear as well water, right?

Wrong. You wouldn't believe the convoluted arguments about who had whom. The debate was unending. "Yeah, he grabbed me, but he didn't say, 'You're my man.' So I said 'One, two, three,' and got him in a headlock. That makes him my prisoner."

"Is that right?" I asked the first captor.

"Hold up, Mr. Bragg. He got it right 'cept for where he got it real wrong. See, when I said 'One, two, three,' he said, 'Okay, man.' That means he gave up."

"No fair. I didn't mean I give up, just that I knew what you meant."

God, give me patience.

Each team also put a lot of thought into where they'd locate their prison area. It had to be defendable, but also safe for the incarcerees. Once, one side located its incarceration area perilously close to beehives. When angry bees began dive-bombing the prisoners, those prisoners took off at high speed, yelling, "Don't worry, we're not running away. We're just quitting; we're out of the game!"

Their captors were infuriated and pursued them relentlessly, eventually returning them all to jail. "Nice try, guys. But we're not buying the bee act."

The prisoners' indignant response of "Act? My ass!" had no effect on the jailers, however.

If you landed in prison, you could be freed by a brave comrade who ran into the prison circle and yelled, "I free this prisoner." You'd automatically be set loose with a free passage. The only problem was that if fifteen captives were in prison only one could be freed. Once the word *free* was uttered, every blessed prisoner would sprint to freedom. If these mass escapees were caught, their vengeful captors would tie them to trees, which looked terrific to any visitors who might drive into camp. Again, I had to decide whom the rescuer intended to free. The fact that the rescuer sometimes changed his mind or contradicted himself and that witnesses could be swayed by candy bars didn't make my job easier. I had hours of this sort of thing to wade through. Gives you a new slant on maybe why some lawyers act a little peculiar.

The main thing I, the judge, had to remember, was that, dammit, it was just a game. Some of Kamp Olympik's generals divided their troops into platoons dedicated to either offense or defense, which to my mind regimented things to just the right degree.

However, it was Rich, with his intense military mind, whose strategy took things to a truly wacky level. It was a given that the most important decision the rival leaders had to work out was the defensive posture of their flag. Rich positioned his flag so that a full regiment with tank and howitzer support couldn't have seized that flag unscathed. He placed his flag in the campfire circle, stacking wood all around it in a teepeelike structure. Nobody with arms thicker than matchsticks could've reached through those sturdy stacks of wood to snatch the flag. And even with thread-thin arms, no invader would've survived an attempt to seize it. My inventive camp director had a surprise lying in wait for anybody who got anything like close to the woodpile. If you crept towards the campfire circle, you would disturb wires connected to small dead trees stacked around the circle. The result? A tree would fall on you. It sounded like something the Celts might do for fun after dinner, but since I didn't want logs bouncing off my campers' heads, I outlawed booby traps, trip wires, and anything that might result in bits of brains being spattered on my cabins' nice cedar-shake siding.

Despite my restrictions, the guys did think up some pretty good stunts—and defense strategies. Once, a couple of counselors found out where the enemy intended to place their flag, so they hid in the cabin closest to it just before we rang the big camp bell to get our war started. They sprang from the cabin, headed for the flag, only to be inundated by campers dropping out of trees, popping out of clumps of weeds, and emerging from other cabins. They never had a chance.

Neither did the bunch who masqueraded as dining hall help, hiding in the designated neutral zone until they leaped out in full attack mode. They were quickly tackled and dragged off to prison.

Once, Rich's brother Magoo spied out where the enemy's flag would be positioned and also worked out a plan that he felt was foolproof. Since he was the waterfront director, he had the keys to the canoe locks. On the day of battle before the sun was up, he took several canoes upstream, then nonchalantly returned to camp. He planned to drift downstream to the flag location, taking the enemy by surprise. I got wind of this and waited with interest for the day to unfold. The opposition placed their flag at the top of the diving tower—whether or not they knew what Magoo was up to, I did not know. But whoever was after that flag would have to deal with campers stationed on each of the tower's three levels. Now, once Magoo learned how thoroughly the forty-foot tower was protected, there'd be only one viable way left for him to retrieve the flag, and that involved attacking the tower with a helicopter. I had a bad moment as I visualized the probable fallout from such a maneuver, but then I relaxed. No, I told myself, even Magoo isn't that crazy.

As Magoo and company floated silently downriver paddling as noiselessly as Duwamish Indian braves, it seemed he'd hit on an effective plan. Bracing for the coming assault, the landing party floated past Tarzanville without a sound. As the invaders drew alongside the diving tower itself, however, the keen-eyed defenders began bombarding them with cannonball dives. With their canoes swamped or upended, Magoo's tactical force floundered out of the water, clinging gratefully to the arms of their captors. All were quick-marched to prison. As they came in sight of the bathhouse, Magoo called out, "Hey guys, I gotta make a quick pit stop."

"Nothing doing, Mr. Waterfront Director. You're going to jail, and you will not be passing Go! You're under *our* control now."

The most unique improvisation that ever showed up in Capture the Flag, though, was the one dreamed up by a counselor who kept a pine snake for a pet. Since only a couple of kids in the entire camp would have anything to do with his serpent, he reasoned that if he marched up to the enemy flag while waving his pet around, he'd be home free. The only flaw in his thinking was that the only other kids who liked snakes were on the other team.

For a while there, he looked rather grandly biblical striding towards his quarry bearing his mystified pet before him while the enemy cringed away. Then the two snake enthusiasts crept up behind him, relieved him of the snake, while the rest of the enemy soldiers smothered the snake charmer with bodies until he was prostrate. Though they tied him to a tree in the prison compound for safekeeping, the two guys with his pet headed for the neutral zone, where they proceeded to scare the hell out of the snake charmer's teammates. Another great idea down the drain, but it nearly worked—in reverse.

No matter how clever the ruses that were dreamed up, only a few flags got captured in over ten years of playing Capture the Flag. That's a miracle, and I attribute it to the fact that both teams were primed to win. The motivating factor? The victors got to feast to their hearts' content on that sugar-sweet treat that's always spelled summer to me: red, ripe watermelons straight from the nearby farms.

Pied Piper with winners of Capture the Flag.

At first we fed the victors in the dining hall, but Yolanda raised Cain about the seeds' speckling her clean floors. She also declared that watermelon seeds were guaranteed to draw the worst class of bugs. So we took our delicious mess to the beach. We could then eat in peace and enjoy a swim afterwards. The only way to determine the winner was an exacting head count of prisoners. And though at first only the winning team received the prize, eventually all the soldiers partook of the spoils of war.

When you get a couple hundred kids scarfing down watermelon, however, it's only a matter of time before another game takes shape, the ultimate food fight. The victors ate first, and it was inevitable that one of them would flick a rind at the vanquished enemy. The enemy would return the favor with chunks of fruit, since they hadn't worked their way down to the rind. A second later, vast quantities of fruit, seeds, and rinds went airborne, blotting out the blue sky with their sheer volume—a veritable melon fog. The kids, the beach, the river—all were covered with juice and spent ammunition. It was a boy's version of paradise, far better than the pillow fights back home. The forest creatures also joined in the fun. The day after the watermelon feed, you'd find pieces of rind well scored by sharp little teeth, and the beach covered with animal and bird tracks. And who can say whether Kamp Olympik's mascot, the Jersey Devil, crept from his lair to enjoy the feast as well by the light of the full moon?

Chapter Sixteen

Although our work at Kamp Olympik was one of the most rewarding chapters in our lives, after ten years of unrelenting labor, Theresa and I were both tired. We realized it was time to move on, and, with incredibly mixed emotions, we decided to sell our camp.

Suddenly I cannot handle the challenge; I fear the devil might take his revenge.

—Don Bragg, "Time Out"

During the time Theresa and I ran Kamp Olympik, we crafted an academic program to bring our campers up to speed in both math and reading, certainly the two most essential elements in building well-educated individuals. Over the years, though, I've occasionally met people who thought we were short-changing the kids. There was one woman who insisted that we should've offered classes in geography, history, the sciences and the arts. *Aahts* was the way she pronounced it, turning up her nose at my description of our arts and crafts program.

"Look, lady," I said to her. "We're talking about a three-week crash course to bring kids up to their proper academic level in the basics. If you can't read, you'll never learn history, and you probably won't give a damn about geography. If you can't divide or multiply, you'll never learn the first thing about physics or astronomy. First things first, don't you agree?" Well, she didn't hear a thing I said, and she went on to describe some enrichment program her kid attended for an entire summer, which is what she really wanted to do in the first place. That was fine with me, but it got me feeling a little defensive. Had we done enough to help our campers prepare for more than a hardscrabble future?

The answer was a resounding "Yes!" But we didn't label what we presented as one more thing the campers were obliged to learn, we just told them we were going somewhere to have fun. Yeah, they had a ball on our field trips, but these mini-adventures gave them an opportunity to ask questions and—even more important—to get answers. I can remember being in school and asking a question about something I thought was fascinating, only to have my harried teacher blow it off because it wasn't on her list of things to cover that semester. Damn, that was frustrating. But our campers were learning about the different kinds of wood and the incredible wealth of animal life that existed not that far from where they lived. That made them hungry to learn more. They learned about life in the colonial days—that got them thinking about things they took for granted. They imagined what it would've been like to captain a schooner trying to reach port in a storm—that helped them to weave dreams about their futures. Most important of all, they learned that there were all kinds of different people out in the world, and most of them weren't too bad. Science? History? You better believe we included that in our curriculum at Kamp Olympik. But we just let learning happen; we didn't beat the kids over the heads with it. That's the main reason they learned all kinds of great stuff in the three weeks they were with us. The lessons stayed with a lot of them, too.

But I've stopped trying to explain that to people who have their own educational axe to grind. When somebody who really doesn't give a damn asks me why I started the camp, I just take a pull on my martini, grin, and say, "Hell, I did it for the money." Then they go away, which suits me just fine.

And that pretty much wraps things up.

Theresa: *And yes, the atmosphere was very male, incredibly macho, constantly competitive, with hot and cold running pranks and antics twenty-four seven.*

But there was so much more.

The eyes of the little ones, sometimes so full of anxiety and doubt when they arrived, glowing with delight at the sight of a mother deer and fawn—I don't care how tired Don and I were, seeing these children figuring out how to plug into the energy of the natural environment was a never-fail pick-me-up. And that was a skill that they'd never lose. They might have their share of troubles, but the colors of a sunset, rich afternoon sunlight filtering down through emerald leaves, the stabbing beauty of light glancing off of a running river: all these things could be sources of comfort and hope in ways that hadn't been possible before they'd experienced the wonder of the Jersey Pinelands.

The children also learned they could understand the natural world, something that might have seemed alien before. They realized they had the ability to assimilate facts that told the why and how of everything around them, from the differences in kinds of wood to how the basic principles of engineering worked. They found out that their questions were important, that they were valuable, precious even, and that there were strangers who were willing to go the extra mile to see that their questions were respected—and answered. Used to classrooms where overstretched teachers simply had no time to explore topics that weren't in their lesson plans, the children thrived in an environment that relished curiosity and gave answers that encouraged exploring young minds. Kamp Olympik was fueled by a sense of competitiveness, but the alchemy of the Pinelands, abetted by a dedicated young staff, transformed that into community and brotherhood.

All those young people who thrived at our camp will always be able to draw on the fund of what they learned there, and being a part of that is what made the work and the worry all worthwhile in the final analysis.

Like Theresa, I knew that Kamp Olympik wasn't defined simply by the crazy pranks and do-or-die competition, nor even by the insane doings that go on when you cram 200 kids into one family. I couldn't really explain what made Kamp Olympik so unique, however, until I remembered something I'd hung on my wall years before. It tells the why of our little corner of paradise in the dwindling forest, that very special place called Kamp Olympik.

A Prophecy and Warning

Duwanish Tribe

State of Washington

1855

President Franklin Pierce

Washington, D.C.

The Great Chief in Washington sends word that he wishes to buy our land. How can we buy or sell the sky—the warmth of the sun? The idea is strange to us. Yet we do not own the freshness of the air or the sparkle of the water. How can you buy them from us?

Every part of this Earth is sacred to my people. Every shining pine needle, every sandy shore, every mist in the dark woods, every clearing and humming insect is holy in the memory and experience of my people.

There is no quiet place in the white man's cities. No place to hear the leaves of spring or the rustle of insect wings. But—perhaps because I do not understand—the clatter only seems to insult the ears. And what is there to life if a man cannot hear the lovely cry of the whippoorwill or the arguments of the frog around the pond at night?

When the buffalo are all slaughtered, the wild horses all tamed, the secret corners of the forest heavy with the scent of many men, and the view of the ripe hills blotted by talking wires—where is the thicket? Gone. Where is the eagle? Gone. And what is it to say goodbye to the swift and the hunt, the end of living and beginning of survival?

Chief Sealth

Duwanish Indian Tribe

However ...

Man's reflections are more angelic and bright than

demonic shadows from campfire's light.

—Don Bragg, "Images"

Printed in the United States
214401BV00004B/5/P